STEP-BY-STEP PUBLISHING GUIDES

BOOKS 1 & 2

STEP-BY-STEP GUIDES

JUDY PENZ SHELUK

Superior Shores Press

Step-by-Step Publishing Guides: Books 1 & 2

Copyright © Judy Penz Sheluk 2024

All cover art by Hunter Martin

Published by Superior Shores Press

Box Set First Edition: January 2024

Published by Superior Shores Press

ISBN e-book: 978-1-989495-73-5

ISBN paperback: 978-1-989495-74-2

Originally published by Superior Shores Press in 2023 and available separately as:

Finding *Your* Path to Publication: A Step-by-Step Guide

Copyright © Judy Penz Sheluk 2023

Edited by Emily Nakeff and Ti Locke

Proofread by Nicky Hill

AND

Self-Publishing: The Ins & Outs of Going Indie

A Step-by-Step Guide

Copyright © Judy Penz Sheluk 2023

www.judypenzsheluk.com

Edited by Emily Nakeff and Ti Locke

PRAISE FOR FINDING YOUR PATH TO PUBLICATION

"Based on experience and extensive research, Judy has created a digestible and easy-to-follow guide for anyone diving into a new world (to them) of publishing. Sometimes it's hard to think of your creative masterpiece as "a product." Judy's guidance both respects your creative process and at the same time presents the realities of the outside world after the writing is done.— K.D. SULLIVAN, AUTHOR OF *A CURE FOR THE COMMON WORD* AND CO-FOUNDER, UNTREED READS PUBLISHING

"If you have ever wanted to write and publish a book, but didn't know where to start, *Finding Your Path to Publication* is for you. Built on years of experience as a successful author and publisher, Judy Penz Sheluk lays out the steps to getting your book out into the world in a simple to follow format—everything from making sure your book is the best it can be, to branding and social marketing, to pitching your baby to potential publishers. If you are new to the world of publishing, this in an excellent guide to making your dreams become a reality."—MIKE MARTIN, CO-FOUNDER, WRITERS FIRST

"A comprehensive resource for anyone interested in the business side of writing and the latest publishing options. Chock full of practical tips and sage advice, Penz Sheluk delivers the information in easily understandable bites with an insider's knowledge. A highly recommended must-read for writers at any stage in their career."— BRENDA CHAPMAN, AUTHOR OF THE HUNTER AND TATE MYSTERIES

PRAISE FOR SELF-PUBLISHING: THE INS & OUTS OF GOING INDIE

"User-friendly and methodically organized: the perfect guide for anyone interested in self-publishing. Answers all the questions you didn't know you had."—LISA TUCKER, THE BOOK COVER, THE BORDERLINE RADIO SOO

"Bestselling author and indie pro Judy Penz Sheluk takes the mystery out of self-publishing for both newbies and veteran authors considering this path. With clear explanations, handy checklists, and invaluable resources, *Self-publishing: The Ins & Outs of Going Indie* offers key information in a supportive but 100% businesslike manner to assist independent-minded authors in making educated, confident decisions. I will wholeheartedly recommend this guide to all of my editing clients interested in learning more about going indie."— LISA MATHEWS, EDITOR, KILL YOUR DARLINGS EDITING SERVICES

"Well-researched, well-organized, easy to read, and very comprehensive. Great both for newbies and old hands. I learned a lot!" —C.J. SHANE, AUTHOR OF LETTY VALDEZ, CAT MIRANDA, AND IRON HORSE MYSTERIES

"A must have for every author embarking upon self-publishing. It's a comprehensive business guide ranging from setting up your publishing identity, to uploading your books to various platforms, pricing, audiobooks, advertising and promotion, and so much more. This handy manual is rich with pro tips from an experienced author who has run the gamut and succeeded."—KEENAN POWELL, MULTI-NOMINATED AUTHOR OF IMPLIED CONSENT, A MAUREEN GOULD LEGAL THRILLER

CONTENTS

BOOK 1: FINDING YOUR PATH TO PUBLICATION
A Step-by-Step Guide

PAVING THE WAY

GETTING DOWN TO BUSINESS

UNDERSTANDING YOUR OPTIONS

MONEY MATTERS

THE WRITE LIFE

ADDITIONAL RESOURCES

BOOK 2: SELF-PUBLISHING
The Ins & Outs of Going Indie

PREPPING FOR PUBLICATION

READY OR NOT?

PUBLISHING PLATFORMS

AUDIOBOOKS

GETTING THE WORD OUT

AUTHOR, AUTHOR

ADDITIONAL RESOURCES

- A STEP-BY-STEP GUIDE -

FINDING *your*
PATH
TO PUBLICATION

SOCIAL

TRADITIONAL

SELF-
PUBLISHING

HYBRID/
ASSISTED

INDEPENDENT
PRESS

JUDY PENZ SHELUK

BOOK 1: FINDING YOUR PATH TO PUBLICATION

A STEP-BY-STEP GUIDE

INTRODUCTION

Each November, regional writing chapters and libraries across North America set up workshops and events around National Novel Writing Month—an annual, worldwide challenge in which writers attempt to write 50,000 words in 30 days. In 2021, after learning that I'd been a NaNoWriMo "failure" on two previous occasions, the adult programming coordinator at my local library asked if I'd consider hosting a virtual "debriefing" on November 30, titled *Failing (and Succeeding!) with NaNoWriMo*.

I agreed. If nothing else, it would encourage me to not only sign up for NaNoWriMo again, and make a concerted effort to reach the lofty 50,000-word mark for the fourth book in my *Marketville Mystery* series.

The 50,000 words didn't happen, though I did come close. Not that it mattered. It turned out the attendees—whether they'd written 50,000 words or not —were far more interested in the publishing process than drilling down on failing or succeeding at NaNoWriMo. Furthermore, the nature of their questions made me realize that the vast majority had absolutely no concept of how to proceed beyond NaNoWriMo. Hint: sending a 50,000-word rough first draft to agents or publishers is *not* the way to proceed!

What really happens next?

I let that simmer for a few days, then approached the programming coordinator with an idea for a virtual presentation that would explore the pros and cons of various publishing options. She loved the concept, and we settled on a title—*Finding Your Path to Publication*—a date, and a timeline: five minutes for introductions, fifty-five minutes for the presentation, followed by a 30-minute Q&A. Because the event was virtual, it would be accessible to anyone who wanted to attend, even if they weren't a library patron or lived outside of the area.

Because the presentation contained so much information, I created a resource document with helpful links for the attendees, the kind of thing I would have loved when I was starting out. It didn't have all the answers, but it was a place to *start*.

Finding Your Path to Publication was both well attended and well received, leading to the creation of a spin-off presentation which was equally successful: *Self-Publishing: The Ins & Outs of Going Indie*.

Fast forward a couple of months, and the Independent Book Publishers Association (IBPA), of which I am a member, sent out a survey asking authors if they had any outside-the-box strategies for business development. I submitted my experience from my two presentations and less than a week later, the Managing Editor of *IBPA Independent* magazine asked if I'd be interested in penning an article for their May/June 2022 issue.

As a former freelance journalist, the idea of going back to my writing roots and sharing my experience held appeal, and so I agreed. Seeing that article in print also gave me another idea. Why not write a book that would demystify the publishing options available, including the steps required for each one? As a mystery author, I'm a complete pantser, never quite sure where the next chapter will lead, let alone the ending. With this project, I'd have my two presentations as an outline to follow.

The result is this book, but with one caveat: if you're looking for advice on which path you should choose, you won't find it here. One path does not fit all.

What you will find is a comprehensive, step-by-step guide to help you understand your options, including a breakdown of publishing and publishers: traditional (Big Five), independent (micro, small, medium, and large), hybrid/assisted, self, and social publishing. Included is information on editors and editing, writing a solid query letter, royalties, understanding copyright, and building your brand.

Throughout these pages, look for the (#AR) symbol, indicating a web link to more information in the Additional Resources section at the back of this book. In the same section, you'll also find Talking the Talk, a comprehensive reference list of terms frequently used in the publishing world.

And now it's time to turn the page and find *your* path to publication.

PAVING THE WAY

DEADLINES & DETAILS

ONE OF THE most common mistakes new authors make is sending their book "out there" before it's truly ready. Of course, the reverse is also true. I've heard of writers who have been editing and revising the same manuscript for years, never quite able to let it go. The question is, when is the time right, and how will you know when that time has arrived?

ARBITRARY AND SELF-IMPOSED DEADLINES

Maybe you've given yourself a timeline to get your project done, a milestone birthday or one year after retirement. Whatever the reason, arbitrary or self-imposed deadlines can be unrealistic. Yes, it's good to have a goal, a date to work towards. It's also important to allow yourself, and your book, the flexibility to change and adapt. Which brings us to…

HONEST AND OBJECTIVE FEEDBACK

Feedback comes in many forms and at various stages of the

writing process. The most important thing to remember is that you are looking for an honest and unbiased evaluation of your work. You won't agree with every comment or suggestion, but you should at least consider each one without becoming defensive. Consider it "thick skin" training for the rejections you're almost certain to face going forward. Let's look at some options:

WRITING CRITIQUE GROUPS

Writers who connect on a regular basis to share their work for the purpose of remaining accountable to their project, exchanging feedback, and improving their craft. While there are no hard and fast rules, these work best if the group is small—three to five people—allowing each member time to read and respond without becoming overwhelmed, while developing an ongoing and supportive relationship with one another.

Ideally, you'll also be working in the same genre. There's no point asking for feedback on your whodunit if your critique partner only reads historical romance and is unfamiliar with the tropes of cozy mysteries. It's also necessary to establish parameters from the get-go, including weekly word count limits and the type of feedback expected. Are you looking for big picture or line edits? Facebook, your local library, and writing associations can be great sources to find an established critique group or connect with people to form your own.

While critique groups can be invaluable for some writers, they should never be the final step in the review process. As you become immersed in your work for months on end, you will lose objectivity. Those intimately familiar with your work will too.

Critique groups also aren't for everyone. I've never belonged to one. Part of that is my own superstition: if I share it ahead of time, it won't come true. But mostly—at least when it comes to my fiction forays—it's because I prefer to focus solely on my work-in-progress without any intervention until the first, and sometimes the second, draft is complete.

Whatever path *you* choose while writing your novel, honest and objective feedback will be required at some point, and that point should be well understood before you start submitting your novel for representation or consider self-publishing. Writing means rewriting and multiple revisions. Be prepared to let go of your favorite passages, scenes, and characters if your readers and editors agree that they hinder the flow of the story. Conversely, you may have to create new passages and scenes to clarify motive and action.

Alpha Readers

Readers who provide detailed and constructive feedback, both positive and tactfully critical, about your book's premise, plot, characters, and other elements. Does the story flow, is it well paced, etc.? This is the place to include readers who have knowledge of the technical elements in your manuscript. You may have done extensive research and even if (for instance) appraising Irish bone china from the early Victorian era is your specialty, having a colleague fact-check your work will prove useful.

Whether you choose to hire a professional, or ask a trusted friend or relative, they should be aware that they are commenting on an unpolished (first) draft. They should also be avid readers of your book's genre or sub-genre.

While a critique group focuses on workshopping with other writers, consider this the first test drive of your overall story from a reader's perspective. This will help pinpoint any big picture problems that need to be addressed.

Beta Readers

Unlike alpha readers who provide first draft review, beta readers (or *betas*) critique finished manuscripts before they are published. As with alpha readers, it's advisable to have betas who are familiar with your genre/sub-genre.

Beta readers can be friends, family members, teachers, members of online writing groups, or other writers willing to do a manuscript swap—basically, anyone who will approach the book as a casual reader, pointing out things they liked and disliked. This will help identify the finer points of your book that may need an adjustment.

"Too many cooks spoil the broth," and this holds true when it comes to betas. Ideally, you'll have no fewer than two and no more than five, allowing for a comparison of opinions without the risk of opinion overload. If one beta reader doesn't understand why your protagonist hates red, that might be a point worth clarifying. If two or more betas don't get it, it's a must-fix.

While betas are an excellent way to obtain (usually free) feedback that allows you to tweak and polish your manuscript, they do not replace the role of a professional editor. There is one school of thought that because traditional publishers pay for editing, there is no need for authors to incur this expense if their intention is to traditionally publish.

Let's look at that statement. Is it true that traditional publishers hire and pay for editing services? Yes. However, it's equally true that agents and publishers receive thousands of submissions from aspiring authors every year. Furthermore, you only have one opportunity to submit to each agent and/or publisher on your wish list. While there are no guarantees, a professionally edited manuscript may increase the odds of acceptance.

On a personal level, I look at hiring the services of a professional editor as an investment in my personal publishing education. For example, I could sign up for creative writing class(es) or I could hire an editor to point out issues that are specific to my work, while helping me to learn and grow for about the same cost.

That said, if you are considering an assisted publishing model where editing and proofreading is part of a paid package, independent services may very well be an unnecessary expense. If you plan to self-publish, however, hiring an independent editor and proofreader is not a corner you want to cut.

Editing and Proofreading (#AR)

Just as there are genres and sub-genres in fiction, there are differences in the types of service editors provide. It's important to understand the nuances of each. Each editor is different, and many will provide a complimentary or modestly priced sample edit of a few pages, allowing both parties the opportunity to evaluate the relationship before signing a formal contract.

Developmental Editing

Also known as substantive or content editing, developmental editing is the first step, focusing on big picture story elements. The developmental editor will also assess and shape draft material to improve flow and organization by revising or reordering content and clarifying plot, arc of action, characters, and/or thematic elements.

Line Editing

Also known as stylistic editing, the line editor focuses on coherence and flow, eliminating jargon, clichés, and euphemisms, while adjusting the length and structure of sentences and paragraphs, and establishing or maintaining the overall mood, style, or voice.

Copyediting

Ideally combined with line editing, the copy editor checks spelling, grammar, punctuation, and usage, and ensures consistency in character names, places, descriptions, and other details. Copy editing also covers fact checking and/or obtaining or listing permissions needed (e.g., use of song lyrics or trademarked products). The copy editor may create or work from a style sheet.

PROOFREADING

Not to be underestimated, proofreading is the final step to catch errors (typos, punctuation, misplaced or missing modifiers, proper capitalization, consistency, and verb or tense usage) and ensure adherence to style. This is not the time to revise or rewrite. At this stage, you should have already completed any *necessary* revisions (though the urge to keep tweaking never truly stops). Proofreading is your final step to making sure your manuscript is clean and ready to be seen by others.

PUBLISHING PATHS

IF YOU'VE GOTTEN this far, you're clearly ready to put in the work. In this chapter, I'll do a quick overview on the types of publishing options available before delving into greater detail. These are not your only options; the publishing landscape is changing daily. But these are the ones we're going to explore and are, to the best of my knowledge, the most popular as of this writing. You'll also find that there are pros and cons to each path, though how you define those will depend on your individual needs, wants, and personality. For that reason, I've omitted a structured pros and cons list. After all, my pro may very well be your con.

TRADITIONAL (TRADE BOOK) A.K.A. THE BIG FIVE

Most aspiring authors dream of signing a contract with one of the "Big Five" traditional book houses (Hachette Book Group, HarperCollins, Macmillan Publishers, Penguin Random House, and Simon & Schuster), publishers with a team of professionals who take care of everything from editing, proofreading, interior book design, cover art, digital and/or print advance review copies (ARCs), book blurbs and uploading to retail, to detailed sales reports to accompany royalty payments, and assistance with advertising and promotion.

Traditional publishers may also pay an advance against future royalties (the author's money to keep, even if the advance doesn't earn out), though in today's world advances aren't guaranteed with a book deal. The amount of an advance, if offered, is typically 50% on signing of the contract and 50% on publication, although terms can and do vary. The amount of the advance offered will depend on how much the publisher wants to publish your book. Authors with a bestselling track record and those with celebrity status or name recognition will reap the largest rewards.

Getting a book deal as an unknown author is far from easy. With rare exceptions, traditional houses do not accept manuscripts from authors directly and will only work with literary agents. This means you must first start the process of finding a reputable literary agent who will represent you and your book, an extensive process that can take months, even years. That's because reputable literary agents do not charge a reading or placement fee. They work on a commission basis, earning a percentage of your royalties (including advances) when you are paid. The good news: they *want* you to get paid, and work hard to make it happen. The bad news: they need to be selective about the clients they take on.

No matter how great your book is, if you're an unknown commodity without celebrity status, name recognition, or some sort of networking "in," you aren't likely to be at the top of anyone's wish list. So, when you're pitching your book to agents, your title needs to stand out to capture their attention. You'll learn more about this process in Getting Down to Business.

Patience is a definite virtue when it comes to landing a Big Five deal. Publication often takes 18 to 24 months from the day you sign on the dotted line, though it can, and often does, take much longer.

Independent Publishers

If being traditionally published is important to you, regardless of your reasons, a contract with an independent publisher is often more attainable. That's because unlike trade book conglomerates, independent publishers (which will later be defined as micro, small, medium, or large press) accept manuscripts directly from the author without the aid of a literary agent, although you'll need to pay attention to their submission guidelines, which vary. In addition, they might have "open" and "closed" reading periods.

Regardless of the size of the press, your contractual agreement should, at a minimum, include paid professional editing, proofreading, cover art, interior book design, uploading to retail, and structured sales reports to accompany any royalty payments. Some will offer a modest advance (think in the low hundreds) against future royalties, again usually 50% on signing, 50% on publication. Other terms vary by press, but all should be clearly identified in the contract.

Some presses will offer digital ARCs (Advanced Reader Copies), though many do not, preferring to fast-track publication in lieu of sending out advance review copies. Authors may also be expected to solicit and/or pay for their own reviews through a review service, and the advertising and promotion budget and support is often minimal. The time from acceptance to publication tends to be faster than a traditional press, typically a few months to a year.

Hybrid / Assisted

Not to be confused with the term "hybrid author" (an author who is both traditionally and self-published), hybrid publishers offer assisted self-publishing, sometimes referred to as "pay-to-play." Years ago, these publishers were known as vanity presses, and there are still plenty of unethical vanity presses out there that will take an author's money and do little to nothing in return beyond getting your book out there, regardless of whether it's ready or marketable. When searching for a hybrid publisher, the importance of careful research cannot be overstated.

In many ways, a reputable hybrid publisher behaves much the same as a traditional publisher. They will vet submissions, publish under their own imprint and ISBNs (International Standard Book

Number) (#AR), adhere to industry standards, and ensure editorial, design, and production quality. They will also publish in both print and digital formats, provide distribution services, and have demonstrated sales.

There are some notable differences, however. Where a traditional publishing company will assume all financial costs related to your book's publication (cover art, editing, interior book design, etc.), a hybrid publisher uses an author-subsidized business model in exchange for a higher-than-industry standard share of royalties. Expect a complete hybrid publishing package to cost several thousand dollars. A small percentage of authors recoup their investment. However, if you're interested in self-publishing without the responsibility of subcontracting editorial and design services, and without the learning curve to upload your book to retail, the hybrid model offers a viable, albeit expensive, alternative.

SELF-PUBLISHING

Self-publishing takes hard work, time, and commitment.

Years ago, the only way to self-publish was to use a hybrid publisher, but today it is easier than ever to upload your book to a variety of retailers and make it available for purchase by libraries and in online and brick-and-mortar bookstores. However, there are some caveats.

Where literary agents are looking for an author with name recognition before investing their time and money, so too are booksellers, librarians, and readers. For the unknown author, gaining recognition in a very crowded and competitive marketplace can be an uphill battle, and not one for the faint of heart.

Another consideration is your own time, money, and organizational skills. As a self-published author, you essentially act as your own contractor, taking on, and paying for, all publishing-related responsibilities. That means editing, proofreading, cover art, interior page design, and more. While your costs will be significantly lower than going hybrid, they will be much higher than if you were to follow a traditional publishing route.

There are upsides, too. Unlike traditional publishing, where the publisher calls the shots (and often dictates the cover art), as an indie-publisher, you have complete control of your book's path to publication from start to finish. Furthermore, any royalties paid are yours and yours alone, no sharing with another party. That said, 100% of nothing is, well…still nothing. A quality product, along with a strong social media platform and marketing plan, are essential for return on your investment. Don't mistake "easier than ever" with easy.

If self-publishing sounds like more than you're willing to take on, and you're not sold on hiring a hybrid service, consider an independent publisher that offers distribution services in exchange for a percentage of your net sales, e.g., a 20% (publisher) 80% (author) split. One such example is Untreed Reads Publishing (#AR).

Social Publishing

Social publishing is an avenue for authors to write, publish, and distribute their work in a public or semi-public forum directly to readers, either by a personal blog or via an established storytelling website. Self-directed, the emphasis is on feedback and growth as a writer, and the pleasure of sharing your words, versus earning writing-based, royalty income.

Social publishing can allow authors to develop their voice while potentially building a fan base. It can also provide a forum to create longer works in a serialized format. It's important to note, however, that any work(s) shared in this matter will be considered previously published, significantly reducing, if not eliminating, any interest by traditional publishers and literary agents for those specific work(s). It will not, however, preclude the author from undertaking an independent or hybrid publication path for those same work(s).

MANAGING EXPECTATIONS

"Of all the learned professions, literature is the most poorly paid." — Dr. *Edward Eggleston, 1890.*

I KNOW what you're thinking…is she ever going to get to the part about finding my path to publication? I promise I will. But before I do, allow me to touch briefly on managing expectations. Yours, to be exact. Because the reality is, very few authors earn a living exclusively from their book royalties. If your primary motivation to get published is to get rich, you might want to consider another line of work.

The following data has been culled from two independent author income surveys, one from the Authors Guild, and the other from Sisters in Crime.

AUTHORS GUILD AUTHOR INCOME SURVEY

Founded in 1912, the Authors Guild is America's oldest and largest professional organization of writers, welcoming traditionally published authors and self-published authors alike in all genres and categories. From June 7 to August 21, 2018, the Authors Guild conducted a survey of U.S. professional writers, generating data from 5,067 book authors, including traditionally published (46%), self-published (27%), and hybrid (traditionally published and self-published) authors (26%). Using the prior year (2017) as the benchmark, 53% of respondents considered authoring books their primary occupation, spending half or more of their work time writing (#AR). This was further broken down by category:

- Genre fiction: 38%
- Academic: 22%
- Literary fiction: 18%
- Nonfiction: 18%
- Undefined: 4%

In addition to the Authors Guild, several other writers' organizations and independent publishing platforms participated in the survey: Romance Writers of America, Society of Children's Book Writers, Sisters in Crime, International Thriller Writers, Textbook and Academic Authors Association, National Association of Science Writers, American Society of Journalists and Authors, Association for Garden Communicators, Independent Book Publishers Association, PEN American Center, Authors Alliance, Next Big Writer, B&N Press, Authors Registry, Ingram Spark, Reedsy, and Lulu.

Of the part-time, full-time, traditionally published, self-published, and hybrid-published authors who were surveyed, the median income for book-related activities was $3,100 in 2017. For all writing-related activities (speaking engagements, ghostwriting, editing, translating works of other authors, teaching and/or presenting workshops on writing, etc.) the median was $6,080. Approximately 25% of all authors surveyed earned $0 in book-related income in 2017.

The Guild and several partners sent out a new U.S. author income survey in February 2023, which ran for approximately two months. Results will be analyzed and reviewed prior to public release later in 2023.

SISTERS IN CRIME: BUSINESS OF BOOKS SURVEY (2022)

While specific to the mystery genre and its member authors, another survey was completed by Sisters in Crime (SinC) in December 2021 (#AR). Formed in 1987 as an activist group with a goal of supporting the work of women crime writers and addressing imbalances in the publishing industry, SinC's mission has expanded to focus on the core values of advocacy, equality, inclusion, and community for all genders.

Titled the *Business of Books Survey Report (2022)*, the survey was open for one month in early 2022, with invitations sent to all members. Responses were submitted anonymously, respondents were allowed to skip any questions they preferred not to answer, and a free-response box was offered with every question. Over 400 members took the survey, which covered the following categories:

- Reading Activities
- Writing Activities
- Short Fiction and Non-fiction Publications
- Book-length Fiction and Non-fiction Publications
- Author Activities
- Member Identities

While only SinC members were eligible to participate, the complete survey is available free to non-members (#AR). Annual income-based results were recorded under Author Activities in three categories: Traditional (including independent publishers), Indie (self-published), and Hybrid (both traditionally and self-published).

At the high end, 5% of all authors reported an income of more than $100,000, with an equal number of traditional and indie authors represented in that category. At the low end, 4% of all authors (3% traditional, 1% indie, 0% hybrid) earned nothing, with 22% of traditional and 41% of indie authors reporting an income of less than $1,000. Here's a breakdown of the rest:

- $1,000 - $9,999: 31% traditional, 30% indie, and 67% hybrid.
- $10,000 - $49,999: 27% traditional, 15% indie, 32% hybrid.
- $50,000 - $74,999: 9% traditional, 3% indie, 0% hybrid.
- $75,000 - $99,999: 1% traditional, 0% indie, 0% hybrid.

Sounds daunting, doesn't it? I'll be honest with you, it can be. But that doesn't mean you shouldn't follow your dreams.

After all, they can't go anywhere without you.

ORPHANS & OTHER REALITIES

REGARDLESS OF THE publisher's size or the length of time they've been in business, authors can find themselves "orphaned" through no fault of their own. "Orphaned" is a term used when an author's publishing contract is terminated. (This is not to be confused with "orphaned work," a term that refers to a book where copyright exists, but where the copyright owner is either unknown or cannot be located. The same term is applied to music, film, and works of art, anywhere that copyright applies and cannot be traced.)

How do authors become orphaned, and can it happen to anyone, even if they are a bestselling author with an ironclad contract? The answer is "a lot of reasons," and "yes."

The technical term is "reversion of rights," which means the publishing rights granted under the terms of the publishing contract are reversed and returned to the author. Once a reversion of rights is complete, the author is free to grant those rights to another publisher.

That's all fine and good, except for one thing: unless past sales numbers are strong enough to support it (think *USA Today* or *New York Times* bestsellers) few publishers are willing to take on an orphaned author's previously published titles. This is especially true (and difficult) for authors who have a series on the go. For example, book 4 in the series may have been written but not yet published. Landing a publishing deal for books 1 to 3, plus book 4 (and possibly subsequent books), while not impossible, can be difficult.

Some authors merely accept that fate as inevitable and give up trying. Some even stop writing altogether. This always breaks my heart. Others persevere and either self-publish or eventually manage to sign with a new publisher. Still others concentrate their efforts on a fresh start and begin a new series.

I've personally been orphaned twice, and very nearly orphaned twice more. And that's just since 2015. In the first case, a multi-author publisher (who had been in business for fourteen years) was faced with the death of her father (a key employee), as well as her own declining, and often debilitating, health. The decision to revert publishing rights back to the individual authors was made from necessity. That didn't change the fact that I was left to find a new home for the published book 1 in my Marketville Mystery series, not to mention the completed, but not yet published, book 2.

Even so, I wasn't concerned. My debut novel in my Glass Dolphin Mystery series had launched in July 2015 by another publisher (let's call them Publisher A), and the sequel was in production and scheduled for spring release. I approached Publisher A, who had thus far been an exemplary partner, and explained my situation. Within a few months, book 1 in the Marketville series was re-released with revised formatting, minor changes, and a new cover.

The plan was to release the second Marketville book the following year, but before we got to the contract signing stage the first warning signs with Publisher A appeared. Delayed communication and royalty reports, ARCs promised, but not delivered, publication dates moved up, authors privately messaging one another with more questions than answers.

With the writing on the wall for a second time, I made the decision to start my own publishing imprint in February 2018— Superior Shores Press. By July, Publisher A announced they were ceasing operation and reversion of rights letters were dispatched. No one was surprised.

In both cases, I was paid all royalties owed in a timely manner. In the case of publisher insolvency, versus voluntary closure, that wouldn't necessarily be the case. I got lucky there.

The cover art and the formatted files were a different story. It turned out copyright for the covers belonged to the graphic artists who designed them, and the files were part of the contractual services (editing, proofreading, interior design) rendered. In other words, they still belonged to the now defunct publishers. Because the copyright for the material belonged to me, I was able to (painstakingly) recreate both manuscripts. Needless to say, it wasn't easy, and took a lot of time I would have preferred to spend writing Marketville 3.

And I was very nearly orphaned twice more. Back in June 2014 I pitched book 1 in the Glass Dolphin series to a publisher's representative at a writers' conference in Toronto. The representative asked for a full manuscript. Before I had the opportunity to send it, I was offered a contract by Publisher A, who'd also requested a full manuscript a few months prior. As you now know, Publisher A has since folded, and while the other publisher remains in business, they have since disbanded their mystery line, orphaning all their mystery authors in the process. Fate (or irony?) at its finest.

The second time was with a publisher I truly coveted. I loved the books in their catalog (of which I'd read many), the cohesively designed covers, the buzz they created, and the awards many of their authors either won or were shortlisted for. I'd even met the acquisitions editor on a few occasions at conferences and was thoroughly impressed. When I narrowly missed a publishing offer, I cried for hours and moped for days. Three years later, that coveted publisher shuttered its doors.

The reality is that many authors I've known, read, and admired (including award-winning and *USA Today* bestselling authors) have been orphaned. Sometimes it's due to a publisher's personal circumstances. Sometimes publishers merge or get acquired and the list must be "culled." It's never personal, even if it feels that way. Don't let the doubt or fear of what "might happen" allow you to give up or discourage you from trying. There's always another light at the end of the tunnel, even if it's not the light you were expecting.

Eyes wide open. Head over heart. Believe.

GETTING DOWN TO BUSINESS

FIVE FIRST STEPS

WHATEVER PUBLISHING path you choose to undertake, there are a few critical first steps to help set yourself up for success. I've broken these down into five main categories: record keeping, writing your author bio, developing a social media platform, building a website, and defining your book.

RECORD-KEEPING

Being an author might sound glamorous, but if you've written a book you already know that it takes hard work and plenty of discipline. Furthermore, your chosen path might change over time. My best advice is to treat this journey like you're the sole proprietor of a business. From the day you decide you want to be a writer, turn up for work and write, network with other authors, and create a budget.

At a minimum, you'll want to keep all receipts and maintain a record of all your writing-related expenses. Think printer ink, paper, pens, computer purchases, software programs such as Microsoft Office or Scrivener, applicable postage and courier charges, webinars and educational courses, internet and cellular phone costs, professional services such as editing, conference or convention fees (including travel, hotel accommodation, and meals), and writing association dues. If you are working out of your home, a portion of business-use-of-home expenses (heat, hydro, water, property taxes, insurance, etc.) are often eligible for write-off.

It is also a good idea to keep a vehicle log. Include the starting and ending odometer readings for the year, as well as the date, return distance, and purpose of any writing-related trip. Going to the library to research historic archives? Need to make a trip to the office supply store for toner cartridge? Track it. The log should also include the cost of gasoline, vehicle maintenance, insurance, vehicle leasing or financing costs if applicable, and so on.

Consult with an accountant to guide you through the tax implications of startup, including what you can and can't write off, and whether or not you should apply for a tax number, set up a separate bank account, and how to register a business name/publishing imprint. While tax rules and regulations vary by location, the consultation fee and any business-related fees you pay an accountant for tax advice, setting up or keeping the business's books, and preparing a business tax return will be tax deductible (#AR).

Writing Your Author Bio

This is always written in the third person and should be succinct and relevant, including as many of the following points as appropriate:

- Recent writing-related publications and/or positions.
- Expertise in the field of your book (this is especially relevant with non-fiction).
- Memberships in any writing associations or organizations.
- A minor personal detail: He lives in North Carolina with his wife and two children. If your book is a memoir, you

would expand on that by adding something along the lines of, *Book Title* is based on his life on the road with his father, an itinerant musician.
- Website URL.

Of course, not everyone has writing-related publications, and that's okay. Here's an example of how to keep it simple:

Jane Doe is the author of Book Title *and an avid reader of fantasy novels. A member of Science Fiction and Fantasy Writers Association (SFWA), Jane lives in North Carolina with her husband and two children. Find out more at www.janedoe.com.*

I'll be addressing social media platforms next, but this also touches on another point which will be addressed later: if there is a local or regional writing association you can join, especially specific to your genre, it is invariably worth the price of admission. Belonging to one or more of these groups tells agents, publishers, and readers that you take your role as an author, and the craft of writing, seriously. For example, I belong to the Independent Book Publishers Association, Sisters in Crime, the Short Mystery Fiction Society, International Thriller Writers, and Crime Writers of Canada, where I served on the Board of Directors for five years, the last two as Chair.

DEVELOPING A SOCIAL MEDIA PLATFORM

It's never too early to start building your social media platform. In fact, agents and publishers will expect you to have an online presence. You don't have to do it all and be everywhere, but rather that you find a lane (or lanes) where you feel comfortable sharing pieces of yourself—at least as it pertains to writing and books.

Because the social media landscape is ever-changing, you'll also need to do your research. Do your books cater to teens and tweens, or older adults? What site is your target demographic most likely to follow? What are their expectations? Video clips or reels? Photo collages? Book reviews? Pictures of your cat or dog? How often should you post? The more you drill down into what works and what doesn't, the more successful you'll be at building your own following.

But social media isn't a one-way street. To be successful at it, you'll need to be a good member of the literary community. It's important to follow and tag writing associations you're affiliated with, as well as other authors—not just the big names or award winners, but those who, like you, may be just starting out. Share, comment, and like others' posts. Learn about hashtags (the best way to do this is by studying others). In short, treat your social media platform like homework, because unless you're already skilled at social media and self-promotion, you've got a steep learning curve ahead of you.

BUILDING A WEBSITE (#AR)

You may not think you're ready but whatever path you choose, your online presence should also include a website, however basic.

There are two ways of going about this. One is to hire a website developer and the other is to use a do-it-yourself website builder, of which there are many. The fun part will be coming up with, and registering, your domain name. More on that in a bit but get your thinking cap on and start googling to make sure "your" domain name isn't already in use. Ideally, a domain name will be your name (plus an extension like .com), but if you have a common first and last name, you'll have to get more creative. That's okay, but don't get so creative you lose your identity. For example, www.JaneDoeCozyAuthor.com could work, whereas www.CozyAuthorJane.com could be anyone.

Now let's take look at your options:

HIRING A DEVELOPER

Probably the easiest approach, it will also be the most expensive.

If you do choose to hire a website developer, it's important to fully understand what that process will entail. Will you have complete control of the website once it's built, able to update and add content quickly and easily yourself? If not, will the developer retain responsibility for some, or all, of the updates? What is included in web developer services vary from one provider to the next. Some offer a set number of maintenance hours in your monthly or annual charge, with work over and above offered at an hourly rate, while others simply charge on a cost-per-change basis.

There's no right or wrong answer here, though the fine print is important. You may want to hand the whole thing off to an expert and be more than happy to do so. Or it might be more appealing to you to take complete charge once the basic structure is set up. Many web developers are open to that and are usually willing to provide additional guidance if required in future.

Only you know the answer that works for you. Just ensure that those answers are fully understood by both parties *and* are covered off in any contractual agreement.

DIY Approach

The second, less expensive, but more time-consuming, option is to use a do-it-yourself website builder. (Don't worry, you won't need to learn how to write code or transform yourself from writer to techie.) And while this is a DIY approach, the end result doesn't need to look amateurish.

Choosing the website builder best suited to you depends on your wants and needs. You'll need to think about what you need now, but don't forget to also consider what you might require down the road so your website can grow with you, rather than having to start from scratch. Start by visiting the websites of authors who write in the same genre as you, and of authors whose work you admire, but again, don't just go with the big names. Check out online bookstores for novels in your genre written by lesser-known authors, then check out their websites as well. Chances are many will have gone the DIY route, and you'll often be able to tell by an imprint and links at the bottom of the page, "Powered by…" or "Developed with…."

Some websites will include a notation with the theme as well as the builder, helpful if you like one particular look (every website builder offers a variety of themes—templates you can build on). For example, my website, www.judypenzsheluk.com, includes "Designed by Elegant Themes / Powered by WordPress" in the footer.

Next, make a wish list of the things you'd like to see on your own website. Not everything needs to be done the first day you go live but can be added as time and energy permits. It's more than okay to start with a basic, functional website, as long as the theme and builder you select allow for future adaption based on your wish list.

Regardless of your wish list, one important consideration (since it's usually one or the other) is your website's landing page—the page readers are taken to when entering your URL. Do you want a home (welcome) page separate from your blog? Or do you prefer that readers land directly on your most recent post? Do you even want a blog? You should also decide whether you'll be using your website as an e-commerce site, selling books and any related merchandise direct to consumer.

The good news is that most website builders offer free trial accounts. Take advantage of that opportunity, and don't worry while you test out various options—your website won't be live until it's activated, so no one will be able to see it but you.

Another consideration is what the website builder offers in terms of registering your domain name and website hosting options. Prices vary for website hosting, so shop around. Keep in mind, there's usually a deal to be made if you're a new customer (including free domain name registration). Website hosting is typically billed on an annual basis; regardless of the deal you make, be sure to review the renewal rates since these can escalate significantly over time. You'll also want to select a host that offers 24/7 technical support via phone and chat. Trust me, when something goes wrong, you want to know that someone will be available to help you fix it quickly. The last thing you want is to lose sales or visitors because of technical difficulties.

Feeling daunted? The internet is your friend when it comes to researching what's out there, and trustworthy online comparisons by industry professionals are a great way to understand the pros and cons of the various services.

DEFINING YOUR BOOK

Think of your book in terms of real estate. If you were selling your home, the listing would include the type of house—detached, semi-detached, townhouse, condo hi-rise, etc.—the number of bedrooms and bathrooms, location, and any other special or unique features. When setting the price, your agent would look for comparable units, both past and present.

Defining your book is much the same, starting with a main category and further defined by sub-categories. A cozy mystery about a female amateur sleuth that works in a restaurant could be categorized as follows: FICTION / Mystery & Detective / Amateur Sleuth, FICTION / Mystery & Detective / Cozy / Culinary, and FICTION / Mystery & Detective / Women Sleuths. If you plan to self-publish, Book Industry Standards and Communications (BISAC) codes will be required at retail upload (more information in Understanding Your Options: Self-publishing), but when it comes to categorizing your book, a review of BISAC codes (listed on their website) is a great place to start (#AR).

If you plan to pitch your book to agents and/or publishers, it's your responsibility to sell them on your book using the appropriate categories, in this case, as a "cozy, culinary mystery about a sous chef who discovers a dead body in the deep freezer. When suspicion falls on her, she resorts to sleuthing to clear her name." I've included more examples under Securing an Agent or Publisher / Loglines later in this section.

Being able to compare your novel to bestselling books that are similar can also help paint a picture but refrain from boasting or making grandiose claims (these scream amateur). A simple statement, such as "similar in style to *Title* by *Author* with humorous undertones and a feisty, likable protagonist" will suffice.

What if your book isn't quite so easy to define as that? I'd like to tell you it doesn't matter, but that's not the reality. If you can't define your book, then no one else will be able to either. That includes agents, publishers, booksellers, and librarians. In short, this is not the time to try to invent a new category.

Hey, if this were easy, everyone would do it.

UNDERSTANDING COPYRIGHT

COPYRIGHT LAW PROVIDES protection for a variety of artistic pursuits, everything from literary to performance to musical works. This chapter will deal exclusively with copyright as it applies to literary works, though I'd be remiss if I didn't mention that you *cannot* use song lyrics in your work (unless it is in the public domain) —not so much as a single line—without express written permission, and more often than not, a *lot* of money. You can, however, reference a song *title* (since the title of any written work cannot be copyrighted). In other words, it's okay to write, "Blue Rodeo's 'Five Days in May' was playing softly in the background."

You should be equally wary of quoting segments from any other copyrighted material, including novels (though once again, referencing a book's title is acceptable). The disclaimers included on the copyright page of a book are meant to be taken seriously. The Berne Convention for the Protection of Literary and Artistic Works, an international treaty ratified by 175 countries (including the United States and Canada) and administered by the World Intellectual Property Organization (WIPO) ensures that copyright is respected in those countries, regardless of where the copyright was filed (#AR).

So, what is copyright? Simply defined, it means just what it says — "the right to copy." The copyright holder (that's you, the author) owns the exclusive right to produce or reproduce your own *original* work, in whole or in substantial part. If the work is unpublished (as yours will be when submitting to agents and publishers), copyright includes the right to publish or grant publishing rights for the work and/or any substantial part of it.

As the copyright holder, you are also automatically protected by copyright at the time of creation, with the following provisions:

- You are a citizen or resident of a treaty country included in The Berne Convention for the Protection of Literary and Artistic Works (#AR). Both the United States and Canada are members.
- The work is first published in a treaty country even if, as the author, you were not a citizen or resident in one of the treaty countries.

Knowing that, you might wonder why you would apply, and pay for, copyright registration, and what you might receive back in return. Not a lot, to be honest, although you will receive a certificate of registration protecting your work, which can be used in court to prove ownership of your book, should the need arise. And yes, you can always frame the certificate to hang in your office. Note: Copyright should always be filed under your legal name, not your publishing imprint or pen name. The exception would be if you were an incorporated business. For example, the copyright listed on bestselling author Michael Connelly's books is Hieronymus, Inc.

There are some exceptions to copyright law, but the biggie is that you cannot copyright a title. That's why you'll see books and movies with the exact same title. That said, titles are important, and the last thing you want is one too closely associated with a universally known classic.

How long does copyright last? In the U.S., copyright protection for authors of an original work exists during your lifetime and for seventy years following your death. In Canada, the term is lifetime plus fifty years. Different rules apply for anonymous works or works for hire.

That also brings up the question of who owns your copyrighted work(s) after you die. In general, as with other property you own, ownership of your copyrighted work will be transferred to the heir(s) of your estate, unless you specify another individual in your will. Once ownership has been passed on, the new owner may generally use and license your works in whatever way they wish, in the same way they can sell or dispose of any of your other belongings. It's best to discuss this with a lawyer specializing in estate law and should be part of the conversation when you're preparing your will.

In closing, there is no need to add the copyright symbol © to your manuscript when submitting it for consideration to an agent or publisher. Doing so will only highlight that you are an amateur. All contracts and direct-to-retail uploads will include a clause where you certify that you are the rightful owner of the copyright. No one else, not your publisher, agent, or retailer, owns the copyright to your work, published or unpublished.

SECURING A LITERARY AGENT OR PUBLISHER

BEFORE WE GET into the nuts and bolts of traditional publishing, I'm going to address first steps. Whether you are seeking agent representation, or taking your pitch directly to a publisher, there are some commonalities you'll need to be prepared for: submission guidelines, loglines, query letters, writing a synopsis, and managing submissions.

SUBMISSION GUIDELINES

Included on an agency or publisher's website, submission guidelines are the instructions that tell you the type of books they accept and how they want your work sent for consideration. They may be called guidelines but consider these hard and fast rules. You are now entering the business side of the writing world, and this is not the time to display your creativity or unique take on things.

This is also the time to READ CAREFULLY. You might be thinking, no problem. I'll format my material once and have my package ready for mass mailing. If that's the case, you might be frustrated at first to find that there are many small differences in these guidelines from one agency to the next. This is intentional.

The reason? Your submission is your application in more ways than one. Agencies and publishers don't only want to see your writing, they want to make sure you can follow instructions and pay attention to details—all things that will give them an idea of whether you would be someone they can consider going into business with.

Pro Tip: Don't pick and choose which submission guidelines you want to follow. You might be tempted to leave your margins the way they are, but even one thing can be a red flag for the person on the other end of your submission.

Now, you might be thinking "it goes without saying," and you'd think so, wouldn't you? Yet from my personal experience as publisher of the Superior Shores Anthologies, I can assure you that is often not the case. Let's look at some examples based on my submission guidelines, and how that might relate to your own submission process:

Formatting: Word document (.doc or .docx), Times New Roman font size 12, double spaced, 1" margins, .5" indent (no tabs), no header or footer (yes, that means no page numbers).

- I received a couple of PDFs, a variety of fonts (Calibri, as I recall, was quite popular, likely because it is the default for Mac users), and several documents with either a header or a footer. The PDFs were returned without being read. The other submissions weren't rejected, but I wondered if the author would be difficult to work with. If the authors couldn't or wouldn't follow formatting instructions, what would they be like when it came to editing?

Another element of submission guidelines you are likely to see includes a wish list, such as this one included in my Call for Submissions for *Moonlight & Misadventure*:

"Sub-genres: Traditional, locked room, noir, historical, humorous, and suspense will be considered; however, do not submit stories with overt sex, violence, or bad language. Speculative fiction, sci-fi, fantasy, and paranormal are **not** of interest for this collection. And please, no werewolves. We really do not care for werewolves."

- I received a couple of sci-fi, one submission that could only be classified as erotica, another loaded with f-bombs, and one story about werewolves that promised to be "different." Each story was rejected without further consideration, including the sci-fi entry which, while well written, simply would not have fit with the overall collection (hence the notation in the guidelines).

Let's look at that from the perspective of an agent or publisher. If their guidelines (or their website) clearly state that they don't accept certain genres or sub-genres and your novel falls into that category, it's time to move on. No matter how polished your manuscript is, you're wasting their time, and your own.

Word count: 1,500 to 5,500 words (though great stories falling "slightly" outside this range will be considered).

- Perhaps the "slightly outside" wasn't definitive enough, however, a story at 750 or 7,500 words pushed the boundaries beyond reasonable limits. There's being flexible, and then there's being an Olympic gymnast.

Would a larger or less forgiving agent or publisher reject a submission because of these discretions? Not necessarily, but it happens. But even if they might be willing to overlook the formatting, why take the chance? Showing respect for the submission guidelines is the first step in demonstrating that you are a professional. And since publishing is hard enough, wouldn't it be better to take a few extra minutes to make sure you're giving yourself the best chance? If you're doing all this work, the last thing you want is for your submission to get rejected without even being read, all because you've sent the wrong format. Be careful, and you'll be showing respect for their time and yours.

Each agent or publisher will have different submission directives. Few will ask for the full manuscript in the first round, rather, they'll want a sample of what's in store: first 50 pages, first three chapters, first 10,000 words, and so on. If you've piqued their interest, you should get a request for a "partial" (the first so-many-words or chapters) and if you've hit it out of the park, a "full" (complete manuscript).

A not-so-subtle reminder: if the formatting, partial, or full request is Times New Roman 12 with 1" margins, do not change it to Times New Roman 11 or narrow the margins to increase the number of chapters you can jam into 50 pages. If your chapter ends at page 48 or 49 and it's a good place to leave the story, then it's acceptable to submit a page or two less.

Pro Tip: If formatting guidelines are not provided, the industry standard is Times New Roman 12, 1" margins all around, double-spaced, with page numbers in the footer, and the author's last name/abbreviated title in header as follows: Penz Sheluk/Plans. Indent the first line of a paragraph at .5" (and don't use the space bar or tab key to do it). The easiest way to do this is to set up auto format parameters in the Format / Paragraph toolbar section of Word.

LOGLINES (#AR)

Imagine that you're in an elevator and an influential person standing next to you says, "Pitch me your book." (Hey, this is your dream, right?) You've got thirty, maybe sixty, seconds, before the doors open. What would you say?

Let's consider another, maybe more likely scenario: you're at a writing conference, one that offers agent pitch sessions. Five minutes or less to convince them to take a chance on you. Perhaps you're doing a pitch contest on Twitter, trying to stand out from the (very crowded) crowd. Or maybe you've decided to indie publish and you're prepping your social media posts to self-promote your book.

Whatever the case might be, you've got one to two sentences max to get the attention of an agent/publisher/potential reader and hook them. Enter the "logline," also known as an "elevator pitch."

Loglines are big business in Hollywood. The good news is that even though you're writing a book, not a screenplay, you can learn from them. Can you guess the name of these popular films based on the logline?

1. "After a tornado whisks a Kansas farm girl to the land of Oz, she embarks on a journey to meet a wizard in the hope of getting back home."
2. "An airhead blonde goes to Harvard Law School."
3. "Two star-crossed lovers fall in love on the maiden voyage of the Titanic and struggle to survive as the doomed ship sinks into the Atlantic Ocean."
4. "A cowboy doll is profoundly threatened and jealous when a new spaceman action figure supplants him as top toy in a boy's room."
5. "The lives of two mob hit men, a boxer, a gangster's wife, and a pair of diner bandits intertwine in four tales of violence and redemption."

What do these five examples have in common? (After all, we know it's not genre.) Let's drill it down:

- Each one conveys the premise in a single sentence.
- None of the characters are named.
- There is no mention of a sub-plot and, unlike a synopsis (more on that later), no nod to the ending.

In summary, a logline needs to be concise, ideally conveying the essence of your plot in one, and no more than two, sentences. You must, however, reference your protagonist in some way, and possibly your antagonist and/or the obstruction(s) to their goal. In our first example, you could add, "Along the way, she befriends a tin man, lion, and scarecrow searching for their own salvation, only to be stopped by a wicked witch on their journey."

Like every other part of your writing journey, perfecting loglines takes perseverance, patience, and lots and lots of practice.

Fortunately, there are a multitude of books, movies, and television shows to practice on, even if you're the only one who's ever going to read (or appreciate) your efforts. Then again, you might make it a game to play with a friend, family member, or critique group.

And now the answers to our logline quiz:

1. *The Wizard of Oz*
2. *Legally Blonde*
3. *Titanic*
4. *Toy Story*
5. *Pulp Fiction*

But you already knew that, didn't you?

QUERY LETTERS

APPROACH your quest for representation the same way you'd approach a prospective employer. Treat the query letter like a cover letter and the submission guidelines and agent/publisher's wish list like the requirements in a job ad.

Most literary agents expect writers to query multiple agents at the same time, though there are exceptions. One example is if the agency's submission guidelines specifically state they prefer that writers avoid simultaneous submissions. Another is if the agent requested an *exclusive* look at your submission at a writing conference or online pitch session (not all direct requests are exclusive). Any specific terms should be clarified at the time of the request.

If you are submitting because of an invitation, your query letter should serve as a reminder, with details of the meeting/session date, place, and terms of the request. (Agents meet a lot of people, and your meeting likely won't stick as clearly in their mind as it does yours.)

Additionally, if your submission is on an exclusive basis, be sure to include a reasonable timeline to protect you from waiting indefinitely for a response. That timeline may be offered on the agent's website (for example, "We respond to all queries within 30 days,") or it may have been part of the pitch session negotiations. If you are left wondering, I'd suggest a period of no less than four and no more than eight weeks. You might not get a response (this is much more common than you might think), but it gives you an opportunity to follow up in a professional and courteous manner. In the follow up, indicate that while you remain very open to working with them, you will now begin querying other agents. This kind of notification is fair to both parties, serving both as a gentle reminder to the agent (which might prompt a response) and as permission for you to continue the process.

Here are a few e-mail query Do's and Don'ts:

DO: Make it clear why you are contacting them, whether through an online form or by email (few agents accept snail mail submissions these days). Follow any submission guideline requirements for the subject line. If one isn't specified, enter "Query, TITLE." If your query is in response to a pitch session request, add, "As per your request." If you've been referred to them by one of their client's, add, "Jane Doe Client Referral." E.g., Query, TITLE, Joe Doe Client Referral.

DON'T: Add extraneous information to the subject line. If there is no referral or pitch session to reference, a simple "Query, TITLE" will suffice.

DO: Address the agent by name and, above all, spell it correctly! Unless you've met the agent personally or via an online pitch session, refer to them formally. In the past, the recommendation would have been to use an honorific (Mr., Ms.) but first names are not always an easy clue to gender, nor does it address the increase in visibility and awareness for non-binary identities. As such, the new standard is to address as First Name Last Name (spell it correctly!). Remember, this is a business communication, not an email to a friend. It is always better to err on the side of professionalism.

DON'T: Address the letter "To Whom it May Concern," or worse, "Dear Literary Agent."

DO: Get straight to the point, e.g., "Jane Doe, I am seeking representation for my [word count] cozy mystery titled TITLE (uppercase, no italics). I believe this novel would be a good fit for your agency because [enter your reason here]."
By entering the word count (which will fall inside the parameters of the submission guidelines) and by giving a reason (something that directly speaks to the agent's wish list), you are showing that you've done your homework.

DON'T: Get gimmicky and write in the voice of your character.

DO: Include your logline, followed by a brief summary (no more than two paragraphs) of your book.

DON'T: Tell the agent your book has been professionally edited; that is already the assumption and highlights that you are an amateur.

DO: Introduce comparables, e.g., "I believe TITLE would appeal to readers of author Jane Doe and her *such-and-such* (italics) cozy mystery series. Note: If the agent represents Jane Doe, all the better, as it once again shows that you've done your homework. Keep comparables down to two or three.

DON'T: Make grandiose claims about how your book is as good as or better than those comparables, or that you're sure that the agent will love your writing.

DO: Read any comparables you reference, just to be sure your book is truly similar in style.

DON'T: Trust back of book blurbs in your search for comparables.

DO: Provide a brief paragraph about yourself, including any pertinent facts. A paramedic might use their knowledge in a medical mystery, a horticulturalist a knowledge of poisonous plants.

DON'T: Include personal information, such as your age, sex, religion, marital status, number of children, etc., unless one or more of these facts are directly relevant to your novel.

DO: End with a professional courtesy, such as "Thank you for your time and consideration," and a call to action, "I look forward to hearing from you." Finish with a "sincerely" or an "all the best," and if emailing (vs. completing an online form) include your full name, telephone number (optional, but advisable), and website URL, if applicable.

DON'T: Make demands, such as, "I expect to hear from you in sixty days," even if the agent's website states that sixty days is their typical turnaround time.

And one final DON'T: Submit more material than requested in the submission guidelines. There's also no need to state you are following the guidelines. That's a given.

While some agents and publishers still accept e-mail queries, more and more are using an online query management system to track queries. In addition to your material, these online forms will request some or all of the following: Name, e-mail address, biography, website, Twitter or other Social Media handle, phone number. You can also expect to answer questions such as: Have you previously published other books? Been previously represented by another agent? Who (name of agent/agency)? Name of referral (if applicable).

The online form will also have a "Tell us about your book" section. This is where you'll copy and paste your text (pay attention to any special formatting guidelines), and enter your query letter, logline, and similar books.

Remember that you've spent months, possibly years, working on your manuscript. Take the time you need to craft a professional query letter, personalized in some way for every agent you approach. It won't be a guarantee of success, but at least you'll have given it your all.

Still unsure? Google "successful query letters" or check out QueryLetter.com for 161 examples of queries that worked (#AR).

WRITING A SYNOPSIS

What is a synopsis, exactly? Derived from the Ancient Greek word *synopsesthai*, meaning "a comprehensive view," a synopsis is exactly that: a summary of your novel's narrative arc, including plot twists and the ending, as well as brief descriptions of major characters. I don't mean details like hair or eye color, unless that's significant to the plot, but rather personality traits that define the character. Take *The Wizard of Oz* as an example. It doesn't matter if Dorothy has auburn hair worn in braids, but it does matter that she's a naïve farm girl from Kansas, a stranger in a strange land. Last, but not least, a synopsis is not the same as a back of the book or retail blurb; spoilers are an expected part of the package.

If there's one benefit to following a non-traditional publishing path, it's that you won't have to write a synopsis. I say that because writing a succinct and compelling synopsis is far from easy. That doesn't mean you need to hire a synopsis writer, though there are writers who specialize in doing just that. Costs for this service vary widely and can be charged on a flat fee or hourly basis. When choosing who to work with, you'll want to make sure the writer's expertise is in synopsis writing for novels rather than scholarly articles or research projects. Ideally, the writer will provide a sample synopsis (free or for a nominal fee) of the first one to three chapters of your novel so you can get a feel for their style and ability level. There are also online courses to help you learn the skill yourself. Review the curriculum to ensure the focus is on synopses for novels before enrolling.

Your synopsis should be:

- Single spaced.
- Between 500 and 800 words (unless otherwise stated in submission guidelines).
- One to two pages, using standard font and sizes, e.g., Times New Roman 12, with normal (1") margins.
- Written in the third person, present tense (even if your book is written in first person, past tense).
- Clear, concise, and neutral in tone. Unlike your novel, you want to TELL not SHOW.

Other synopsis standards include:

- Putting the title at the top of the page, e.g., *Skeletons in the Attic*: Synopsis, with your name on the line below.

- Naming your file with your novel's name_synopsis.doc, e.g., Skeletons-in-the-Attic_synopsis.doc (or abbreviated as SITA_synopsis.doc), vs. simply "synopsis"—you want your document to stand out.
- Putting main character names in uppercase (most common) or bold font (acceptable) when first introduced, along with their age in parentheses and a brief description, e.g., Single city girl CALAMITY (CALLIE) BARNSTABLE (36) inherits a house in Marketville with the proviso she move into the house and investigate her mother's murder thirty years before.
- Keeping setting details to a minimum while painting the picture, e.g., *Skeletons in the Attic* is set in Marketville, the sort of town where families with two kids, a collie, and a cat move to for a bigger house, a better school, and soccer fields.
- Limit the number of named characters. Your protagonist and antagonist, and if applicable, sidekick(s), are essential. Beyond that, it's better to write "the bartender," vs. "the bartender, BETSY EHRLICH." When it comes to the synopsis, less is more.

There are any number of ways to begin but approaching your initial attempt as a first draft can alleviate the pressure. Without worrying about word count, here are a couple of ways to do that:

1. Write one, and no more than two, explanatory sentences for each chapter. What is the chapter's purpose or pivotal scene? That's what you're trying to capture, no more and no less. Let's say the average per chapter is 20 words (as are the first two sentences of this bullet point, to give you a quick reference point). With 50 chapters, you'd be looking at 1,000 words. Over your target, yes, but on review you'll look for elements that, while important to the novel, can be excluded in your synopsis.

2. Tell the story from beginning to end in the same way you might tell the story to a friend over coffee. This is a talking-out-loud exercise, and you'll want to record yourself using your phone or computer. You'll probably find yourself stopping and restarting, and that's okay. Then transcribe the recording into a Word document, and let the editing begin.

As FAR AS the structure of your synopsis, you'll want to include major plot points in the following order:

- Introduction of your protagonist and their mindset/current world, addressing the five "W's. (Who/what/when/where/why).
- Reveal the inciting incident while emphasizing the protagonist's motivation. In *The Wizard of Oz*, Dorothy wants to get home to Kansas. The Wicked Witch of the West wants to stop her.
- Continue with the rising action or sequence of events that build tension until you reach the height of the action (also referred to as the crisis or climax), at which point the protagonist typically decides on a course of action or faces the truth.
- Conclude with the falling action (denouement), tying up loose ends to reach the final resolution, closing both plot and narrative arc.
- Restate the protagonist's motivation (Dorothy finds her way home).

Here are a few simple do's and don'ts:

DO: Introduce major characters in order of appearance.

DON'T: Get bogged down with sub-plots and secondary characters.

DO: Touch on the overarching theme of your novel without getting too deep into the weeds. Let's use *The Wizard of Oz* once again, which includes several underlying themes, each important to the story. However, if you were limited to one, either good versus evil or the power of friendship would work.

DON'T: Include dialogue. Remember you are relating the story in a factual manner.

DO: Touch on the genre/sub-genre of your book while making every word count, e.g., "a fast-paced political thriller" can be boiled down to "a political thriller" because, by definition, thrillers are fast-paced.

DON'T: Add unnecessary details. It doesn't matter if your character favors blue because it matches her eyes.

DO: Run your synopsis by one or two beta readers before sending it out.

DON'T: Ask rhetorical questions, e.g., "Calamity is faced with a decision. What would you do?"

Summing up 80,000 words into 800 or less can be a challenge, but don't let that intimidate you. It's all about taking it one step, and one version, at a time.

MANAGING SUBMISSIONS

There are subtle differences between Agent Submissions and Publisher Submissions, and tips that are applicable to both. Even if your preference is strongly skewed to one path or the other, don't let your personal bias or desire stop you from considering every angle.

AGENT SUBMISSIONS (#AR)

Start by compiling a master list of agents currently accepting submissions that meet your criteria (genre/sub-genre and word count). I like to use an Excel spreadsheet, but you may find it easier to use a Word document, or an online program, such as QueryTracker.net or PublishersMarketplace.com (but realize online resources will not have all agents/publishers in their databases).

It's also important to note that it's considered bad form to query two agents from the same agency, which makes sense. Would you send your CV to two managers at one company for the same position? Of course not.

Because this is your master list, it should include the names of thirty to fifty agents, ranked or sorted in the order of your preference. I know that sounds like a lot of names, but if you're already doing the homework, you may as well compile a list worthy of the effort. In fact, I'd encourage you to compile a separate list of agents/agencies you'd considered, but eliminated, with the reason for your decision. At the very least it will save you from retracing your steps.

Your master list should include the name of the agency, the agent's first and last name, website URL, and a brief note on their guidelines (first three chapters, first 50 pages, one-page synopsis, etc.). Additionally, you'll want a column for the date you sent your submission, date acknowledged (not all agents will acknowledge receipt), and a Y/N for their response.

If it's a no: Include any feedback, such as whether it was a form letter or a personalized rejection. Form letter rejections are easy to spot because they tend to be generic in the wording. A personalized rejection will include references to your novel and/or query letter. While a rejection will sting, any advice or suggestions offered can only serve to assist you going forward, and a positive comment or two can make it sting a little less. Resist the urge, however strong, to respond, unless, and *only* unless, the agent has invited any questions or comments. Instead, cross that agent off your list and move on to the next.

If it's a yes: Do a happy dance, then record the response for a full or partial manuscript and reply promptly with the requested material, submitted in the manner they request (font, spacing, etc.). Update your submission log accordingly. If they ask for an exclusive, refer to the query letter section that addresses this and follow the same process. If they don't ask for an exclusive, keep on querying. It can take several months to a year (or sometimes more) to hear anything back, and although you've cleared a massive hurdle, it still might be a rejection.

Now, you might be thinking: what if this is my dream agent, and another agent offers me a contract before I hear back? The good news is this provides a legitimate opportunity to follow up with Agent #1. Advise them that while they remain your top pick, you have received an offer from another agent, and would therefore request an update on the status of your submission. They should either bow out or jump in, though they may still be months away from a final decision. At that point, it's up to you to decide whether to go for a sure thing or hold out for the dream. As far as communicating with Agent #2, not only is it acceptable to ask for two weeks to review and consider the offer, it's expected and advisable. I'll cover contracts off in greater detail in Money Matters.

The prevailing wisdom is to send queries out in batches of six to eight. There's good reason for this—if your initial batch is met with some positive response, you've got the first step down. Conversely, if your first batch is rejected without a single request for additional material, and worse, only with form letter rejections, odds are your query letter is lacking. Rather than lament about what could have been, take the necessary time to review and revise your query, then get back out there with your second batch.

Should you resubmit your edited query to an agent you really want to work with? Some agents will consider a heavily overhauled query after rejection, but the odds are against you.

Which agents to send queries to first? If you're convinced your query letter is rock solid, why not start with your A list? If you're at all uncertain, or less of a gambler, consider starting with a mix of your A, B, and C-ranked agents. A positive response from any one of them will bolster your confidence, and if the entire batch is rejected, at least you haven't burned through every one of your top picks.

Last, but by no means least, agents earn their income from a percentage of your royalties, typically 15 to 20% of your earnings. They will never charge reading fees or a fee to represent you. If you receive an offer that requests either, run, don't walk, in the other direction (#AR).

PUBLISHER SUBMISSIONS

The first step is to compile a master list of publishers currently accepting unagented submissions that meet your criteria (genre/sub-genre and word count). Make sure to indicate the estimated size of the press (micro, small, medium, large). This can best be determined by their catalog and the number of authors they represent.

Once again, I'd encourage you to compile a separate list of publishers you've reviewed, but eliminated, with the reason for your decision. Additionally, your master list should include the name of the publisher, main contact, website URL, dates submitted/responded, with a place for additional notes, and a brief note about their guidelines and any open or closed reading periods (it's not unusual for publishers to establish date parameters for submissions).

Unlike agented submissions, independent publishers willing to look at unagented submissions often accept full manuscripts, sometimes using an online portal for uploading. Follow the instructions and wait. In the publishing world, patience is a much-needed virtue.

At this point you might be asking, "Where do I get the names of agents and publishers?" It's a fair question, and there are several ways to find names, starting with a simple internet search for "List of Literary Agents" or "List of Mystery Publishers." There's also Publishers Marketplace (#AR), a good starting place.

Additionally, many associations will maintain a list, some available to the public, and others as a members' only benefit (see The Write Life for more information on associations).

Magazines geared to writers are another good resource, many with online databases. Yet another is querytracker.net, an online search engine that offers free and premium (paid) services (#AR).

*Pro Tip: Authors often thank their agent and publisher in their acknowledgments. Check books in your genre for possible names.

And now it really is time to get down to business. It's time to turn the page and look at publishing paths in greater detail.

UNDERSTANDING YOUR OPTIONS

TRADITIONAL (TRADE BOOK) PUBLISHERS

A.K.A. THE BIG FIVE

THESE ARE the publishers most likely to be stocked at brick-and-mortar stores. That's because the Hachette Book Group, HarperCollins, Macmillan Publishers, Penguin Random House, and Simon & Schuster, or "Big Five," as they are collectively known in the biz, control roughly 80% of that market and account for approximately 90% of the titles on bestseller lists. That leaves 20% of the brick-and-mortar market (and 10% of bestseller lists) for independent, hybrid, and self-published authors combined. It's worth mentioning that the odds of self-published books finding space in a physical store are slim to none. If nothing else, these are statistics to remember going forward, if only to keep your expectations realistic.

The bottom line? The Big Five rule the book publishing world, and few unknown writers get past their very stringent gatekeeping. Of those who do, one in five will earn back their royalty advance.

A tough business, to be sure, and it's getting tougher.

There was a time when the "Big Five" were the "Big Six," and, most recently, they almost became the "Big Four."

Mergers and acquisitions have been altering the publishing landscape since the 1990s. They may not seem relevant to you as a writer, but the reality is fewer players erode the dwindling traditional publishing opportunities available for unknown authors.

In August 2022, Stephen King's disapproval over the proposed merger between Penguin Random House (PRH) and his own publisher, Simon & Schuster, led him to voluntarily testify for the U.S. government in an anti-trust trial aiming to stop the $2.18 billion merger. The lawsuit argued that the acquisition would create a publisher with too much influence over books and author payments. The planned merger was blocked by Judge Florence Pan of the United States district court for the District of Columbia on October 31, 2022.

A (Deeper) Dive into the Big Five

Each of the Big Five represent smaller publishers who in turn represent dozens more publishing interests, known as imprints. Here's a quick look at the current state of the market (#AR).

Hachette Book Group (HBG): Headquartered in New York City with offices in California, Colorado, Massachusetts, North Carolina, Oregon, Pennsylvania, Tennessee, as well as Hachette Book Group Canada, Inc., a marketing and publicity company based in Toronto, HBG publishes approximately 2,600+ books each year. Publishing groups include Grand Central Publishing, Hachette Audio, Hachette Nashville, Little, Brown and Company, Little, Brown Books for Young Readers, Orbit, Perseus Books, and Workman Publishing. A few dozen imprints fall under each of these groups. HBG works exclusively with literary agents, and will not consider or respond to unsolicited submissions, manuscripts, or queries.

HarperCollins: Headquartered in New York City, HarperCollins has publishing operations in seventeen countries and more than 120 branded imprints around the world, publishing approximately 10,000 new books every year in 16 languages, with a print and digital catalog of more than 200,000 titles.

MACMILLAN PUBLISHERS (MACMILLAN): A division of the Holtzbrinck Publishing Group, a large family-owned media company headquartered in Stuttgart, Germany, Macmillan is a global trade publishing company operating in more than 70 countries, with imprints in the United States, Germany, the United Kingdom, Australia, South Africa, and India. The company operates eight divisions in the United States: Celadon Books, Farrar, Straus and Giroux, Flatiron Books, Henry Holt and Company, Macmillan Audio, Macmillan Children's Publishing Group, St. Martin's Press, and Tor Publishing Group. None accept or respond to unsolicited manuscripts or queries.

PENGUIN RANDOM HOUSE (PRH): Headquartered in New York City with operations in more than 20 countries across six continents, Penguin Random House is home to about 275 international publishing imprints, annually publishing more than 70,000 digital and 15,000 print titles, with 100,000+ eBooks available worldwide. The PRH website offers advice on getting published, but it's nothing you don't already know. Find an agent. Be patient. Lather, rinse, repeat.

SIMON & SCHUSTER: Founded in 1924, Simon & Schuster is owned by ViacomCBS, which publishes such imprints as Atria, Scribner, and Simon & Schuster. With multiple bestselling authors to their credit, Simon & Schuster does not accept unagented submissions. They do, however, suggest that writers who want to pursue self-publishing check out Archway Publishing, a subsidiary of Simon & Schuster. Proceed with caution: Archway is outsourced to Author Solutions, a vanity press with several imprints.

DREAMING THE DREAM

Despite the almost insurmountable odds, thousands of aspiring authors share the dream. But dreaming isn't going to grab a top-notch agent's attention, and that's exactly what you'll need to land a Big Five contract. Beyond a fresh concept and killer manuscript, you'll need a combination of luck (right place, right time), dogged determination, and months, if not years, of concerted effort.

LUCK: My mother always told me, "The harder you work, the luckier you get." She wasn't right about everything, but she was right about that.

A FRESH CONCEPT: Not as easy as it sounds. To quote Mark Twain, "There is no such thing as a new idea. It is impossible. We simply take a lot of old ideas and put them into a sort of mental kaleidoscope. We give them a turn and they make new and curious combinations. We keep on turning and making new combinations indefinitely; but they are the same old pieces of colored glass that have been in use through all the ages." Twain aside, if you write with the view of cashing in on this year's hottest trend, remember that those books would have been acquired two to three years earlier. Chances are that market is already saturated, and the trend has started to spiral downward. (How many people thought they could write the next *Twilight* or *50 Shades of Grey?*)

DOGGED DETERMINATION: It's hard enough to land an agent, and not all agents are created equal. You want someone who can submit to and get an audience with a trad publisher. Publishing houses only work with agented authors, and those agents tend to be people they know and trust. Polish your manuscript, synopsis, and query letter until they shine, make your list of agents as recommended in Getting Down to Business, and start pitching with this in mind.

CONCERTED EFFORT: Kathryn Stockett spent five years writing *The Help*. It took another three years, numerous revisions, and a whopping 60 rejections before she landed an agent. That's a concerted effort. Writing your first draft during NaNoWriMo and sending it to ten agents on December 1st is not.

TIMELINES

The best agents will use their expertise to suggest edits to your manuscript and proposal *before* approaching publishers. This process takes time and there is no guarantee that your manuscript will be picked up by a publishing house. Even in the best-case scenario, submissions seldom lead to an offer right away. Manuscripts can take months, sometimes years, to find a publisher.

Let's say you are one of the lucky chosen few. Average advances (a royalty paid based on projected sales) for a new, unknown author vary widely. But with a traditional publisher you can optimistically expect an amount starting in the low thousands, and quite possibly more. Of course, a new author with name recognition (celebrities, sports legends, etc.) will earn upwards of $250,000, which might seem unfair unless you weigh the percentage (rather than the dollar amount) of financial risk taken by the publisher. I've gone into more detail on advances, royalties, and royalty structure in Money Matters.

Once the deal is sealed the publisher takes over, controlling and financing every step of the publishing process. This includes everything from editing and book design to distribution and promotion. I use the word controlling, instead of managing, because that is the reality. Expect to relinquish all rights: hardcover, trade paperback, mass market, digital, audio, foreign, film, etc. The characters you've created, the fictional world they might live in, will all belong to the publisher. Even a short story featuring your protagonist cannot be published elsewhere without their permission. In other words, the trad publisher literally controls the narrative, not only because they've paid you well for the privilege, but because they have a team of experts who are skilled at doing so. If you're the sort of person who needs frequent updates, wants to take an active role, or expects to approve every editorial change, a trad publisher is the wrong dance partner.

EXCEPTIONS TO THE RULE

While it's true that traditional publishing houses don't accept unagented submissions, some imprints or divisions within imprints might. The only way to find out is to check out the website for every imprint under a Big Five umbrella and start digging. Even if your search yields a potential publisher, you're still going to need patience. There may be periods when they are closed for submissions or limited-time mentorship programs for debut or underrepresented voices. Response times may be lengthy. Some may only respond if they are interested, and that interest could take upwards of a year—they're not in a rush to make your dreams come true.

As is the case with independent publishers, not all imprints make it for the long haul. You may or may not have heard of Random House's digital imprints Hydra (sci-fi, fantasy, horror) and Alibi (mystery/thriller), or their romance/women's fiction lines, Loveswept and Flirt. That's because they only lasted a few years before they were closed. Other imprints that may once have accepted unagented submissions, such as Macmillan's Farrar, Straus and Giroux, discontinued the practice because of the sheer volume of unsolicited manuscripts, proposals and query letters received daily.

But all is not lost. Heartdrum, an imprint of HarperCollins, self-described as a "Native-focused imprint of HarperCollins Children's Books," is open to submissions from unagented Native writers. Yen Press, a publisher of graphic novels, which Hachette co-owns with Kadokawa Corporation, does (or did at the time of publication) accept unagented queries. They also actively seek qualified Japanese and Korean translators for their Manga, Manhwa, and Light Novel books. Also under the HarperCollins umbrella is the Write for Harlequin website (#AR).

NO DEAL DOESN'T MEAN NO HOPE

By now you've accepted the reality that most unknown authors won't land a Big Five publishing contract, but that doesn't mean your book can't find a good home, and it doesn't mean your only option is to self-publish. There are many reputable independent publishers who offer traditional publishing paths on a smaller scale. Most don't require an agent. We'll take an in-depth look at your options, from micro to large press, next.

INDEPENDENT PUBLISHERS

MICRO, SMALL, MEDIUM, AND LARGE

LET'S FACE IT. Landing a deal from one of the few remaining traditional publishing houses is a bit like winning the lottery. You might get lucky, but odds are you'll play the same numbers for a decade and never win much more than a free ticket. Yet for many writers, true validation will only be achieved by signing a traditional publishing contract. The self-, hybrid-, or social-publishing routes are not for them. Somehow, those other options don't seem "worthy." It could be they just want their work to be considered, no matter how remote the chance, for an award or newspaper review from which self-published authors are still often excluded. Or maybe they just want to avoid the self-publishing stigma that still exists in many circles.

I get it. You want to be part of the club. I was one of those writers myself and I'm not ashamed to admit it. After all, knowing a publisher believes in you, and in your words? That's powerful stuff. And if my first indie publisher hadn't believed in me back in 2014, I honestly don't know where I'd be today. Maybe in the same place. Maybe not. I do know I will be forever grateful for how I got my start, even if "The End" wasn't exactly how I'd envisioned it.

Which brings me to the "independent" publisher, a segment of the book publishing market that has grown in leaps and bounds as Print on Demand (POD) has become not only more accessible, but the norm. Furthermore, independent publishers play an important and powerful role in today's publishing landscape.

Before we get too far ahead of ourselves, let's define the term "independent publisher" which, ironically, is not the same as "independently published." And, yes, I know what you're thinking: whoever coined these terms (along with "hybrid author" and "hybrid publisher") should have purchased a thesaurus. Alas, it's too late now.

So, back to our definitions, such as they are. An *independently published author* (also known as an "indie" author) is a fancy way of saying self-published. An *independent publisher* is independently owned and managed, not part of any larger publishing house and in no way associated with any of their smaller imprints.

But defining an indie publisher doesn't stop there, because if there's ever a case to be made for "one size does not fit (or in this case, define) all," this is it. You're about to learn the differences, from micro to large independent. But before we go there, a few words of caution: reputable publishers, no matter their size, never advertise looking for authors. With rare (and I do mean *rare*) exceptions, they will never contact you out of the blue, and certainly not with an ironclad offer of representation.

Sadly, there are any number of scams and scammers out there that have no hesitation in luring unsuspecting authors into their net (#AR). Before you sign with *any* independent publisher, research them online and get answers to these important questions:

- What sort of gatekeeping do they employ with submissions? This doesn't have to mean agented, but there should be a review process of some kind. If everyone who submits gets accepted, you are dealing with a vanity press, *not* an independent publisher.
- Is the website professionally designed and frequently updated? Does it promote authors and their books, or is

the focus on promoting the press and what they can do for authors? The first is a positive, the second a warning sign.

- How long has the company been in business? Who are the owners and/or staff members and what are their credentials? A well-intentioned mission statement isn't enough. For an example, read "Whatever Happened to Catstone Books?" on the Writer Beware website (#AR).

- Have any complaints been registered on sites such as Writer Beware? What about comments on Querytracker.net? Online in general? Here again, the internet is your friend.

- How many authors does the press represent? It never hurts to contact individual authors for their feedback. In my experience, most authors are upfront in this regard. Even those who are more cautious speak volumes if they decline to comment.

- How many books are in their catalog? None yet? Then tread with extreme caution. A handful? Are they older or recent releases? How often do they publish? Extended gaps in production may be an indicator of past or present financial difficulty. Select a handful of titles and check their reviews, rankings, and ratings on Amazon. Read the "look inside the book" excerpts to see what the editing is like and get a sense of the quality of the material. I always check Goodreads as well.

- Where are the books being distributed? Do they publish on retailers outside of Amazon (Barnes & Noble, Apple Books, Kobo, etc.)? If it's Amazon only, move on. You can do that yourself for half the cost and probably twice as well.

- Has the publisher been vetted by a writing association? For example, Mystery Writers of America has an Approved Publisher List (#AR), which requires a publisher to uphold professional standards of good business practice and fair treatment of their authors. NOTE: In this section, I'll be referring to contracts and royalty structures. Money Matters explains both in detail. Feel free to skip ahead and come back when you're ready.

Back already? Okay then, let's look at the options:

Micro Press

A micro press is typically a one- or two-person operation, often started as a way of self-publishing their own work(s). As a rule, there are no paid employees, which can mean:

- Editing, proofreading, interior page design, cover art, and accounting (preparation and payment of royalty statements) will either be done in-house by the principal(s) (owners) or farmed out on a work-for-hire basis.
- Quality and delivery of published materials will vary widely.
- Promotional support and budget will be minimal to non-existent.
- An advance on future royalties is unlikely.
- No Advance Reader Copies (ARCs).

Self-publishing takes hard work, commitment, business acumen, and a certain amount of cash flow. Operating a micro press increases those needs tenfold. While some micro publishers may "grow up" to become small presses, most, like the ill-fated mom-and-pop diner competing with the big money of restaurant chains, will fail within the first year. Eighty percent will shutter their doors within five. Because of that, you will want to ensure that any contract you sign has a straightforward, fair, and clearly defined reversion of rights clause in the event of insolvency or closing of the business. Even with that, know that the odds of recouping any royalties owed to you are remote if the micro press does close. Legal action is expensive, and chances are there would be no money in the coffers to pay you regardless.

Since the value-add of signing with a micro press is limited (truthfully nothing more than you can do yourself with a modicum of effort), your share of royalties earned should reflect that, e.g., an equal 50/50 split between publisher and author on net royalties for print and e-book. Additionally, do not give up any publishing rights where there is no reasonable expectation of the micro press following through, such as film, foreign, mass market, hardcover, or audiobook rights. You may be able to sell those rights elsewhere.

Warning: if you are asked to contribute towards any of the costs of production (as outlined in the first bullet point), you're not dealing with a micro publisher, but a hybrid publisher and possibly a vanity press.

The same holds true for marketing. Regardless of publication path, the bulk of advertising and promotion will undoubtedly fall on you, the author. This will be even more evident with a micro press who, by their very nature, are not flush with cash or marketing savvy. That said, advertising and promotional options should *never* be payable to the publisher from a fee-for-service menu, but rather to an independent and completely unrelated third party, e.g., social media ads, bookmarks, etc.

One final caveat: be watchful of contracts that require a bulk purchase of your books. POD publishers (which all micro presses use) can print as few as one copy of your book, or as many as you desire. At a bare minimum you should receive one free author copy in all digital formats, as well as print. Lastly, author copies, if you wish to order some for friends, family, or a book launch, should be discounted to 50% off the list price (plus shipping and tax). The press won't make money on those, but they won't lose money either. And isn't that what partnerships are supposed to be about?

Have I scared you off micro publishers yet? While it might seem that way, my intent is to apprise you of the potential pitfalls, of which there are many. But there are solid micro presses out there, too. My own imprint, Superior Shores Press, which I use to self-publish my books, also qualifies as a micro publisher for the multi-author Superior Shores Anthologies of mystery and suspense. Did the contributing authors take a chance on me, especially those who were featured in the first multi-author collection, *The Best Laid Plans: 21 Stories of Mystery & Suspense*? Without question.

To be fair, I paid the authors a flat fee per story, was transparent about the process, and had a solid reputation as an author adept at promotion. That said, solid or not (just like so many well-intentioned and passionate micro presses) I *am* and remain (by choice) a one-woman band. If I cease to publish, whether through death or desire, the music will simply stop playing.

Would I consider publishing books by individual authors? Not a chance. The anthologies were a labor of love. Publishing other authors? That's a full-time business, and burnout or disillusionment, probably within a couple of years, is virtually guaranteed.

Whether you choose to sign with a micro press is a decision only you can make. Like any business, they can grow, and you might be getting in on the ground floor of the next big thing. And just like the stock market, where early investors often reap the greatest rewards, every successful independent press had to start somewhere.

SMALL PRESS

Many of the cautions mentioned under micro press also apply to small press publishers, albeit to a lesser extent. Their roster of authors will be greater, the length of time in business longer. Even so, a massive author list, which may seem impressive, can also mean the publisher isn't very selective and/or is trying to grow the business too quickly. The latter isn't a factor if the press has the financial resources and staff to support and manage the growth.

How do you know if a small press is adequately funded and staffed? Checking the "About Us" section is a start, but the truth is there's probably no real way for you to find out beyond taking the precautionary steps we've already talked about.

Once you've done your research and feel adequately reassured, it's time to focus on the benefits of a small press, not the least of which is providing opportunities for unagented authors seeking traditional publication. That's not to say that small presses won't accept agented submissions. Some will, some won't.

In addition to providing all the services outlined in the first bullet point, a small press should provide digital ARCs (print ARCs are unlikely) at least four months prior to the release date, though it may be up to you to find reviewers to send copies to. That said, some small presses will ask their other authors to "blurb" an upcoming release (praise for a book included inside or on the cover).

The time from your book's acceptance to publication varies but is almost always less than that of a larger press, and often less than a year. This is both good and bad. Good in that you aren't waiting in the wings wondering if your book will sell. Bad, because a tight timeline can mean less time to get reviews. It can also mean a rushed editing and proofreading process. Long production times don't necessarily equal improved quality, but any deadline of six months or less, and something is going to give. If that's what you're being offered, question the publication process before signing.

A small press should also share a galley proof (a preliminary, formatted version of your soon-to-be-published novel). Galley proofs are meant for the author, editor, and proofreader to review a book on a chapter-by-chapter basis, and either approve or suggest changes. I've been previously published by two small presses. One required me to participate in the galley proof review. The other did not allow their authors the opportunity to collaborate, preferring to fast track the editing and proofreading process, often with less than desirable results. Suffice it to say I would never again agree to be excluded from the galley proof process, and nor should you. After all, it's your name on the cover. You should have a say in the final product.

When it comes to advertising and promotion, a small press offers minimal support—even though they stand to benefit from every dollar you as the author invests independently towards an ad campaign, a fact that I'll readily admit annoyed me when I was a published by a small press; surely if they reap the royalty rewards, they should contribute their fair share? Not so, I'm afraid, though maybe such a policy will one day become an industry standard.

It's not all doom and gloom, however. Small press publishers worth their salt will hold book sales (where titles in their catalog are discounted for a limited period) one or more times each year. These sales arc typically based around the publisher's anniversary or another special occasion or holiday. When accompanied with publisher-prepared artwork, these book sales are an easy way for authors to promote their work on social media with a new hook at no cost (beyond reduced royalties on discounted sales).

Which brings us to royalties.

Small press publishers typically pay royalties based on net receipts (also known as net sales). Based on one of this reporting format, royalties should be in the 30 to 50% range, reported and paid on a quarterly or semi-annual basis, with an expectation of lower royalties for print, and higher for digital.

MEDIUM PRESS

The closest thing to a large independent, the medium press publisher tends to favor agented submissions, though there are ways for an unagented author to find another way into the fold.

One of the best ways is to have a prior business relationship, and by that I don't mean a novel, but rather a short story or stories included in anthologies published by the press. Many medium presses publish multi-author collections, either for their own imprint, or on behalf of a conference, convention, or charitable initiative. For example, Bouchercon, an annual mystery convention, releases a multi-author anthology in conjunction with their event, as does Malice Domestic, another annual mystery convention. Both anthologies are published by independent presses. (More on Conferences and Conventions in The Write Life.)

Another "in" is to have written exactly what their submission wish list is currently looking for. If that's the case, you'll want to ensure your query letter drives that point home. You'll also want to include a brief, but solid, marketing plan, and any other information which will tell them you're the real deal. Refer to Query Letters in Getting Down to Business.

Medium press independents typically pay royalties in the same way as their small press counterparts, on net receipts with the percentage (royalty rate) paid varying by publisher and often by author. In general, the larger the press, the stronger the sales and marketing support, the higher the advance, and the more units (books) you will sell. With that comes the likelihood of a lower royalty rate than you might receive from a smaller press.

LARGE INDEPENDENT

The closest thing to a contract with a traditional "big five" publishing house, most large independent publishers accept unagented submissions, though agented submissions will always take preference. Getting a referral from one of their published authors, while helpful with any publisher you approach, is especially valuable when the stakes are higher. It might even move your submission up from the slush pile to the "soon to be read" pile.

There is also a harsh reality (don't shoot the messenger): the larger the press, the more submissions they are likely to receive from other hopefuls—hundreds, if not thousands, every year.

Let's be conservative and guess that's one submission a day. Even the largest of the large independents can't publish 365 titles in a year. Because of that (and not necessarily because of the quality of your submission) the odds of rejection intensify tenfold. Most will take it one step further, adding a disclaimer on their website. Here are a couple of actual examples:

> "We receive hundreds of submissions each year, please allow six months for a response. If you do not receive a response within six months, you can assume that the submission has been rejected. Please no phone calls or follow up emails."

"Please allow at least three months for a response. Please do not call our office. If you do not hear back, assume your project doesn't fit our current editorial needs."

In other words, don't call us, we'll call you. Maybe.

Discouraging? It can be. But understanding the business is the first step in setting you apart from the rest.

HYBRID/ASSISTED PUBLISHING

I KNOW several authors who had their pick of publishing path options and chose to go the assisted publishing route. One was even shortlisted for a prestigious "Best Unpublished" manuscript award. She has since gone on to win (and be shortlisted) for numerous North American awards for her hybrid-published historical novel. Another is a well-known book reviewer with a hefty number of "industry in's," should he have elected to play that card. Last, but by no means least, is a talented author I met at a library event when I was first starting out. He believed in his book but accepted that wanting a fast track to publication, along with the demands of a growing family and a full-time job, would eliminate the possibility of traditional paths or self-publishing.

For each of these authors, going this route was *their* best path to publication...with one caveat. They all did their due diligence before signing with a hybrid publisher.

The Award Winner mentioned above compiled a list of her own expectations and determined her "top pick." She then reached out to a handful of authors who had used their services and asked for the unvarnished truth. It helped that, in addition to reading their books, she'd developed a relationship with these authors through writing associations and social media connections. There's no reason you can't apply the same strategy.

The Reviewer routinely receives hundreds of books every year, in the hope that he will write a favorable review. He made a note of every publisher, doing his own homework. He knew he wanted to self-publish. He also knew he didn't want to do the grunt work. One hybrid publisher stood out for consistent quality, and that's the one he selected for his own debut novel.

What all three authors knew, and what I can't stress enough, is the need to proceed with extreme caution. For every legitimate hybrid publisher out there, there are more with the wrong intentions and a polished website. An easy "yes" should never be your benchmark. Trust your intuition when it comes to red flags and, if unsure, ask. There are plenty of forums, including social media, where you can check in with other writers if something seems too good to be true (we talked about that, remember?). And that brings us to the vanity press.

VANITY PRESS A.K.A. THE DREAM STEALERS

Here's a heads up: Vanity press publishers often *look* legitimate, with slick websites and promises of TV and radio ads, social media prowess, bogus testimonials, and so much more. Sometimes they even look more legit than legit publishers. Regardless of their online persona, they will never use the term "vanity" to describe their services, though they will use the term "hybrid publisher" liberally, which can entice the unwitting and uninformed.

Sadly, the claims of a vanity press will be greatly exaggerated and, in most cases, outright fabrications. Their desire to part you from your hard-earned money without any thought or care for you as the author, all while doing virtually nothing to earn their exorbitant fees, is the stuff of legends—in the worst way. That's why I call vanity press operators dream stealers. Because that's exactly what they're doing. Stealing your dreams.

Do *not* let them steal yours.

FINDING THE REAL DEAL

How will you differentiate between a vanity press and a legitimate hybrid publisher?

A legitimate hybrid publisher offers the five fundamentals of trade publishing and self-publishing: editing, proofreading, book design, cover art, and uploading to retail, while adhering to the same industry standards and attention to quality as their traditional counterparts.

While there are ethical and reputable hybrid publishers, there are more bad actors in this arena than well-intentioned companies. Doing your research cannot be overstated!

Even those that mean well might charge premium prices for the services provided, well above the cost you would incur with self-publishing. Let's take book distribution as an example. If you opt to self-publish, you will be responsible for uploading your book to the various retailers, such as Amazon (KDP), Barnes & Noble (Nook), Rakuten KOBO (Kobo), etc., or through an aggregator like Draft2Digital. There's no charge to do this, beyond the time you invest in the process.

But time is money, and it would be unrealistic to expect free book distribution under a hybrid publishing model. Some offer fee-based book distribution packages. Others include book distribution as part of their overall publishing package but make no mistake: included does not mean free. The same can be said for every service provided, from editing to book design and beyond. It's a bit like hiring a professional renovator. The renovator supplies the materials needed—drywall, two-by-fours, paint, etc.—but there will be a markup on the materials, as well as a cost per hour to do the work.

The bottom line? Carefully vetted, hybrid/assisted publishing can be a viable, albeit more expensive, option for those who want greater control of their publishing path without doing all the heavy lifting. That said, there are no guarantees that you will earn back your investment, and few authors will. This isn't a reflection on the hybrid publisher model, either; even traditional publishers lose money on four out of five authors signed. That's just the nature of the business.

FINDING THE RIGHT HYBRID FIT

Let's start by stating two facts: no matter how it's presented, this isn't a partnership—it's a business arrangement. They are the business. You are the client. They are *assisting* you in your path to publication.

It's important to differentiate between a hybrid publisher and a print on demand (POD) publisher. The latter does not offer in-house editorial services before sending it out into the world, they are simply the conduit to publishing your pre-formatted manuscript to retail in print and/or e-book format. For more on POD publishers, see the Self-publishing section.

When searching for a hybrid publisher, start with the Independent Book Publishers Association's (IBPA's) *Hybrid Publisher Criteria*, available for free download (#AR).

The Association's first point, that a hybrid publisher must "define a mission and vision for its publishing program," while important, should not be relied on too heavily. After all, even the worst vanity presses (or perhaps, especially the worst) offer this, often quite convincingly.

Here are a few other areas worth consideration:

TRANSPARENCY: From the editing and design to retail uploads and royalty payments, the publisher's website should be transparent about cost and services offered. Ideally, there will be a sample contract online or made available upon request. (Contract terms and review options are covered in Money Matters.)

REPUTATION: By reputation, I don't mean online testimonials. While some may be legit, they can easily be faked and, let's face it, no company is going to post negative reviews on their website. Instead, visit sites that expose fraudulent publishers and/or rate legitimate ones. Two excellent resources are The Alliance of Independent

Authors' (ALLi's) *The Best Self-Publishing Services (And the Worst)* and Writer Beware by Victoria Strauss (#AR).

CATALOG: This should be online, broken down by category, and easily accessible. Have you heard of any of their authors in your genre? Does the publisher seem to specialize? If so, does that specialty align with yours? Taking the research one step further, consider selecting a half-dozen or more names and titles in the catalog and checking the Amazon and Goodreads reader reviews and ratings. Don't be put off by the occasional 1-star rating; reading is subjective. I'd even go so far as to suggest disregarding any 1-star rating that doesn't include a review citing the reason for it. Instead, look at the number of ratings (an indicator of sales) and overall average rating (an indicator of quality). Take the time to read the reviews; it's there where you might find reader comments about editing or other quality issues.

MANUSCRIPT EVALUATION: An unbiased review of your novel's strengths and weaknesses prior to accepting your book for publication. The gatekeeping won't be as strict as that of a traditional publisher, but there will be a general commitment to quality. Manuscripts determined to require additional editing will usually be offered alternate options. These may include a referral to onsite editing or an affiliate partner, or a referral to recommended freelance editors. If this happens to you, take a moment or two to wallow, and then be grateful for their candor. A vanity press would have accepted your not-quite-ready-yet work without question.

PROFESSIONAL EDITING SERVICES: Your options should include developmental, copy, and content editing, as well as proofreading. Some hybrid publishers offer a pay-per-service model. Others offer an all-inclusive publishing package that excludes editing but includes a final proofread. If you've gotten past the gatekeeper stage, a final proofread might be enough. That said, additional coaching or editing services may be suggested, and in some cases required, by the publisher before moving to the publishing stage. Before you dismiss the advice, however difficult it may be to hear, remember this: a vanity press won't care, a legitimate hybrid publisher will. Don't let your ego get in the way of putting your best book forward.

COPYRIGHT: Always remains with the author. Don't confuse copyright with publishing rights, which is what you, the author, assign to a publisher to publish your novel. Refer back to understanding copyright in Getting Down to Business.

DESIGN SERVICES: Professional cover art (e-book and print) and interior book layout. Check out covers from the publisher's online bookstore, paying special attention to those in your genre. Are they innovative and eye-catching? Or uninspired and unremarkable? Note: some hybrid publishers will allow you to supply your own hi-resolution artwork or photography. Don't be afraid to inquire about options if that's something that interests you.

PUBLISHING PROTOCOL: Legit hybrids use their own ISBNs (International Standard Book Number) and imprint(s) for publishing. They will never use "free" ISBNs assigned through any book retailer and there should be no expectation for you to supply your own. I've included more on ISBNs in the Self-publishing section.

RETAIL DISTRIBUTION: The publisher must be able to upload to retail in print and e-book formats. Some publishers have an upload fee per retailer, others have a flat rate. Both are a cash grab since they are going to make a percentage off every book you sell. Before you sign on the dotted line, take the time to see what current retail royalty rates are for each individual bookseller and compare that with what the publisher is offering. You may also be encouraged to purchase book return insurance for print copies. While returns can be expensive (see Understanding Royalties in Money Matters), book return insurance will likely be even more expensive. After all, hybrid publishers are not in the business of losing money.

Author Copies: IBPA's *Hybrid Publisher Criteria* says it best: "If an author is asked to subsidize *or* pay for the full cost of print runs, they should own the physical copies outright and should therefore not be required to pay a 'percent off-list price' amount when ordering copies." While IBPA doesn't specifically address Advanced Reader Copies (ARCs), the same rules should apply. Do not hesitate to ask how ARCs and author copies are handled. You have a right to know, and to understand.

Royalties: Must be completely transparent on the publisher's website and clearly defined in your contract. Further, because you are paying for publishing services, royalties should be significantly higher than what you would be paid by a traditional or independent publisher, who incur the cost of editorial, design, production, etc. There should also be an increased royalty rate for any publisher-operated bookstore purchases, though few sales will be generated from this source. More information on royalties can be found under Traditional Publishing and Independent Publishing in this section, as well as in Understanding Royalties in Money Matters.

Support: It goes without saying that there will be support before you sign with a publisher (and likely no end to friendly conversation), but what about after the fact? How and who will you contact if you have a question or concern during the publishing process?

While there are many positives to this path, one consistent negative associated with hybrid publishers are the high-pressure sales tactics, especially when it comes to marketing and promotion. You will be told that getting your book noticed will be difficult, and that's true.

You'll also be told you need a targeted marketing campaign—also true, regardless of path—but they will "help" you with a plethora of ways to spend your money. Let's look at some possible examples:

BOOK CATALOG: Your book listed in the publisher's latest catalog, possibly even a coveted cover spot, might sound like a great opportunity, but at what cost? Be wary of hype promising bestseller status or undefined distribution numbers, and *always* ask for statistics. How many digital downloads per month on average? What's the click-through rate on individual titles? How many of those clicks result in a direct sale? How, what, and where are print copies distributed? Those statistics should be available, and you have a right to know the answers.

PRESS RELEASES: A pre-packaged statement about your book and all pertinent details, distributed to relevant newspapers and magazines. It should include anything unique about the story or you as an author as a hook to entice the outlet to include it in their limited space. Sometimes outlets will run the release exactly as-is, and on rare occasions they will contact you for an interview to do an expanded story with a different angle. If picked up for publication, it can be great free exposure to a wide audience. However, there are never any guarantees that a press release—even one you paid for—will get any further than languishing in an editor's inbox. (For more on this, see Money Matters: Advertising and Promotion.)

VIDEO BOOK TRAILERS: If you're hopeless with creating videos, this may be a worthwhile investment, but it wouldn't hurt to do some comparison shopping. There are a lot of talented people out there offering comparable, and possibly better, rates. You'll also need to think of how and where you'll promote the book trailer.

LAUNCH PARTIES: This is another area to do some comparison shopping. Many blog tour companies also specialize in virtual launch parties.

One final caveat: unless you have unlimited funds, most of the advertising and promotion will fall on your shoulders. Make sure you have enough time to successfully market your book, and you're planning ahead to keep track of all the moving pieces.

An assisted publishing route should mean exactly that: assistance with your path to publication. At a minimum, signing with a hybrid publisher should offer an expectation of professional editing and design services, publishing to recognized industry standards, effortless print and digital retail distribution, and higher than industry average royalties. As for the optional add-ons, preparing a cost-benefit analysis of each one is a good place to begin (#AR).

SELF-PUBLISHING

IF YOU ARE an organized individual who wants control over every aspect of your writing journey, from inception to publication to publicity and beyond, self-publishing may be a good option for you. However, if you think self-publishing is a fast, easy, and inexpensive way to get your book to market, think again. Yes, the costs associated with getting your book out there will be considerably less than what you would incur with a hybrid publisher, but that doesn't mean there aren't expenses. Remember, in this role you are no longer the author, you are the PUBLISHER, which means accepting financial responsibility as well as complete accountability for the quality of the book. After all, it's your name on the cover and, ultimately, your reputation.

But back to the expenses. At a bare minimum you will have paid for professional editing (do not, I repeat do NOT, skip this step), proofreading (ditto), and, unless you're a gifted graphic artist, cover art. There are also the interior design elements of the manuscript required for retail and wholesale upload. While I encourage you to learn to format your books yourself, you will need to purchase formatting software (#AR). You'll also need a unique ISBN for each format of your book (e-book, hardcover, trade paperback, mass market). (More on formatting and ISBNs will follow later in this section, under BOOK BASICS.)

There's also going to be a learning curve. Not to mention ongoing advertising and promotion. All of that is going to take not just money, but many, many hours of your time.

Will you recoup your investment? According to WordsRated (#AR), a non-commercial, international research data and analytics group, the numbers look like this:

- 300 million self-published books are sold each year.
- The average self-published book sells 250 copies.
- The average self-published author makes $1,000 per year from their books.
- 33% of self-published authors make less than $500 per year.
- 90% of self-published books sell less than 100 copies.
- 20% of self-published authors report making no income from their books.

On the plus side, the same study reports that:

- More than 1,000 self-published authors made $100,000 last year from Amazon.

Of authors who have published their first book in the last 10 years:

- 1,200 traditionally published authors have earned $25,000+ a year.
- 1,600 self-published authors have earned $25,000+ a year.

I'm not trying to talk you out of it. Self-publishing can be a rewarding and personally enriching experience, one that I've embraced and benefitted from. That said, I'm not buying a chateau in France any time soon.

There's also the stigma that still exists when it comes to self-published work. There are some conferences that won't offer panel spots to indie authors. Likewise, some writing awards exclude self-published work. That said, many conferences and awards now treat indie and traditionally published authors with equal respect, and acceptance in the market continues to grow.

Can self-publishing books hit number 1 on Amazon and other retailers? Absolutely, and in multiple categories, though I know firsthand that, bragging rights aside, the achievement is by no means default entry into a celebrity book club endorsement or a movie deal.

Can self-publishing be a stepping stone to movie deals or signing with one of the Big Five? The answer is yes, though fair warning: they are a far cry from an everyday occurrence. Two well-known examples are *Still Alice* by Lisa Genova and *50 Shades of Grey* by E.L. James.

But we're getting ahead of ourselves. Before any of those scenarios can happen, you're going to have to do the work.

BUSINESS BASICS

I've titled this section Business Basics because that's exactly what self-publishing is, a business. *Your* business. While you can list the publisher of your book as your name, e.g., Judy Penz Sheluk, I strongly encourage you to set up a publishing imprint, which adds a layer of professionalism to your product (and yes, your book is a product). For example, my publishing imprint is registered as Judy Penz Sheluk (Sole Proprietor) DBA (doing business as) Superior Shores Press, which is renewable for a fee every five years. On the copyright page of all my books, the publisher is listed as "Superior Shores Press, copyright © (year) Judy Penz Sheluk."

When selecting a name, you'll need to do a search to ensure the name isn't already registered, and it shouldn't be part (or all of) your name, e.g., Judy Penz Sheluk Press. Starting an online search which will help narrow the possibilities, and both Google and Amazon are good entry points for this. But you'll also need to search national trademark name databases to make sure the name you finally decide on isn't legally registered to someone else (#AR). Once you've registered your name, you may want to go the extra mile and have a logo developed, either by the same person you'll hire for your cover art, or a logo designer. (A quick online search will provide plenty of options.)

Because rules and regulations for small business vary by country, as well as state/province, consult with an accountant who can provide guidance with setting up a publishing imprint and provide advice on registration, tax implications and requirements, and acceptable business write-offs. Note I said "guidance with" versus "can set up a" publishing imprint, because it's usually fairly straightforward to register a business. You'll have enough expenses going forward, no point paying an accountant their hourly rate PLUS the business registration fee.

You'll also need to set up a separate bank account with checking privileges, as well as a solid record-keeping system for income and expenses. The latter is something you've probably already thought about, but what you may not have realized is that income tax slips may not be provided for royalty income. The same holds true for grant programs and contest winnings. Despite that, you are required to declare that income at tax time, in the same way you would as a freelance writer or consultant. Of course, your accountant should have already told you that. If they didn't, find another accountant.

Because the United States and Canada have a reciprocal income tax agreement, each U.S.-based retailer will require Canadian authors to complete a W-8 BEN form (#AR) to certify that your country of residence for tax purposes is in Canada, and that you agree to abide by Canadian tax laws for any royalties earned. In return, you won't have a portion of those royalties withheld to pay U.S. taxes, and you won't need to file a U.S. tax return. Seriously, who wants to pay income tax to two countries?

Book Basics

I've structured this sub-section in the order I'd suggest taking care of things, rather than alphabetically (though it's not a hard and fast rule).

I've covered copyright basics earlier, but to recap: technically, you own the copyright the minute your work exists, which means you are not required to file (and pay a fee) for copyright protection. Personally, I recommend filing the paperwork, at least for novel-length material, if for no other reason than peace of mind, but the decision is yours to make.

You will also need a copyright page which includes your disclaimer, e.g., "This is a work of fiction," copyright year/name, publisher, editor, proofreader, cover artist, edition number, and ISBNs. Easiest way to figure this out? Open a few books, review the disclaimers, and take it from there (#AR).

Author Bio & Photo

Your bio (#AR) should be written in third person, be 100 words or less, no more than two paragraphs, and keep it relevant. Even if your book is science fiction, this is not the time to mention that you're a Trekkie. If you've written a legal thriller and you're a lawyer or a paralegal, that's relevant. You should also have a professional author photo taken to include with your bio.

ISBNs

An International Standard Book Number (ISBN), the barcode at the back of a book, is a unique number assigned to each version of a book. In Canada, ISBNs are free (#AR). In the U.S. ISBNs must be purchased through the Bowker Agency (#AR), the only official source of ISBNs in the United States. Because part of the ISBN coding identifies the publisher of record, traditional, independent, and hybrid publishers should supply the ISBN. Self-published authors will need to obtain (in Canada) or purchase (in the U.S.) ISBNs under the name of their publishing imprint. Note: The International Book Publishers Association (IBPA) offers a member discount on Bowker purchases.

Once you get to the book upload stage, you'll discover that many retailers, including Kindle Direct Publishing, Barnes & Noble Press, and some Print on Demand (POD) services will provide a "free" ISBN. The catch? You can't use that ISBN with any other publisher. You'll also need to list the issuer of the free ISBN as the publisher, and not your publishing imprint. Not exactly sounding free anymore, is it?

FORMATTING

As an author, you've learned to properly format a manuscript, but readers aren't going to purchase your Word document. They'll be buying your e-book, or a printed paperback or hardcover copy. Because of that, you'll need to have your book formatted before uploading it for sale. There are three ways to do that:

1. Reformat your Word document to meet specific conversion requirements. Kobo Writing Life has an excellent tutorial on how to do this, but writer be warned: this option is far from simple (#AR). Draft2Digital also offers free formatting, and they will allow you to use the formatted files on other platforms (#AR).
2. Purchase formatting software. Be sure you select one that will allow you to format an unlimited number of books (always think ahead, never restrict your options!) for *multiple* retailers, in print and digital versions. There should be an option to upload sample material or an offer of a free trial period. I stress the word multiple because a "free" formatting option will probably restrict where you can sell your book. Examples of formatting

software include Atticus, Vellum, Adobe InDesign, and Scrivener (#AR).

3. Hire a book formatting service. A good option for the tech-averse, though the cost to do this will probably be as much as or more than purchasing your own software, especially if you plan to publish additional books (#AR).

ARCs (Advance Reader Copies)

Unless you have already uploaded your book to retail, you won't be able to supply print ARCs, but once you've formatted your book, you should have digital copies (PDF, EPUB, and MOBI versions) to email to reviewers.

Advance reviews are used for "blurbs" on the back cover and inside as "praise for" (you see this a lot in e-books since they don't have a back cover). You may also choose to include a blurb on the front cover.

*Pro Tip: It's okay to take a snippet of a longer review and use it as a blurb.

If you've been networking through writing associations, conferences, or conventions, you may have an author or two willing to blurb your book. You can also try your local paper, though the reality is fewer and fewer newspapers offer book reviews, and most won't even consider self-published novels. You may have better luck with a small community paper; this is discussed in more detail in Money Matters: Advertising and Promotion.

There are also review sites which charge a fee, such as Kirkus Reviews and Midwest Book Reviews though, in the interest of their reputations, neither can guarantee a positive review (#AR).

Finding "known" authors or experts to blurb your book can be a challenge. Improve your odds by allowing six to eight weeks for the blurb. It's perfectly okay if it's still in the final editing/proofreading stage. Minor mistakes are expected in an ARC. It's even okay if all you have is a temporary placeholder as the cover. Just be sure the cover of your ARC is clearly marked as ADVANCE READER COPY – Uncorrected Author Proof, Not for Resale — and that the same wording is used on the copyright page.

Ideally, you'll have two or three blurbs, but worst-case scenario, you can always publish without any. Don't let a lack of reviews become an excuse to give up.

Cover Art

We're not supposed to judge a book by its cover, but let's face it, we do, and good covers help sell books. Period.

Let's look at the nitty gritty. Print templates are available at no cost from your POD publisher. Each publisher uses a different template and has different rules, but the templates are based on the size of your book, paper, and page count. You will need to include an ISBN. Because you may want to change the retail price of your book in the future, never include the price on the cover.

Ideal e-book covers have a height/width ratio of 1.6:1, with 1,600 x 2,650 pixels as the optimum size, created as a jpeg or TIFF file.

When it comes to cover design, you have two options:

1. Hire a professional graphic artist who specializes in print and e-book covers. Be sure this is treated as work-for-hire and that you own the copyright to the artwork. Some writing associations offer discounts and/or recommendations for this service. Always credit the artist on the copyright page.

2. Do it yourself. Unless you're a graphic artist, this can be tricky. Yes, there are inexpensive online options (Canva comes to mind) which may be helpful for e-book covers, but that won't help you when it comes to POD templates. You can also use free templates from KDP, but that will restrict you to using that cover only on Amazon. In both cases, you will need to own the copyright to any images you use or purchase a license to use them.

Jacket Copy / Retail Blurb / Back of Book Blurb

The sales pitch, also known as the jacket copy, back of the book blurb, or retail blurb, is the one thing you really need to get right, so take your time with it. What is it you want the reader to know? What is it you want to tease? What's the message you want them to take away? Remember, no spoilers (which means you cannot include some clever diddy you wrote in chapter 19). Unlike beta readers, the more input you can get on this, the better, and test-driving different versions can be a fun way to interact with potential readers on social media, all while drumming up interest in your soon-to-be released book.

Retail Basics

Direct to Consumer

As a self-published author, you have three main ways of selling your books direct to consumer:

1. On your website: You will need to set up an e-Commerce platform. Unless you're tech-savvy, it will mean hiring someone to manage this for you. You'll also be responsible for delivery, customer service questions (can't open file, package not received, etc.) If you choose to do this, do it in conjunction with one or more of the other online sales options.
2. At a market, book launch, library event, or other in-person venue: If you're the outgoing sort who loves to meet and mingle with readers, these can be fun while providing good networking opportunities, but in my experience, they are seldom lucrative.
3. On consignment: Arts councils, independent bookstores (including used bookstores), and local businesses will often accept books on consignment; some offer "Meet the Author" days. Since margins on print books are slim,

and consignment fees range from 20% to 40%, this is not the road to riches, though it can help you gain recognition in your community and, in turn, help to build a loyal following.

AGGREGATORS, RETAILERS & DISTRIBUTORS

You have your final formatted files and cover art and are ready to get your book in the market. You now have two options: put it on pre-order or publish immediately. For established authors or those with lots of advertising cash, pre-orders can be a way to generate buzz for an upcoming book. Big Five publishers in particular use pre-orders very effectively as a marketing tool.

For first-time authors who haven't built up a huge following—or advertising budget—there's no real benefit in holding off. Even readers who are interested in a book often won't pre-order, preferring instead to wait until release date. That said, there's no right or wrong approach, and the length of the pre-order period can be weeks or months, during which time you can upload new files if necessary. Because pre-orders aren't sales, you won't be paid royalties and, apart from a social platform like Goodreads, books cannot be reviewed or rated prior to release.

There are three main avenues to get your book out there. For each option, you will have an opportunity to review your book as it will be seen on the various platforms before approving for sale.

AGGREGATORS

An aggregator is a one-stop online distributor that will list your book with several online booksellers, as well as library and subscription services. An excellent example of this is Draft2Digital (D2D) (#AR), whose digital storefronts (D2D's term for retailers and subscription services) include Amazon, Apple Books, Baker & Taylor, Barnes & Noble, bibliotheca, BorrowBox, Hoopla, Kobo, Overdrive, Palace Marketplace, Scribd, Smashwords, Tolino, and Vivlio.

While D2D may be the easiest option for e-book distribution, at minimum, I'd recommend setting up a direct account with Kindle Direct Publishing (KDP for Amazon), as well as two or more of the more popular e-book retailers in the U.S. and Canada (see Online Retailers, next).

Setting up a Draft2Digital account is free, though you'll need to provide banking information, tax ID, etc. Once you've done that you can upload your book (at no charge) and select the digital storefronts you want them to distribute on your behalf. Any royalties will be paid directly to D2D by each individual storefront. In turn, D2D will coordinate those reports and submit one combined monthly royalty statement and payment to you. Their cut is approximately 10%. I've covered royalties in some detail in Money Matters.

Additional information can be found on the D2D website, and I've personally found their customer service to be excellent. Another nice feature is their Universal Book Link option through Books2Read (#AR), where you can create (and custom name) one link for multiple storefronts. Here's an example for my Glass Dolphin Mystery Series box set: https://books2read.com/GlassDolphin.

ONLINE RETAILERS

As with D2D, there is no charge to set up individual accounts or upload book content because the storefronts earn a portion of your royalties. The main e-book retailers (also known as storefronts or digital storefronts) in the U.S. and Canada are: Amazon (KDP), Google Play (Google Play Partner Center), Kobo (Rakuten Kobo), Barnes & Noble (B&N Press), and Apple (iTunes Connect). Each of these retailers have different royalty rates and payment terms, defined on their websites (#AR). There is usually a minimum payment threshold (anywhere from $10 to $50). If it's too overwhelming for you in the beginning, I'd suggest D2D for all but KDP, which also offers a Print on Demand (POD) option.

PRINT ON DEMAND (POD) WHOLESALE DISTRIBUTORS

As a self-published author, Print on Demand (POD) wholesale distributors are your only option when it comes to printing and distributing your book. The term "on demand" also means just that. Your book will be listed as available online and in catalogs but will not be printed until one (or more) copies of your book are ordered. Note: a POD publisher only sells direct to qualifying businesses and institutions, such as bookstores, libraries, and other retailers. They do not sell to consumers, though as an account holder you are able to order author copies at a discounted cost.

While D2D has recently included POD publishing to their service offerings, IngramSpark (#AR) is probably the best-known POD publisher for wholesale global distribution of print books to libraries and brick-and-mortar bookstores. Though account set-up is free, there is a charge to upload your book's interior and cover, as well as a cost if you want to revise either after you've uploaded and approved.

Pro Tip: Some associations, like the Independent Book Publishers Association (IBPA), offer a limited number of free IngramSpark codes. I encourage you to check out the member benefits of writing associations you might consider joining before uploading to Ingram.

Although you can use IngramSpark for e-books as well as POD, their longer-than-industry-average payment terms (90 days) and lower royalty rates (40%) make this a less attractive option than D2D or going direct.

While IngramSpark will supply books to Amazon, you can also use KDP's print option for paperback copies to be sold exclusively on Amazon (you would use the same ISBN as you'd use for IngramSpark).

KDP also offers an "Expanded Distribution" option, however many libraries won't order from Amazon, and bookstores are unlikely to order from their competition. Because KDP, Ingram, and

D2D all use the same distribution channels, do not use the Expanded Distribution option if you are using another POD distributor.

KEYWORDS & CATEGORIES

Regardless of where you upload your book, you'll be asked for keywords, usually limited to seven words or a certain number of characters. Note that a keyword can also be a phrase, e.g., antiques shop mystery. The idea is to think of words or phrases that will lead readers to your book when doing an online search. An excellent article, *How to Select Keywords for Your Book* can be found on Babelcube.com (#AR).

You will also be required to select categories for your book. Each retailer operates a bit differently, but you'll be asked to pick a primary subject heading and one to three sub-categories. The basis for the subject heading and categories is derived from Book Industry Standards and Communications (BISAC) codes. For example, the primary subject for this book is LANGUAGE ARTS & DISCIPLINES and the sub-categories are LANGUAGE ARTS & DISCIPLINES / Publishers & Publishing Industry (BISAC code LAN-027000) and LANGUAGE ARTS & DISCIPLINES / Writing Authorship (BISAC code LAN-002000) (#AR).

PRICING

Determining a book's price depends on many factors, not least of which are estimated royalties, a figure that will be provided at the time you upload your book and enter price information. But there's more to pricing than how much money you might make, emphasis on the *might*. Overprice your book and you'll limit sales. Underprice, and you risk giving the impression your book isn't very good. It's also worth noting that some vendors (like Amazon), charge a significantly higher vendor fee for e-books priced below $2.99 or above $9.99.

You may want to put your e-book on sale in the future. A discount from $5.99 to $0.99 is much more appealing than $2.99 to $0.99. Start by doing a price comparison of books in your categories on Amazon and find a happy medium. The good news: it's easy to change the price at any time and doesn't require re-publishing.

I've gone into much more detail (including mathematical examples) on book pricing, vendor charges, and sales in Money Matters: Understanding Royalties.

ROYALTY-BASED SERIALIZED PUBLISHING

Wattpad and Inkitt offer select paid publishing options and both platforms are covered in more detail under the Social Publishing section. While there may be other royalty-based options available, at the time of publication Kindle Vella is the most viable (#AR).

A KDP initiative, Kindle Vella was launched in July 2021 and limited to U.S. authors and readers. Stories uploaded to Kindle Vella are meant to be released in a serialized format with 600 to 5,000 words per episode, with new episodes uploaded on a regular, and frequent, basis.

Compensation on Kindle Vella is royalty- and bonus-based (bonuses are based on customer engagement and activity). The first three episodes of all books are free, then readers purchase tokens to access the rest of the Kindle Vella content. More information on the program and Kindle Vella payment structure can be found on the KDP website under *Kindle Vella - Royalties, Reporting, and Payments*. To publish using Kindle Vella, you will need to create a KDP account. While there is no requirement to do so, completed books can also be published as paperback, e-book, hardcover, and audiobook, with some restrictions.

POST-PRODUCTION

You knew it was coming: marketing. While every author, regardless of publishing path, will need to familiarize themselves with the ins and outs of promotion, as a self-published author 100%

of this will fall on your shoulders. I've covered several possibilities in Money Matters: Advertising & Promotion.

In summary, self-publishing isn't free and no matter what you believed before reading this section, you now realize that it's hard work...and not for the faint of heart. Is it the right path for you? Only you can answer that.

SOCIAL PUBLISHING

THERE ARE any number of reasons for wanting to get your words out into the world. Feedback. Growth. Affirmation. Validation. A forum. Social publishing is one way to do that. In short, it's publishing content directly for your readers with little to no gatekeeping and minimal costs, if any.

This does not mean that all social publishing platforms will be a fit for your work. Some, such as Booksie.com, have minimum age requirements and restrict mature (erotic) content. Whichever platform you choose to use, you'll find commonalities between them and, regardless of platform, your success will depend on your ability to grow a following. While traditional publishing is part of a deeply rooted establishment and process, the community-focused social publishing is a newer format, and one that continues to evolve.

It began with the most obvious example, blogs. The wave of blog popularity and direct link to the success of many authors is undeniable, but it was only the beginning. Social publishing has now branched out to websites and mobile apps tailored to sharing and reading all manner of writing, from poetry to essays to fiction. Some are more professional than others, and most don't offer compensation for writers, so if your goal is purely financial this won't appeal to you. But most do have forums and groups to connect with readers and contests, all to help you hone your craft as a writer. What sets it apart from other publishing paths is the direct reader feedback you get.

WEBSITES & BLOG POSTS

No matter how much you want to simplify it—even if all you want to do is write a weekly blog for a handful of followers—at the very least you'll still need a website and a web provider. Fortunately, there are plenty of options (#AR) and, once again, the internet will be your friend when it comes to choosing the best fit for your current needs. That said, you might want to adjust your vision beyond today and consider the possibilities of tomorrow. After all, your future depends on you and the choices you make now.

When it comes to bloggers, much has been made of the success of the late Julie Powell, famously known for her 2002 food blog, the *Julie/Julia Project*. The blog chronicled her year-long journey recreating every one of Julia Child's 524 recipes in *Mastering the Art of French Cooking: Volume I*. According to *The New York Times*, Powell's blog received more than 400,000 page views that year. Three years later, Little, Brown, and Company published *Julie & Julia: 365 Days, 524 Recipes, 1 Tiny Apartment Kitchen* (later retitled *Julie & Julia: My Year of Cooking Dangerously*). In 2009, Nora Ephron's screenplay *Julie & Julia* (based on Powell's memoir and Child's autobiography, *My Life in France*, written with Alex Prud'homme) hit theaters, garnering multiple nominations and awards for Streep and Ephron, and further acclaim for Powell.

It's a wonderful story, the stuff dreams are made of. But it's also important to put things into perspective.

In 2002, blogging was a "shiny new thing" captivating a growing audience, but still very much in its infancy. Fast forward to today, when there are a reported 1.9 billion (and growing) websites worldwide, approximately one-third—or 600 million—with blogs.

It's estimated that six million blog posts are published every single day, meaning roughly 2.5 billion each year. That's *a lot* of competition. Not to mention a general feeling of blog fatigue among followers. Where blog subscribers might once have read every word, they're now often skimming the content, if not skipping it altogether.

Don't get me wrong, I'm not trying to discourage you from blogging. I'm just saying that cooking up an idea doesn't mean anyone's going to come sit at your table. Then again, maybe you don't care about the number of followers you gain (or maybe you're just an optimistic sort). In that case, you'll want to define the type of blog you want to create *and* the reason you want to create it.

Maybe your purpose is one of passion, a cause you believe in, with a mission to spread awareness. Or maybe, as a writer looking for agent representation or independent publication, it might be about building your brand and adding content to your website to prove you're the real deal. There's nothing wrong with that, in fact it's an admirable pursuit. Just remember that dedication and a will to succeed may not be enough.

Next, you'll need to decide how many hours you're willing to commit to blogging. That time commitment will be a direct reflection on the frequency—daily, weekly, bi-weekly, monthly—and length of your posts.

While there are varying opinions on the magic number, I'd suggest monthly isn't going to be enough to build a following, and daily can be a grind. It's one reason why many authors have taken to forming multi-author blogs. Not only do they provide fresh voices every day, joining others alleviates the burden of writing daily posts.

Microblogging, a Twitter-like concept that's become trendy, is another option, essentially a brief message along with a photo. Which reminds me. Remember our copyright section? Copyright applies to photographs, too. Make sure you have the right to use whatever you post.

What about posting content like short stories or excerpts from your book-in-progress? Now you're treading into a gray area. As the author, you own copyright, which gives you the legal means to publish them. That said, if you're considering converting your blog into a full-length book eventually, even Julie Powell didn't just compile a list of blog posts and recipes—she wrote a memoir about her entire *Julie/Julia Project* experience. It's also worth keeping in mind that this isn't 2005. Memoirs have become plentiful, and most are a tough sell. Jane Friedman's "Why Your Memoir Won't Sell" serves as a stark reminder of why, and while there are always exceptions, her article is well worth consideration (#AR).

What if you aren't writing a memoir, but a novel? Will excerpts draw readers in? Perhaps. But be wary of how much you post. A Twitter-length snippet on social media is fine, but a chapter or two and agents and publishers will likely consider the work already published and available to the public. As my mother used to say to my teenage self (admittedly in an entirely different context), "Why buy the milk if the cow is free?" In publishing jargon, this translates to "Already published, no paying market."

What if you've had a short story or two published, and the publishing rights have reverted to you? Adding a sampling as a free value-add to your website might demonstrate expertise, or at the very least, publication credits (though you should be sure to list them that way). Posting an unpublished story? Well, now we're back to our cow scenario.

Most importantly, remember that every hour you invest in blogging will be time taken away from your current work-in-progress, or your efforts to get otherwise published. If all you're looking for is validation and feedback, blogging might be enough. But something tells me you purchased this book to do more.

So do more.

SOCIAL STORYTELLING PLATFORMS (#AR)

The social publishing platform provides a forum for your work to be read and critiqued. Is that enough or do you want more? If so, what does "more" mean to you? Financial success? Recognition, awards, and accolades? Maybe it's simply honing your craft in a community of like-minded individuals.

Whatever your objective, there are pros and cons to every publishing platform, and social publishing is no exception. The best advice I can give you is to always read the fine print before publicly sharing your work.

Here we'll look at a few of the more well-known options in more detail, beginning with the one that started it all: Wattpad.

WATTPAD

There are several alternatives to Wattpad available today, but that certainly wasn't the case when Canadian co-founders Allen Lau, an entrepreneur, and Ivan Yuen, a computer engineer, launched Wattpad in 2006. A self-defined "social storytelling platform where new voices write and share," Wattpad provides an online portal for writers to upload and share their work with readers. Wattpad currently boasts a community of 93 million users —and counting—who collectively spend 23 billion minutes on Wattpad each month, with stories available in 50 different languages.

It wasn't always that way. In October 2012, *The Lit Platform* offered an insightful interview into Wattpad's backstory (#AR). In the article, Lau admits that early traffic was "depressing" with a few hundred users at best, though he's quick to point out the company's primary focus of mobile e-reading at the time was a challenge before the era of Kindle and smartphones. Materials available on Wattpad were comprised of works available in the public domain (works no longer subject to copyright).

Today's Wattpad catalog goes well beyond the public domain. In addition to creating new stories using the online portal, writers can submit their work to brand-sponsored writing contests under the Wattpad Brand Partnerships initiative, and enter the annual Watty Awards, which offer a variety of categories in multiple languages, though winning is far from a sure thing with an estimated 300,000 writers entering each year. There's also Wattcon, an annual, one-day conference where writers and readers can meet and mingle. As a Wattpad writer you can also monetize your work in one of two ways: Paid Stories and the Creators Program. Both are by invitation only. There is no financial compensation for writers who are not included in either program.

Whether you've written a short story, novella, or novel, content must be posted chapter by chapter, and not as one single file. In fact, Wattpad recommends publishing in a serialized format, with updates two to three times per week. Content can also be edited after uploading.

This publish-as-you-go format allows readers to follow stories, read new chapters as they're made available, and provide feedback while the story is in progress. Wattpad's Story Statistics metrics measure reader engagement in three ways:

- Total Reads (the number of times a story has been read; a single reader can account for multiple reads).
- Unique Readers (the number of individual readers).
- Engaged Readers (unique readers with 5+ minutes of time spent reading your story).

Wattpad's serialized, publish-as-you-go format isn't unique to Wattpad. As mentioned in the self-publishing section, Kindle Direct Publishing (KDP) offers a similar model under Kindle Vella, although as a self-publishing (vs. social publishing) platform, authors are paid royalties. Additionally, content posted on Kindle Vella cannot be *freely available* elsewhere on the web. Note the wording: not available freely (meaning at no cost) but freely available (meaning accessible). In other words, you can't publish the same content on Wattpad (or anywhere else, including your own website or social platforms) and Kindle Vella.

The question you might be asking is, "is there traditional publishing light at the end of the Wattpad tunnel?" Truthfully, the odds are slim. The most recent statistic I could find referenced 665 million story uploads to Wattpad, representing 70 million writers. That doesn't mean it can't happen. Success stories include *My Life with the Walter Boys* (Sourcebooks, Netflix) by Ali Novak, *White Stag* (Macmillan) by Kara Barbieri, *Follow Me Back* (Sourcebooks) by A.V. Geiger, and *The Kissing Booth* (Penguin Random House, Netflix) by Beth Reekles. Interestingly, all four are Young Adult novels, although perhaps not surprising; the average age of a Wattpad user is 20; 90% are between the ages of 13 and 40.

INKITT

Imitation is the sincerest form of flattery, and the success of Wattpad continues to spawn alternatives. One of the fastest-growing platforms that also offers author's compensation is Inkitt.

Founded in 2014 in Germany, Inkitt is a self-described "reader-powered publisher." Submissions must be written in English, German, or French, with copyright belonging to the submitting author and, at least at the present time, categorized as fiction. A short story submission video provides an easy-to-follow tutorial for those unfamiliar with the platform.

Content (short story, novel-in-progress, or complete novel) must meet a stringent set of community and writer's guidelines. Only after a story passes this quality assurance—a process that takes about 48 hours—will it be published onto the Inkitt platform. As with Wattpad, writers are allowed to revise and edit their work. The site also offers monthly contests, a blog which includes writing advice, and community groups.

Writers are also privy to the following:

- Chapter Reads (when a reader starts or continues a story).
- Collected Data (a bar showing how much data has been collected).
- Reviews (reader feedback).
- Demographics graphs (by age, gender, country, where provided by reader).

- Binge rate (the percentage of readers who immediately continue to the next chapter).

Inkitt's algorithm analytics also measures more than 1,200 reader behaviors. Books considered to have bestselling potential are offered a publishing contract with Inkitt's sister app, GALATEA. These authors are provided with cover design, professional editing, royalties, and a marketing team to promote their story.

According to the website, GALATEA has active readers binging over 40 million chapters per month. A section titled *Success Stories* lists *The Millennium Wolves* by Sapir A. Englard, first published in October 2018. Described as an erotic werewolf fantasy, *The Millennium Wolves* passed the one-million-dollar sales mark within ten months of publication, and five million in sales within the first two years. There are now 15 books in the series, all of which have been translated into multiple languages.

While GALATEA is one potential option, it's not an obligation. Because Inkitt authors retain 100% of their rights, they are free to publish their stories on other platforms concurrently, or sign publishing contracts outside of Inkitt.

What are the odds? While Inkitt's user base is a fraction of Wattpad's 93 million (at last check, the Inkitt number was listed as "more than two million readers and writers"), there is still potential to build a strong fan base. Who knows? You might even find a smaller playing field allows you to stand out from the crowd. How you leverage that fan base is up to you.

GOING BEYOND SOCIAL

There are, of course, other social publishing alternatives to blogs, Wattpad, and Inkitt. Much like defining comparables for your book, understanding these three business models can serve as comparables as you delve deeper into the social publishing arena. Remember: due diligence!

But select success stories aside (because we know they are the exception, rather than the rule—even if we dare to hope otherwise), can social publishing hurt or help the average writer? I posed the question to one of my writing association groups. Here's what these authors had to say:

"My romance books were very successful on Wattpad. Based on those statistics, I queried a mystery series with romantic overtones. The series was picked up by an independent publisher, however, the contract required that the mystery series be written under a name not used on Wattpad."

"I received a traditional publishing contract, but not for the work posted on Wattpad. The terms of the contract included removing all their work from Wattpad and any other online platform, including blogs."

"Speaking just for the St. Martin's unpublished mystery novel contest (#AR):
    1. The excerpt/story posted is no more than 10% of the novel's wordage;
    2. The story/excerpt is not for sale in any manner whatsoever, and;
    3. That it is the ONLY appearance of part of the novel in any publicly accessible format."

"My opinion is that regardless of where the story was posted, the work would be considered previously published."

"Every publisher (or competition) has different rules regarding previously published work. However, there often rules that specify that you can post a small excerpt somewhere, not for sale."

"Some publishers will say that posting on a platform like Wattpad is a no-go, but a personal blog is fine, providing that blog has fewer than a certain number of page views a month.'"

"I would suggest that an author should err on the side of caution. If the writer is seeking traditional publication, then don't post that particular story, or an excerpt (beyond snippet length) of a novel you want to pitch, on ANY site."

My personal takeaway from the comments is that if you've established a fan base, those statistics might be meaningful in a query letter. Just don't expect that "already widely read for free novel" you toiled over to generate a book deal.

MONEY MATTERS

CONTRACTS

I'VE SIGNED a few publishing contracts in my time, but I'm not a lawyer, and I'm far from an expert in contract law. What I do know is that the terms of your publishing agreement will determine the *control you retain over your work* for the duration of the contract, however long that might be. Some contracts are two years, others three, five, or seven. There is no "standard." Most contracts (though not all) will automatically renew on an annual basis unless the author requests termination in writing. The contract will also include a clause ("reversion of rights") in the event of publisher bankruptcy or insolvency.

So, what does "control you retain over your work" mean? In a nutshell, these are the rights you will keep (known as the "publishing rights granted") for trade paperback, mass market, hardcover, audio, film, and foreign distribution, etc. of your book. Pay special heed to this section. Before you sign away publishing rights for film, find out if the publisher has ever optioned a book for film. If not, then why would you allow them to control (own) the film rights? This, then, is a publishing right you would (and should) retain control over. Don't be afraid to negotiate.

The contract will also dictate how much and when you'll be paid (e.g., 50% of net sales, quarterly), including any advance on future royalties.

A contract inevitably favors the party who initiates it (publishing is a business, after all). Don't let your desire for representation intimidate or sway you. If something feels wrong or "off," you are well within your rights to question it before signing on the dotted line, and reputable agents and publishers will always allow you time to seek advice. This is because publishing contracts should be a two-way street, open to reasonable (emphasis on reasonable) negotiation on *both* sides, without fear of reprisal. Once you've signed, however, there are no do-overs. Your novel will be subject to the terms, timeline, and conditions set forth in writing. When you get to the contract stage, proceed with equal measures of optimism and caution.

Because of the complexity of contract law, this section is only an introduction to sources listed below that are better equipped to answer any questions you may have. These sites have been listed in alphabetical order, not in any order of preference (#AR).

ALLIANCE OF INDEPENDENT AUTHORS (ALLi)

A non-profit professional association for authors who self-publish, ALLi offers members downloadable templates and annotated contracts, including publisher, ghostwriting, author and/or artist partnership agreements, and reversion of rights. At the time of publication, ALLi is not offering literary agent/author templates. However, in addition to other member benefits, ALLi offers general legal and business advice, as well as free contract review, which includes literary agent/author contracts.

If you're not a member (and even if you are), ALLi's *Understanding and Negotiating Book Publishing Contracts* is a good resource (#AR).

INDEPENDENT BOOK PUBLISHERS ASSOCIATION (IBPA)

IBPA offers two members-only resources regarding contracts.

The first, *A GUIDE TO THE BOOK PUBLISHING AGREEMENT* (#AR) is a seventeen-page sample author/publisher contract listing forty-two distinct clauses, which are broken down into nine sub-sections. Each numbered clause contains the language typically used in a standard publishing contract, along with a detailed definition of the clause. It's a great way to further your understanding of the elements of a contract—you can never be too familiar with the vernacular.

The second is an online discussion forum. Under the broader umbrella of Publishing Law on the website, members can search for previously posted contract advice, or start a new thread with questions or helpful insights.

For non-members and members alike, IBPA's *Hybrid Publisher Criteria* (#AR) includes eleven key elements required to be categorized as a hybrid (versus vanity press) publisher, along with additional points to consider. Available online and in a five-page downloadable PDF, the data contained within it can provide food for thought should you decide to ink a deal with a hybrid publisher.

The Authors Guild

With more than 12,000 members, the Authors Guild is the oldest and largest professional association for writers in North America. It's important to note, however, that there are strict eligibility requirements for joining (#AR).

In terms of publishing contracts, members are provided access to a legal team who will review a contract line by line at no charge to help authors understand what they are getting—and giving away—before signing. Comprehensive written reviews include traditional publishing, e-publishing and self-publishing, agency agreements, multi-media and film options, and freelance agreements.

Both members and non-members can access the Authors Guild's *Model Trade Book Contract* (#AR) which emphasizes fair practice and provides detailed commentary in thirty-five sub-sections. You might not consider such things as the possibility of publisher insolvency or termination of an agreement, but the Authors Guild has it covered, along with a breakdown of more pleasant topics, like royalties and advances. There is also a similar model contract for Literary Translation Rights. Both are backed by two webinar videos (roughly an hour each), available to the public. Last, but not least, there's an op-ed article regarding morals clauses in contracts.

REASONABLE EXPECTATIONS

Timelines for free contract reviews vary, but a good rule of thumb is a turnaround of ten business days. In other words, don't join the day you get a contract offer and expect to get a contract review the next day. As keen as you might be to receive an answer and get signing, it's unlikely you'll be the only one on any association's list. If timing is of the essence, hiring a lawyer who specializes in literary contract law may be another option, though again, you might not be first on their docket.

Whatever path you choose, and however long the feedback takes, remember: it's okay to ask questions, okay to negotiate in good faith, and okay to protect as many publishing rights as you can. If your publisher has never brokered a single foreign rights language deal, why would you agree to transfer those rights to them? From personal experience I can say that opportunity comes in many forms, and you never know who might come knocking on your door down the road.

The offer of a publishing contract is exciting, but now is the time to think with your head and not your heart. Embrace the possibilities, absolutely, but pay attention to the warning signs, and weigh every single pro and con. Only then will you be able to make an informed decision. I've said it before, and I'll say it again. Publishing is a business, not just "theirs," whoever "they" might be, but yours too. And your business is every bit as important as theirs.

UNDERSTANDING ROYALTIES

BEFORE WE GET STARTED, there are a few things you need to know as an author: agent, publisher, wholesaler, aggregator, and digital storefronts—everyone, and I do mean everyone, gets a piece of your royalty pie. Here's how it works (and don't stress if it seems confusing. I've included examples later in this chapter):

DIGITAL STOREFRONTS & WHOLESALE POD DISTRIBUTORS

All sales distribution channels report royalties to the publisher on a monthly basis. This is known as the royalty period. The royalty report will include all book sales from that period, e.g., a March royalty report would include the royalty period of March 1 to March 31.

A percentage (anywhere between 30 to 70%) is deducted from each reported sale as the distributor's share.

Payment to the publisher (Publisher Compensation) for the royalty period is made once per month (provided monetary thresholds are met) and range from approximately 30 to 90 days after the date of sale, depending on the storefront/wholesale distributor, e.g., sales recorded from March 1 to March 31 will be paid to the publisher between April 30 to early July.

AUTHOR PAYMENTS

Payment to the author is calculated from the amount received by the publisher. In other words, they can't pay you until they get paid. Terms of author payments vary by publisher and will be stipulated in your publishing contract (e.g., quarterly, semi-annually, annually) and royalty rate (percentage). There is no "standard" term or percentage, though e-books typically earn a higher royalty rate than print. If you are self-published, you are considered the publisher.

Literary agents are paid the contract-designated percentage, e.g., 15% of your royalties, including any advances. This amount is deducted from your share of royalties, *not* the retailer, wholesale distributor, or publisher's share.

ADVANCES

Most writers assume that contracts include an advance against future royalties, paid on signing (or a percentage on signing and the balance on publication) but, at least according to the *Sisters in Crime Business of Books Survey* (2022) (#AR), that's not always the case. In fact, 50% of published authors and 90% of pre-published (debut) authors did not receive an advance.

Of course, that's just one survey, but it's still worthy of mention. If you are paid an advance, and don't earn it out, you won't have to repay the amount, but you also won't receive any further income from that book, regardless of timeline.

Let's take an advance of $1,500 as an example. At the end of five years (or any length of time), your book earned just $800 in royalties. You won't have to pay back the $700 difference (the publisher accepts that as a loss), but you will also not be paid any additional money. Be grateful. You were paid $800 for sales you didn't make.

And Before We Get to the Nitty Gritty...

Unlike a "regular" job where no one would dream to ask you how much you earn, you *will* be asked, because no one thinks it is an inappropriate question. I'm not talking about sharing with other authors over drinks at a conference or reporting your annual sales as a means of combating pay incquity. I'm talking about nosey neighbors, your best friend's husband's cousin, even strangers you meet at a backyard barbecue. Be prepared to be asked the question, often when you least expect it. How, or if, you choose to answer it, is your call.

Calculating Royalties

Traditional and/or hybrid publishers calculate royalties in one of three ways: Net Receipts, Gross Receipts, or Cover Price. Details on (royalties based on) Cover Price are included under "When It's Not POD" a bit later in this chapter. For now, here's a breakdown on Net and Gross Receipts:

Net Receipts (also called Net Sales): Net Receipts are defined as the total dollar amount received by the Publisher (aka Publisher Compensation) from the wholesale or retail sales of the work during that royalty period, minus any fees (such as PayPal, wire transfer, and other bank fees associated with the sales). In the first example I've assumed that the author is unagented.

EXAMPLE
Publisher Compensation $50.00
Less Bank Fee ($10.00)
Net Receipt $40.00
$40.00 (Net Receipt) x 30% (Royalty Rate) = $12.00
Author Earns: $12.00

Gross Receipts: The total dollar amount that is received by the publisher (Publisher Compensation) *without* deductions. In the next example, I've assumed the author has an agent.

EXAMPLE
Publisher Compensation $50.00
Gross Receipt $50.00
$50.00 (Gross Receipt) x 30% (Royalty Rate) = $15.00
Less 15% Agent Commission ($ 2.25)
Author Earns: $12.75

PUBLISHER COMPENSATION

You, as the author, will either be paid based on your publisher's net receipts (also known as net sales) or gross receipts. Unless you are self-published (and therefore acting not only as the author, but also the publisher), you will only earn a percentage of the Publisher's Compensation. That percentage will be clearly defined in your contract.

At this point you might be wondering how Publisher Compensation is calculated, and the answer is, "it depends."

DIGITAL/E-BOOK ROYALTIES

The online bookseller is the first in line to take a piece of your royalty pie. Online booksellers include Apple Books, Kindle (Amazon), Kobo (Rakuten Kobo), NOOK (Barnes & Noble), and others.

E-book royalties are based on the sale price of the book, e.g., a book regularly priced at $9.99 but discounted to $2.99 for a promotion will earn a royalty based on the $2.99 sale price.

Additionally, e-book royalties typically have tiered pricing, once again based on the sale price of a book. Here are two examples:

E-BOOK PRICED LESS THAN $2.99 OR MORE THAN $9.99

- Online seller deducts 65% of the sale price of the book
- Publisher compensation = 35% of the sale price of the book

EXAMPLE A (<$2.99)
Sale Price $1.99
Bookseller deducts 65% = $1.29
Publisher compensation @ 35% = $ 0.70

EXAMPLE B (>$2.99)
Sale Price $12.99
Bookseller deducts 65% = $8.44
Publisher compensation @ 35% = $4.55

E-BOOK PRICED BETWEEN $2.99 AND $9.99

- Online seller deducts 30% of sale price
- Publisher compensation = 70% of sale price

EXAMPLE
Sale Price $7.99
Bookseller deducts 30% = $2.40
Publisher compensation @ 70% = 5.59

Note that where an aggregator (a multi-distribution sales channel, such as Draft2Digital) is used, the aggregator will reduce Publisher Compensation by approximately 10%. Aggregators are often used for less common markets, as well as subscription-based digital services, and for e-book distribution to libraries and institutions.

PRINT-ON-DEMAND ROYALTIES

Independent publishers operate on a print-on-demand (POD) basis; they simply can't afford to sponsor huge print runs in the hope your book will sell in massive quantities. The same holds true for hybrid publishers. And, of course, if you choose to self-publish, POD is the most viable option in your arsenal, though there are independent printers you can hire for print runs. When determining POD royalties, you'll need to factor in two additional steps:

PRINT CHARGE: The actual cost to print the book, calculated by page count (cost per page) and type of ink (standard black and white or upgrade to color). Trim size (e.g., 6" x 9"), cover finish (matte or glossy), and choice of interior paper color (white or cream) do not impact the cost. The quality of the paper (regular, recycled, or premium) will.

WHOLESALE DISCOUNT: The percentage of trade discount off the suggested retail price, offered to booksellers to purchase your book for the resale market. For print-on-demand (POD), the recommended trade discount is 55% (40% to the retailer and 15% to the POD publisher.) Any amount below 55% is known in the industry as a "short discount," and reduces incentive to stock your book. However, unless you have a reasonable expectation for a large volume of brick-and-mortar orders, it can be worth going "short." That's because even if a bookstore won't stock your book on their shelves (and let's face it, unless you are a known commodity, they aren't about to, no matter how great the discount or what else you might be told), they will almost always order a non-returnable copy in at a customer's request. You'll still need to offer a reasonable wholesale discount, e.g., 40% (meaning 25% to the retailer and 15% to POD publisher).

POD EXAMPLE

This example assumes a retail list price of $21.99, a page count of 400, and a print charge of $6.88 per book.

Retail list price $21.99
Less wholesale discount @55% = ($12.09)
Wholesale price = $9.90 (retail less discount)

Minus print charge = ($6.88)
Publisher compensation: $3.02 (wholesale less print charge)

Your jaw may have dropped by this point. Surely for a book that sells for $21.99 the publisher must earn more than $3.02? Because that would mean an author with a POD publisher would earn only a percentage of that amount. Sadly, it's true. In most cases, the print royalty percentage paid by a publisher will be 40% or less, meaning author earnings on a book retailing for $21.99 will be, at best, $1.21.

Eye-opening, isn't it? It also explains why the cost of paperbacks has escalated so rapidly in the past few years. A 400-page trade paperback retailing at $29.99 will have the same print cost of $6.88 as one retailing for $21.99.

But take heart. Even if all an author earns is *one single dollar per sale*, a book that becomes a million-copy bestseller will make that author a millionaire. Sure, the odds are long, and maybe they even seem insurmountable, but you didn't come this far to give up on the dream, did you? Believe in the dream, and maybe, just maybe, it will believe in you.

WHEN IT'S NOT POD

POD has become the gold standard for most independent publishers, regardless of size, but that's not the case with traditional publishing houses, aka the Big Five, which produce print runs versus print on demand. That said, they expect to lose money on one out of every five books they publish (meaning they've printed more copies than they will sell at a profit). Because of that, you might assume the percentage of royalties paid per sale are significantly less than their independent counterparts.

But are they?

These contracts typically pay an author anywhere from 4% to 8% of the print cover price. Simple math tells us that 4% of a book selling for $21.99 will net the author $0.87 per book. At 8%, the author will earn $1.76 per copy—roughly the same as your POD publisher. The difference? Your odds of selling a million copies are far more likely if you've landed a "Big Five" contract and the marketing machine behind it. Your odds of landing a Big Five contract...well, that's another story.

WHAT ABOUT RETURNS?

You've probably returned a book or two in your time without giving it much thought. Now that you are thinking of it, though, it makes sense that if you return a book, the publisher would be charged back the original amount of compensation. That's true for e-books, but when it comes to print, things can get more expensive.

Let's take our previous print example, where the publisher compensation was $3.72. In that case, the publisher would be charged back the wholesale price of $9.90. However, if the publisher allowed physical returns (vs. an option of Return/Destroy) there will be an additional shipping and handling charge, and the quality of any returned books will not be guaranteed. Because book returns can be costly, the decision to opt in should be carefully considered. However, unless you are self-published, it's unlikely the decision will be left to you. This is especially true of large presses, where returns are an inevitable part of life, though it may also hold true for independent publishers.

Whatever your situation, the terms regarding returns will be clearly outlined in your publishing contract, e.g., "Net copies sold shall mean the number of copies sold, less any returned (including copies destroyed or otherwise deemed destroyed) or those sold at or below publishing cost." The latter refers to those clearance bin copies you'll find at bookstores, where the price has been marked down to a fraction of the original list.

You might be offered "book return insurance" by a hybrid or small, independent press. Since there are no insurance companies that offer this type of coverage, the "insurance" is provided by the publisher in exchange for a set amount (upfront and usually quite steep) paid by the author. Exercise extreme caution before purchasing, and before you do, ask yourself: Do you anticipate multiple bookstores nationwide to stock your book in large quantities? If you're a known commodity and the answer is yes, then go for it. If your expectations are more modest, save your money. Make your book non-returnable (despite any pressure tactics to the contrary) and move on. There will be better ways to spend your hard-earned cash.

ADVERTISING & PROMOTION

TALKING about advertising and promotion might seem a bit like putting the cart before the horse, especially if you're planning on following a traditional publishing path, but the one thing many authors struggle with most is marketing.

True, if you land a contract with a large press, odds are a publicity team will put together a solid package for you. That said, the A-listers will get the bulk of time, money, and attention, and you'll still be required to do more than your fair share of the heavy lifting (and paying). That "fair share" increases exponentially as the size of the press decreases. Hybrid publishers can and do offer marketing support, however that will get costly. The more you can take control of on your own, the better. Should you decide to go indie, it will all fall on you.

AUTHOR PHOTO

You'll use this for many things: your website, inside your book, guest blogs, newspaper articles, conference catalogs…the list goes on. A professional headshot is a worthwhile investment, and while you want to put your best face forward, ask them to go easy on the filters and photoshopping. The idea is to be recognized from your author photo.

BLOGS

Whatever publishing path you choose, a personal blog can be the first step in building a following. Even better, outside of the time invested to write the posts, it's free. While it's never too late, having an active blog before you begin the querying process can count as a point in your favor. "Here," an agent or publisher might think, "is an author invested in their future."

Even if you don't have a blog, following one or more writing/genre-related blogs can allow you to gradually cultivate a relationship with those bloggers by sharing their posts on social media and/or leaving insightful comments on posts that resonate with you. When the time comes to celebrate your own book news, you can legitimately approach that blogger for a spot or tag them in a social post, which they will (hopefully) share. Start by following as many writing-related or genre-specific blogs as you can comfortably handle without turning this exercise into a part-time job, understanding that the expectation is never that you interact with, or share, every single post. This is following, not stalking.

In addition to individual blogs, there are also blog tours and blitzes. Blog tours are an online version of a traditional book tour, designed to promote books that have already been, or are about to be, published. Much more popular since the COVID-19 pandemic, these typically run for a period of five to ten days, with each post offering original content. Blitzes, on the other hand, feature several blogs posting the same content at the same time. Both can be arranged by a blog tour company, of which there are many, which will find willing hosts. Here's the sticky wicket: you, as the author, will be required to create the content, which takes time and effort. There are no free lunches on the promo circuit.

Because blog tour companies list links to their current and upcoming tours and blitzes, you'll have an opportunity to vet them using your own specific criteria, e.g., were the blog hosts a good fit for the novel being promoted, or were they just trying to fill up available slots, regardless of the genre or sub-genre?

The bottom line? You may not use a blog tour service for many months yet, if at all, but at the very least you'll gain a better understanding of the blog and blitz tour business. As a rule, tours trend towards gaining visibility vs. selling books, and it's unlikely that you'll break even on your investment, however modest.

ONLINE/SOCIAL PRESENCE

Never underestimate the power of social media, or the effort you'll have to put in to keep up with the changing times (there's always something newer and shinier…remember MySpace?) and understand your target demographic. Facebook remains a favorite with an older crowd, and, at the moment, TikTok tends to attract a younger demographic. Nevertheless, social platforms like Instagram, TikTok, Twitter, Facebook, and others can be a great way to connect with readers. In fact, BookTok (a term coined for the book-related content on TikTok) has been credited with bumping print sales in 2022, and Instagram's bookstagrammers have become an integral part of the bookish community.

While regular social media posts are free, there are always options to pay for advertising or boosting a post beyond your existing followers. Targeting criteria makes it easy to get your content in front of individuals with specific interests that line up with your book to find new readers. Targeting can also be defined by a specific geographic area, which can be helpful when promoting in-person events. Before you head down this path, you'll need to understand audience targeting, the difference between clicks, impressions, and clickthrough rates, and the cost of each. Here's a quick primer:

- Clicks: The number of people who click on your ad.
- Impressions: The number of people who saw your ad.
- Clickthrough Rate (CTR): Clicks divided by impressions.

- Example: CTR = 50 (Clicks) ÷ 1,000 (Impressions) = 0.05 x 100 (percentage) = 5% CTR

While there is no hard and fast rule, a CTR of 4 to 5% is generally considered good, and 3% or less means something is lacking. In the above scenario of 1,000 impressions at 5%, it also means that 950 people who saw your ad did not click on it.

A few pennies per click can also add up quickly, and it's important to remember that not all clicks equal sales. How often have you inadvertently clicked on an ad? Or clicked on it and then thought, "no, I don't think so." And you really don't want to pay per impression.

While some authors have success (meaning they'll recoup their investment and make a few dollars), advertising on social media can be a bit like going to a casino. At the end of the day, the house usually wins.

There are ways, however, to increase your odds. Creativity (whether that's a static post or a clever video), not salesmanship, is also essential. Repeated "enough about my book, here's more about my book" campaigns will turn off readers. In my experience, balancing personal posts and/or writing quotes/wisdoms with promotion is the most effective strategy to build a strong and engaged social following that benefits you. Don't forget, it doesn't have to go viral to be effective. A post that resonates with people, whether a book review, something about your writing journey, or a piece of writing advice, that gets shared by enough people can work wonders in attracting potential new readers to your account and building your dedicated following.

I'd also suggest collaborating with other authors to promote each other's work. One way to do this is to join or create what's known as a "street team" (a dedicated group of readers who like your work and are interested in helping promote your books) (#AR). I'm often more inclined to purchase a book recommended to me by a friend or author whose books I enjoy, than when the author is pitching their own book. My guess is, you're much the same.

THIRD PARTY MARKETING

Yet another option is to hire a book publicist or a promotion or marketing firm, someone who will take care of the vetting and promoting for you (and may even write some, or all, of the content for an added fee). Because this involves the most hands-on involvement by a third party, it should also be the most personalized. As such, it will be your most expensive option, often in the thousands of dollars.

As with any marketing plan, prices vary widely and results are mixed. Obtain references and examples of past promotions and ensure that expectations on both sides are clearly defined in writing. A publicist is usually focused on traditional media, whereas a marketing firm will consider multiple promotional avenues.

YOUTUBE

There are several advertising alternatives to blogging, including paid advertising, newsletters, and promotional materials, such as pens, postcards, and bookmarks. And if you're in a better position to invest time than money, YouTube is another great option that can provide some variety to your creative outlets and be an effective way to put a face to your author brand. Here you can explore the same variety of content as on a blog—book trailers, writing tips, and day-in-the-life videos are just a few examples of how viewers can get to know you and your book, and they're easy to share on social media.

BOOK LAUNCHES

It's fun to dream, right? Even pre-publication, put some thought into the kind of book launch event you'd like to have. More and more, these are happening virtually, which has its benefits. Namely, no cost to rent a location or feed your guests in attendance, as well as broadening your potential audience from local to global. But there is no shortage of benefits for in-person launches either—book signings, on-the-spot purchases, face-to-face interaction with readers, and the potential for local media coverage (the best kind of free advertising). If you're unsure of the right fit for you and your book, the best way to learn what you do—and don't—like is to attend some book launches and see for yourself. As an added bonus, you'll be supporting a fellow author, and it's never too early to start networking.

GOODREADS

Many readers, including me, use Goodreads to rate and review books. Setting up an author profile is free, as is adding your book's information to the website. If you have a blog, you can link that directly to your Goodreads author profile page. There's also an area on your profile for questions from readers you can answer (or make up a couple of your own), as well as multiple reader groups you can join (typically defined by genre of interest, e.g., cozy mystery), as well as other promotional opportunities. If you aren not reviewing books on there already, now's the time to start. It's a free and easy way to be a good and active member of the literary community, and besides, you shouldn't expect reviews if you're unwilling to give them yourself (#AR).

AUTHOR CENTRAL

You've read author bios and editorial reviews of books on Amazon, but did you know those were created using Amazon's Author Central? In addition to providing book stats, the platform allows you to post your bio, photos, and share your blog feed (#AR).

BOOKBUB

Start by joining as a reader, reviewing, and recommending books. Once your book is published, creating an author profile is free. BookBub also offers a Partners blog with advice on marketing, as well as paid advertising options (#AR).

MEDIA

There are many choices at your disposal when it comes to media, which range from bank-breaking to completely free.

When I worked as a magazine editor, I appreciated a professionally written press release, but that didn't mean the magazine used every one that landed in my mailbox, whether it came from a PR professional or an individual. In fact, regardless of the magazine, press releases were considered "filler," a way to fill in a blank spot that had been left open in the hope a last-minute ad might be booked. As such, relatively few were used (unless, of course, our sales team could talk the PR pro or individual into a paid ad). Before you choose the paid PR route, ask for PDFs of recent examples, including which newspapers and/or magazine the press release appeared in.

My personal experience is that local media will usually include a press release of mine if I direct it to the correct individual and personalize the request as a local author. But hey, I'm a writer, so I write my own. Then again, so are you.

You can also look at paid advertising with newspapers and magazines. If you aren't a graphic designer yourself, most outlets offer creative work at an hourly fee in addition to the cost of the ad space. And with so many newspapers moving to digital platforms, there are plenty of options for reasonably priced digital ads on their websites and newsletters that are more affordable than print ads. These can also be hyperlinked directly to your online store or website. Digital ads also often have a longer shelf life than print ads in say, a weekly or daily paper, giving you more bang for your buck.

While press releases have no guarantee of getting published, advertorials do. Often overlooked but a common tactic in marketing, these are paid articles that appear in a newspaper as regular content but give you more control over the messaging of the story. Ever notice the words "sponsored content" at the top of a news article? It's this cleverly disguised form of advertising. The cost varies by publication, and by length, but you may decide this tactic is money well spent.

Other potential options include regional television or radio; a cable TV provider might have a channel in search of local news, a local radio station might offer programming to showcase authors.

Podcasts are also popular, and they are growing in leaps and bounds. Many smaller start-ups are looking for content. Some writing associations and libraries have a dedicated YouTube channel that includes interviews with members or local authors. You might even consider trying to do your own.

You are not there—yet—but it never hurts to research your best resources going forward. If nothing else, you can spend a few hours daydreaming, and there's nothing wrong with that.

One final caveat: always do your due diligence *and then some* before hiring any outside firm or individual. Starting the process pre-publication can protect you from being rushed or pressured into making an uninformed decision.

Promises are cheap. Advertising isn't.

THE WRITE LIFE

ASSOCIATIONS

IT SOMETIMES SEEMS as if there are as many writing and author-related associations as there are writers, and deciding which ones to join can be overwhelming. National or regional? Big or small? Most organizations charge a membership fee, but the fees can be considered a tax-deductible business expense.

The first thing to remember is that while some associations offer lifetime memberships, joining one doesn't have to be a lifelong commitment. Associations most valuable to you as an emerging author may hold less value to you post publication. The reverse is also true. Start with a trial membership, if offered, and an annual membership if one is not. A partial list of writing associations can be found in Additional Resources: Resources by Section.

From international, North American, and national to regional and local levels, the breadth and depth of associations varies widely, as do the types of membership benefits. Your local arts council might have a critique group that meets on a regular basis. A larger organization might offer grants for professional development, educational programs, and webinars and presentations. Beyond the craft, larger organizations like the Authors Guild offers helpful resources to help writers at any point in their career understand the more complex, but no less important, aspects of the business, such as copyright and contracts.

Here's a sample of members-only benefits you might find:

- Access to liability and/or health insurance.
- Author bio page on association's website.
- Blog page.
- Contract advice.
- Critique groups.
- Directory of additional resources.
- Discounts on professional services (editing, design, printing, etc.).
- Discounts on writing-related magazine subscriptions.
- Educational courses.
- Genre-related reports.
- Grants for professional development.
- In-person and/or virtual meetings.
- Lending library for writing-related reference books.
- Marketing memos.
- Member magazines and/or newsletters
- Membership badge (for website use).
- Members' directory.
- Members only website access for exclusive content.
- Mentorship programs.
- Online discussion forum (such as discussion boards and online digests, such as Groups.io).
- Online and/or brick-and-mortar store for book sales.
- Reciprocal membership discounts.
- Regional/local chapters.
- Reports and/or surveys on publishing.
- Social media promotion.
- Sponsorship of events, conferences, and conventions.
- Virtual meetings.
- Webinars.
- Weekly write-ins.
- Workshops.

- Writing awards (for published novels and/or unpublished manuscripts).
- Writing contests.
- Writing tips and advice.

A less tangible benefit, but equally important consideration, is that memberships can serve as proof to agents and/or publishers that you are serious about your craft. Be sure to include any affiliations in your bio and query letter.

Many associations also actively seek volunteers to work on committees and special projects. Some even offer select positions on their Board of Directors for unpublished authors, so don't be afraid to ask if you're interested in getting involved. Volunteering can be an invaluable experience when it comes to networking and understanding the behind-the-scenes world of book publishing.

Points to Ponder

Top Five: Write down a list of the five must-have elements you want from a writing association membership. Think of this exercise in the same way you might approach buying a house (must have three bedrooms and two bathrooms). These are your non-negotiables.

Mushy Middle: This is your wish list (I'd really like granite countertops and stainless-steel appliances, but I could live with laminate and a white fridge and stove.)

Bottom Five: Finally, list your "Never gonna use it/don't care" list (e.g., soundproofed, musician-friendly garage).

Once you've made your lists, consider the following:

Membership Type: Look at the membership categories the association offers, specifically those offered to unpublished authors. Do benefits pander more to the published, with a trinket or two to the aspiring, or is it an equal split? Are there other opportunities (such as volunteerism)? How easy will it be to commute your membership to "Published Author" status?

COST OF ADMISSION: Are there trial memberships? Do they have a refund policy? Are pro-rated annual memberships available if you join mid-year? Is there a way to test drive your membership?

TERRITORY: National, regional, or local? Is the association genre-specific (e.g., mystery), geared to independently published and/or self-published authors, or is the focus broader, all-encompassing? What's more important at this stage of your career? Can one membership satisfy all (or at least most) of your wants? Or are you ready to mix and match by joining two or more associations?

VOLUNTEERISM: Local arts groups often require a minimum number of volunteer hours as part of the membership requirement. Are you ready for that commitment? On the other hand, larger associations may not offer volunteer spots to unpublished authors (though many do).

There are no right or wrong associations, and no right or wrong answers. There are only the answers that work best for you at this point in your writing journey.

After all, this is *your* path to publication.

"FREE" MONEY

Contests, awards, and grants. The very thought of them conjures up images of "free" money and skyrocketing to professional success. But submitting to contests and awards usually requires an entry fee, and grants often require an extensive application process. Here's a quick look at what to expect:

Writing Contests & Awards

A good place to start your search is the *Poets & Writers* website. Not only does it showcase a fairly comprehensive list of the contests out there, *Poets & Writers* (#AR) reviews the practices and policies of each contest before including it, which is helpful (sadly, not all writing contests are legit). Many writing associations, especially those that are genre-specific, also sponsor awards, usually without a membership requirement. But are they worth entering?

They can be. Winning, being short- or long-listed, even getting an honorable mention, can make a nice addition to your bio. Additionally, some competitions will offer a brief critique to non-winning entries of unpublished manuscripts or short stories. If they do, put a checkmark in the plus column. Honest professional feedback is invaluable as you continue to hone your craft.

Points to Ponder

Your Why: Are you looking for validation? Feedback? Prize money? Bragging rights? Honest evaluation? Or just someplace to send your stuff to say you tried?

Application Process: Rigorous and time-consuming? Or simple and straightforward?

Entry Fee: If not free, does the reward, financial or otherwise, justify the cost?

Judging Process: Judges' names are often anonymous, but the process should be clearly defined and transparent.

Past Winners: Legitimate competitions list the names of past winners, and often the names of those who were shortlisted.

Who: Who is sponsoring the contest? How long have they been doing it? What's *their* reason for supporting it?

Fine Print: The part where you usually just scroll down and click "I agree" without reading it? Read it. Then treat it like a contract— because it is. What publication rights are you signing away by entering? What about if you win or are shortlisted? The devil really is in the details.

Grants

Writing-related grants typically come in two forms: project-based or professional development. Whether backed by local, regional, or federal government initiatives or non-profit foundations, eligibility is often measured by your publication track record, meaning unpublished authors need not apply. That said, there are always exceptions. An excellent primer on grants and grant writing (which is a skill in itself) can be found on Jane Friedman's website (#AR).

POINTS TO PONDER

REQUIREMENTS: Do you have the qualifications required for eligibility?

CHANCE OF SUCCESS: What percentage or number of applicants receive grants? Are certain ethnic or diverse groups or geographical areas (e.g., those in rural or remote regions) given priority?

APPLICATION PROCESS: In doing a time/cost benefit analysis, does the amount of a (possible) grant warrant the time spent to complete the paperwork?

MENTORSHIP PROGRAMS

Mentorship programs are popping up more and more online. These can be a great way to build your network with fellow writers as well as connect with industry professionals who can lend some insights into how you might follow in their footsteps.

These programs are often free to enter and have different opportunities for specific genres or underrepresented authors. Finished manuscripts can be submitted for consideration, much like pitching literary agents, and participating mentors will select projects they feel they can help to improve with one-on-one coaching.

POINTS TO PONDER

ASSOCIATIONS: Many writing associations offer mentorship programs. If this is important to you, look for that as a member benefit when researching which one(s) to potentially join.

SCAMMER ALERT: Be mindful to watch for scams whenever fees are requested. I can't say it enough, always do your due diligence.

WRITING CONFERENCES & CONVENTIONS

As an aspiring author, you've probably been given advice to attend a writing conference or convention. Well-meant, but not that helpful, given the sheer number to choose from. As with associations, your wants and needs will evolve over time. So, too, will your expectations from a writing conference or convention. If you're unpublished, you may be looking for an opportunity to pitch your book to an agent, whereas once published, you'll be looking for ways to promote your book to readers.

While the terms are often used interchangeably, there are differences between the core objective of conferences and conventions. Let's begin by defining those differences:

CONFERENCES

The primary purpose of an industry-specific and, in the case of writing, usually genre-specific, conference is the exchange of information with an educational component, a venue where attendees can learn and better themselves professionally. For example, in addition to networking opportunities, a conference might offer master classes, craft-related seminars or workshops, breakout sessions, presentations, manuscript critiques, author-led panel or roundtable discussions, and live agent and/or publisher pitch sessions.

Most conferences also host a debut author program or an awards banquet and dinner. Both offer excellent opportunities, even if you're not a debut author or eligible for award consideration. A debut author may be very willing to share their publishing journey with you. As for the awards nominees and winners, reading award-nominated books and meeting those who penned them can be an education in itself. In my experience, authors in all stages of their careers are more than willing to take a few minutes to chat.

Registration for conferences is open to readers, authors, and aspiring authors, with a bestselling guest (or guests) of honor on the program to draw attendees. They typically take place over three to four days. Some offer one-day passes or fee-per-session options. Conferences are usually held in the same city each year.

CONVENTIONS

Most writing conventions are billed as fan-based, meaning the primary objective is to introduce readers to authors and vice versa. In addition to author interviews, there are author-led panel discussions, however the emphasis generally falls on showcasing attending authors vs. educating attendees. Some conventions will include an educational component, such as a workshop, seminar, or master class, but these are typically held prior to the start of the convention so as not to interfere with scheduled programming.

Similar to conferences, most conventions also host a debut author program and awards banquet and dinner, and the same networking parameters found in conventions also apply.

As with conferences, convention registration is open to readers, authors, and aspiring authors, with bestselling guests of honor on the program to draw attendees. They typically take place over three to four days, and some may offer one-day passes. A key difference is that conventions are often held in a different city each year, with discounted or group sightseeing excursions offered to attendees. At the end of the day, conventions are more about entertainment than education.

POINTS TO PONDER

LOCATION: Do you want something close to home? Or would you prefer to combine business with pleasure and visit a place on your travel wish list, perhaps combining it with a family or solo vacation? Your accountant can explain the ins and outs of what you can write off, but registration fees, travel, hotel accommodations for the length of the conference or convention, and a portion of meals are, in general, tax-deductible expenses. Sightseeing excursions and additional nights or expenses are not.

TOTAL COST: Think registration fee, travel, travel insurance, hotel, meals. Registration fees are usually tiered, with early-bird pricing that escalates as you get closer to the event. The earlier you book the less you'll pay, but you'll want to check the cancellation policy. Terms and conditions vary widely. Some conferences offer scholarships based on financial need, though there will be an application process, and it's not guaranteed.

NETWORKING: Both conferences and conventions offer networking opportunities, though a smaller venue is generally more conducive to making one-on-one personal connections.

YOUR #1 WHY: Pitching to an agent or publisher? Honing your craft? Mix and mingling with other authors, both published and aspiring? Defining your *why* is essential to the planning process to get the most out of your experience.

TYPE OF EVENT: Are you interested in writing in general, or would you prefer an event that has a genre-specific focus (e.g., romance, mystery, sci-fi)? In my experience, there are far more that are focused. Additionally, genre-specific events will introduce you to like-minded individuals, providing an opportunity to network with readers and other authors, aspiring and published.

WARDROBE: You can't go wrong with business casual (this is a business meeting, after all), with layers to accommodate unpredictable conference room temperatures which can range from frigidly air conditioned to hot and stuffy. Bring something a bit dressier for the banquet evenings. Not wedding fancy, but a step up from your daytime duds. I'd also recommend comfortable shoes.

VIRTUAL OR LIVE: Many conventions now offer virtual options. The good news is the cost will be minimal (no travel-associated costs). The bad news is networking opportunities are minimal or non-existent. That said, virtual offerings are a way to dip your toe in the water to get a feel for the experience without diving into the deep end.

Pro Tip: Conference and convention organizers will book a block of rooms at the host hotel to offer discounted pricing, but the number of available rooms will be limited and booking at the time of registration is usually recommended. Since most networking takes place after the day's scheduled programming ends, staying at the host hotel (if financially feasible) may enhance your overall experience. At the very least it will allow you a place to take a quiet (and often much-needed) break between sessions. Don't discount this as a value-add: conferences and conventions can be exhilarating, but being "on" 24/7 for three or four days is also exhausting.

FINDING YOUR FIT

By now you've made your list of wishes, wants, and whys, and are ready for the conference/ convention when and where. But where do you start?

If you're on social media or part of an online writing group, that's a good place to pose the question. Associations, too, will often endorse, sponsor, or supply a list of conferences and conventions. A simple Google search with keywords like "mystery conference" and the year is sure to bring up a laundry list of suggestions. Too many? Filter your search by adding defined geographic areas.

Attending conferences or conventions isn't for everyone, especially in view of the time and cost considerations, not to mention that the truly introverted writer might find it all too intimidating. But remember this: once you've been published (and that's the dream, right?) you may be required (or plan) to attend one in the future, and be invited to be part of a panel discussion. Watching and learning from the sidelines is a painless way to start planning for your turn.

Let the journey begin.

ADDITIONAL RESOURCES

TALKING THE TALK

Advance: The payment paid by a publisher on signing and/or publication in advance of any future royalties (monies) earned.

Advertorial: Paid newspaper article that appears as regular content, often used in marketing strategies. Rates vary per publication, and the purchaser has final say on what is published.

Aggregator: A one-stop online distributor that will list your book with several online booksellers, as well as library and subscription services.

Alpha readers: Readers who provide detailed and constructive feedback on your unpolished first draft about premise, plot, characters, and other technical elements.

ARCs: Advanced reader copies.

Author bio: A brief description about the author written in third person, including information relevant to your story or work as an author, often found at the back of a book.

Beta readers (betas): Readers familiar with your genre/sub-genre who critique finished manuscripts before they are published.

Blog: A website or webpage that is updated regularly with content from one or more writers on a specific topic or theme.

Blurb: Praise for a book included inside or on the cover.

Book Industry Standards and Communications (BISAC): These are codes that indicate the categories and subcategories of your book to retailers, distributors, and librarians so they know where it should be shelved. BISAC codes are generated by categories chosen by the publisher prior to retail upload.

Book launch: Virtual or in-person event or series of events to promote the release of your book.

Brick-and-mortar: Refers to the physical location of a business where products are sold.

Clicks: The number of people who click on your ad.

Clickthrough (CTR): The number of people who click on your ad, divided by the number of impressions (people who saw it).

Climax: The final battle in a manuscript that determines who (or what) wins established conflicts.

Comparable titles: Also called "comps," these are books that are similar to yours in tone, theme, setting, vibe, etc., ideally published within the last five years, and with a proven track record. Comp titles are typically included in query letters and pitches to agents and publishers.

Conference: Virtual or in-person event with an educational component for attendees to learn and better themselves professionally. Often include networking opportunities, master classes, smaller seminars or workshops, manuscript critiques, author-led panels, live agent/publisher pitch sessions, and more.

Contract: Legal agreement detailing the exchange of products and services.

Convention: Fan-based in-person or virtual event usually taking place over several days to introduce readers to authors and vice versa, with the emphasis on showcasing authors. Activities usually include author interviews, author-led panel discussions, and networking.

Copyright: The exclusive legal ownership of artistic material. Laws vary from one country to the next. Permission is required by the copyright owner to copy or use these works.

Closed for submissions: Period in which an agent or publisher is not accepting new pitches. You should not pitch to an agent or publisher during this time.

Critique group: Writers who connect on a regular basis to share their work for the purpose of remaining accountable to their project, exchanging feedback, and improving their craft.

Critique partner: Writer you connect with on a regular basis one-on-one to exchange feedback on each other's work, encouragement, and remain accountable to your respective projects.

Denouement: Following the climax, this is the final part of the narrative arc where the different threads of the story come together, and conflicts are resolved.

Direct to consumer: Sales method from author to customer with no middleman, e.g., at a book fair.

Domain name: A website address (e.g.: judypenzsheluk.com). For authors, it is ideally your name, plus an extension like .com, but if you have a common first and last name, you'll have to get more creative.

Earn out: When book sales equal or exceed the advance paid to the author.

E-commerce site: A website that has the function for people to buy and sell physical and digital products and services, like paperback books, e-books, and related merchandise.

Elevator pitch: A way to effectively share your expertise, credentials, and project quickly with agents and/or publishers.

Falling action: The period between denouement and climax.

Full: A request from an agent or publisher for the complete manuscript.

Galley proof: A preliminary, formatted digital version of your soon-to-be-published novel.

Genre: Category of story, e.g., mystery, romance, science fiction.

Hybrid author: An author who is both traditionally and self-published.

Hybrid publisher: A reputable publisher that offers assisted self-publishing, sometimes referred to as "pay-to-play," with editorial standards and gatekeeping. Not to be confused with vanity publishing, though some vanity presses will identify themselves as hybrid publishers.

Impressions: The number of people who see your ad.

Inciting incident: The event that sets the action in motion, often leading your protagonist on a new course.

Independently published author: Writer who has self-published their book(s).

Independent publisher: Independently owned and managed, not part of any larger publishing house and in no way associated with any of their smaller imprints.

ISBN: International Standard Book Number is a unique code assigned to each commercial book that contains the publication details of each edition and format.

Jacket copy: Also known as the retail blurb or back of book blurb, this is a teaser meant to hook readers.

KDP – Kindle Direct Publishing: Amazon's publishing platform.

Landing page: A standalone web page potential readers will be redirected to from linked ads, emails, or other digital locations.

Loglines: Concise, engaging summary of the essence of your plot in one to two sentences.

Manuscript evaluation: An unbiased review of your novel's strengths and weaknesses.

Microblogging: Similar in content to a blog, with a photo and brief message on a specific topic or theme, often shared via social media.

Micro publisher: Typically a one- or two-person operation, often started as a way of self-publishing the owner's work(s).

Narrative arc: The chronological structure of one single story or a connected series that includes the exposition or starting action, inciting incident, rising action, climax, falling action, resolution, and denouement.

Orphaned: A term used when an author's publishing contract is terminated, also known as reversion of rights.

Orphaned work: A term that refers to a book where copyright exists, but where the copyright owner is either unknown or cannot be located.

Partial: A request from an agent or publisher for a partial manuscript, e.g., first 50,000 words.

Pay-to-play: Another term for "hybrid publisher," which offers assisted self-publishing.

Pitch: A concise presentation of your idea to generate agent and/or publisher interest.

Pitch contest: Often on social media platforms like Twitter, authors are invited to pitch their story to participating agents or publishers for consideration of representation or publication.

Pitch sessions: Done virtually or in person, these are opportunities for unagented authors to pitch their book in a controlled setting with more direct access to agents and/or publishers than submitting based on their submission guidelines.

Platform: Your vehicle to reach your readers with news about your work. Platform can be comprised of one or more channels, such as a website, social media account(s), and/or blog.

Press release (PR): A pre-packaged statement about your book and all pertinent details, distributed to relevant newspapers and magazines.

Print-on-demand (POD): A publishing platform where books are printed when ordered, without minimum quantity requirements.

Protected work: Artistic work that falls under copyright laws.

Public domain: All creative work that no longer falls under or is protected by copyright; permission is not required to copy or use these works.

Publisher Compensation: The amount a publisher is paid by the digital storefront or distributor.

Publishing imprint: Smaller branches of a larger publishing company to market to different audiences (e.g., Berkley is an imprint under Penguin Random House) and/or the brand used to publish books.

Query letters: Similar to a cover letter when applying to a job, this is a formal letter sent to agents or publishers with a pitch of one specific project when seeking agent representation or publication.

Reversion of rights: Publishing rights granted under the terms of the publishing contract are reversed and returned to the author.

Rising action: Series of events within the narrative arc of a story that outline the roadblocks and conflicts to be overcome.

Royalties: What an author is paid from book sales.

SASE: Self-addressed stamped envelope.

Scrivener: A paid word-processing and outlining program for authors.

Serialized format: Publishing longer work in smaller segments, often done through social publishing platforms, such as Wattpad, Inkitt, or Kindle Vella.

Simultaneous submissions: When an author or agent submits their book for consideration to multiple agents or publishers at one time, without waiting for acceptance or rejection letters.

Social publishing: An avenue for authors to write, publish, and distribute their work in a public or semi-public forum, directly to readers, either by a personal blog or via an established storytelling website.

Street Team: A dedicated group of readers (fans) who like your work and are interested in helping promote your books.

Style sheet: List prepared by an editor with important style and spelling rules throughout your book to maintain consistency.

Sub-genre: A more specific way of categorizing your story type within each genre, e.g., cozy mystery or historical romance.

Submission: The package sent to an agent or publisher for consideration of representation or publication.

Submission guidelines: Included on an agency or publisher's website, instructions that tell you the type of books they accept and how they want your work sent for consideration.

Synopsis: A summary of your novel's narrative arc, including plot twists and the ending, as well as brief descriptions of the key personality traits that define your major characters. Always written in third person, present tense, regardless of how your book is written.

Traditional (Trade Book) Publishers a.k.a. "The Big Five": Major publishing houses Hachette Book Group, HarperCollins, Macmillan Publishers, Penguin Random House, and Simon & Schuster make up the Big Five. Also called "Trad publishers."

Unagented submissions: Pitching your project directly to a publisher without agent representation.

Vanity press: Also referred to as a vanity publisher or subsidy publisher, a disreputable publishing company with limited (usually no) editorial or creative standards, with the sole intent of exploiting the writer. Not to be confused with reputable hybrid (assisted) publishers who vet submissions, though many vanity presses will adopt the hybrid label.

Website developer: Outside company (or individual) hired to build a website. Costs and services vary widely from one developer to the next.

Wish list: List of desired stories or topics that an agent or publisher is interested in receiving.

Works for hire: Creative work made by an employee or independent contractor under an employment contract commissioning the work.

RESOURCES BY SECTION

This is a list of resources only; no endorsement is being made for any of the firms or services listed.

PAVING THE WAY

SELF-PUBLISHING (MANAGING EXPECTATIONS)

2018 Authors Guild survey of U.S. professional writers
https://authorsguild.org/news/six-takeaways-from-the-authors-guild-2018-authors-income-survey/
*Survey to be updated in 2023

Sisters in Crime *Business of Books Survey (2022)*
https://www.sistersincrime.org/page/2021BoBS

GETTING DOWN TO BUSINESS

FIRST FIVE STEPS

Book Industry Standards and Communications (BISAC) codes
https://www.bisg.org/complete-bisac-subject-headings-list

UNDERSTANDING COPYRIGHT

The Berne Convention for the Protection of Literary and Artistic
Works
https://www.wipo.int/treaties/en/ip/berne/

SECURING A LITERARY AGENT OR PUBLISHER

Association of American Literary Agents
https://aalitagents.org/canon-of-ethics/

Canadian Literary Agents
https://www.writersunion.ca/literary-agents

QueryTracker.net
https://querytracker.net/

QueryLetter.com
https://www.queryletter.com/post/161-examples-of-successful-
query-letters-from-famous-author

Publishers Marketplace
https://www.publishersmarketplace.com

UNDERSTANDING YOUR OPTIONS

TRADITIONAL (TRADE BOOK) PUBLISHERS A.K.A. THE BIG FIVE

Current state of the market
https://www.publishersweekly.com/pw/by-topic/industry-news/
publisher-news/article/89038-over-the-past-25-years-the-big-
publishers-got-bigger-and-fewer.html

Write for Harlequin
https://www.writeforharlequin.com/

INDEPENDENT PUBLISHING

Scams and scammers
https://writerbeware.blog/scam-archive/?utm_source=mailpoet&
utm_medium=email&utm_campaign=the-latest-post-from-the-
writer-beware-blog_154

Writer Beware by Victoria Strauss
https://writerbeware.blog/

Article: *Whatever Happened to Catstone Books?*
https://writerbeware.blog/2022/11/11/whatever-happened-to-
catstone-books/

Mystery Writers of America: Approved Publisher List
https://mysterywriters.org/how-to-become-a-member-of-mwa/
approved-publisher-list/

HYBRID/ASSISTED PUBLISHING

The Independent Book Publishers Association's *Hybrid Publisher Criteria* free download
https://www.ibpa-online.org/page/hybrid-publisher-criteria-download

The Alliance of Independent Authors' (ALLi's) *The Best Self-Publishing Services (And the Worst)*
https://selfpublishingadvice.org/best-self-publishing-services/

Cost-benefit analysis of assisted publishing add-ons
https://online.hbs.edu/blog/post/cost-benefit-analysis

SELF-PUBLISHING

- *FORMATTING & SOFTWARE*

Adobe InDesign
https://www.adobe.com/products/indesign.html

Article: Kindlepreneur
https://kindlepreneur.com/how-to-hire-a-book-formatter/

Article: Kobo Writing Life
https://kobowritinglife.zendesk.com/hc/en-us/articles/360058975512

Article: Selfpublishing.com
https://selfpublishing.com/book-formatting-software/

Atticus
https://www.atticus.io

Draft2Digital
https://draft2digital.com/knowledge-base/

Scrivener
https://www.literatureandlatte.com/scrivener/overview

Vellum
https://store.vellum.pub/

- *SALES STATS*

WordsRated
https://wordsrated.com/self-published-book-sales-statistics/

- *TRADEMARK NAME DATABASES*

U.S.: https://www.uspto.gov/trademarks/search

Canada: https://www.canada.ca/en/services/business/start/
choosing-a-business-name-2.html

- *TAXES*

W-8 BEN form
https://www.irs.gov/forms-pubs/about-form-w-8-ben

- *COPYRIGHT*

U.S. General: https://www.copyright.gov/
U.S. Registration: https://www.copyright.gov/registration/

Canada General: https://www.canada.ca/en/services/business/ip/
copyright.html
Canada Registration: https://copyright-application-online.com/
apply/

- *ISBNs*

U.S.: https://www.bowker.com/isbn-us

Canada: https://www.bac-lac.gc.ca/eng/services/isbn-canada/
Pages/isbn-canada.aspx

- *REVIEW SITES*

Kirkus Reviews: https://www.kirkusreviews.com/

Midwest Book Reviews: https://www.midwestbookreview.com/

- *E-BOOK RETAILERS/DISTRIBUTORS*

Amazon (Kindle Direct Publishing): https://kdp.amazon.com/
en_US/

Apple (iTunes Connect): https://itunespartner.apple.com/books/

Barnes & Noble Nook (B&N Press): https://press.
barnesandnoble.com

D2D https://www.draft2digital.com/Path

Google Play https://play.google.com/books/publish/u/0/

Kobo (Rakuten Kobo): https://writinglife.kobo.com

Untreed Reads https://www.untreedreads.com/additionalservices/

Universal Book Link
https://books2read.com/links/ubl/create/

Print on Demand – IngramSpark
https://www.ingramspark.com/

Article: *How to Select Keywords for Your Book*
https://www.babelcube.com/how/select-keywords

Book Industry Standards and Communications (BISAC) codes
https://www.bisg.org/BISAC-Subject-Codes-main

- *SERIALIZED PUBLISHING*

Wattpad: https://www.wattpad.com/

Inkitt: https://www.inkitt.com/

Kindle Vella: https://kdp.amazon.com/en_US/help/topic/
GR2L4AHPMQ44HNQ7

- *SOCIAL PUBLISHING*

Article: *How To Choose the Best Website Builders*
https://www.wpbeginner.com/beginners-guide/how-to-choose-the-
best-website-builder/

Article: *Why Your Memoir Won't Sell* by Jane Friedman
https://www.janefriedman.com/memoir-wont-sell/

Article: Wattpad's backstory
https://theliteraryplatform.com/news/2012/10/wattpad-building-
the-worlds-biggest-reader-and-writer-community/

St. Martin's unpublished mystery novel contest
https://mysterywriters.org/about-mwa/st-martins/

MONEY MATTERS

CONTRACTS

Alliance of Independent Authors
PDF download (free) *Understanding and Negotiating Book Publishing
Contracts*

https://www.authorsalliance.org/wp-content/uploads/2018/10/
20181003_AuthorsAllianceGuidePublicationContracts.pdf

Authors Guild
https://authorsguild.org/news/authors-guild-issues-model-trade-
book-contract/

Independent Book Publishers Association
*A GUIDE TO THE BOOK PUBLISHING AGREEMENT (members
only)*
https://www.ibpa-online.org/page/fullcontract-members-only

Hybrid Publisher Criteria
https://www.ibpa-online.org/page/hybridpublisher

The Authors Guild *Model Trade Book Contract* (members only)
https://authorsguild.org/resource/model-trade-book-contract/

UNDERSTANDING ROYALTIES

2021 Sisters in Crime Business of Books Survey (Released December
2022)
https://www.sistersincrime.org/page/2021BoBS

ADVERTISING & PROMOTION

Goodreads: https://www.goodreads.com

Author Central: https://author.amazon.com/

BookBub: https://partners.bookbub.com and
https://insights.bookbub.com

Street Team: https://www.writersdigest.com/publishing-insights/
develop-street-team-book

THE WRITE LIFE

Associations (Partial List)

Alliance of Independent Authors: https://www.allianceindependentauthors.org

Canadian Society of Children's Authors, Illustrators and Performers: https://www.canscaip.org

Crime Writers of Canada: https://www.crimewriterscanada.com

Historical Novel Society: https://historicalnovelsociety.org

Independent Book Publishers Association: https://www.ibpa-online.org/default.aspx

Romance Writers of America: https://www.rwa.org

Science Fiction and Fantasy Writers of America: https://www.sfwa.org

Sisters in Crime: https://www.sistersincrime.org/default.aspx

https://www.sistersincrime.org/page/guppy-online-chapter

Society of Children's Book Writers and Illustrators: https://www.scbwi.org/

Writers' Union of Canada: https://www.writersunion.ca

Grants

Grant Writing 101 – Jane Friedman
https://www.janefriedman.com/grantwriting-101/

RESOURCES BY CATEGORY

AGGREGATORS, RETAILERS & DISTRIBUTORS

Amazon (Kindle Direct Publishing): https://kdp.amazon.com/en_US/

Apple (iTunes Connect): https://itunespartner.apple.com/books/

Barnes & Noble Nook (B&N Press): https://press.barnesandnoble.com

D2D: https://www.draft2digital.com/Path

Google Play: https://play.google.com/books/publish/u/0/

Kobo (Rakuten Kobo): https://writinglife.kobo.com

Untreed Reads: https://www.untreedreads.com/additionalservices/

AWARDS, CONTESTS & GRANTS

Poets & Writers
https://www.pw.org/grants

St. Martin's unpublished mystery novel contest
https://mysterywriters.org/about-mwa/st-martins/

EDITING & PROOFREADING

Editorial Freelancers Association
https://www.the-efa.org/

Editors Canada
https://www.editors.ca/ode/search

Chartered Institute of Editors and Proofreaders
https://www.ciep.uk/directory/

GOVERNMENT LINKS

Copyright – Treaty Countries
https://www.wipo.int/members/en/

UNITED STATES
https://www.copyright.gov
https://www.copyright.gov/about/fees.html

Register a Business Name
https://www.sba.gov/business-guide/launch-your-business/register-your-business

Taxes
https://www.irs.gov/businesses/small-businesses-self-employed

CANADA

Copyright Canada
https://www.canada.ca/en/services/business/ip/copyright.html
https://www.ic.gc.ca/eic/site/cipointernet-internetopic.nsf/eng/
wr04196.html

Filing for an HST Number
https://www.canada.ca/en/revenue-agency/services/tax/
businesses/topics/gst-hst-businesses/account-register.html

ISBN Canada
https://www.bac-lac.gc.ca/eng/services/isbn-canada/Pages/isbn-
canada.aspx

Register a Business Name
https://www.canada.ca/en/services/business/start/choosing-a-
business-name-3.html

HELPFUL BLOGS & WEBSITES *some resources not
referenced in text

Career Authors
https://careerauthors.com/

Jane Friedman (reports on book publishing industry)
https://www.janefriedman.com

Kobo – Glossary of Self-Publishing Terms
https://kobowritinglife.zendesk.com/hc/en-us/articles/
360059385491-Glossary-of-Self-Publishing-Terms

NaNoWriMo
https://nanowrimo.org

Ngrams

https://books.google.com/ngrams

QueryLetter.com
https://www.queryletter.com

The Passive Voice
https://www.thepassivevoice.com/contact/

Using Music in your Book
https://www.pdinfo.com/public-domain-music-list.php
http://www.judypenzsheluk.com/2022/01/22/lets-talk-about-writing-using-lyrics/

Writer Beware by Victoria Strauss
https://www.sfwa.org/other-resources/for-authors/writer-beware/

Writers First
https://writers-first.com

PUBLISHERS & PUBLISHING PLATFORMS / INFORMATION

Literary Marketplace
http://www.literarymarketplace.com/

Publishers Marketplace
https://www.publishersmarketplace.com

Query Tracker
https://querytracker.net/

Article: The Odds of Getting Published
https://wordsrated.com/odds-of-getting-published-statistics/

IMPRINTS

Heartdrum: https://www.harpercollins.com/pages/corporate-for-authors-submit-a-manuscript

Yen Press: https://yenpress.com

SELF-PUBLISHING

BOOK REVIEWS

Kirkus Reviews: https://www.kirkusreviews.com/indie-reviews/

Midwest Book Review: https://www.midwestbookreview.com

SOCIAL PUBLISHING

Booksie: https://www.booksie.com/

BookieSilk.com: https://www.booksiesilk.com/

GALATEA (Inkitt sister app) https://getgalatea.com

Inkitt: https://www.inkitt.com/

Kindle Vella: https://www.amazon.com/kindle-vella

Wattpad: https://www.wattpad.com/stories/website

TRADITIONAL PUBLISHERS

Hachette: https://www.hachettebookgroup.com

HarperCollins: https://www.harpercollins.com/

Macmillian Publishers: https://us.macmillan.com

Penguin Random House: https://www.penguinrandomhouse.com/

Simon & Schuster: https://www.simonandschuster.com/

WRITERS' TOOLBOX

DESIGN

Canva
https://www.canva.com

FORMATTING

Adobe
https://www.adobe.com/products/indesign.html

Atticus
https://www.atticus.io

Draft2Digital
https://draft2digital.com/knowledge-base/

Kindlepreneur
https://kindlepreneur.com/how-to-hire-a-book-formatter/

Scrivener
https://www.literatureandlatte.com/scrivener/overview

Vellum
https://store.vellum.pub/

BUILDING A WEBSITE

WPBeginner
www.wpbeginner.com/beginners-guide/how-to-choose-the-best-website-builder/

How to Write an Author Bio

LiveWriteThrive
https://www.livewritethrive.com/2022/01/31/how-to-write-the-perfect-author-bio

Loglines

NFI
https://www.nfi.edu/logline-examples/

AUTHOR'S NOTE

Ten years ago, I made the decision to write a novel. I'd been working as a freelance journalist for a decade, and in addition to contributing to multiple North American consumer and trade publications, I was the Senior Editor of *New England Antiques Journal* and Editor of *Home BUILDER Canada*. I thought my reputation in the industry would help pave the way to publication.

It didn't, and despite my knowledge that publishing was, first and foremost, a business, it also didn't prepare me for the road ahead. Like every naïve author, I too made the requisite number of mistakes along the way. Fortunately, I've been guided by many established authors on my journey, authors who agreed to lend an ear, offer advice, or blurb my books, and I will be forever grateful for their insights and inspiration.

The publishing world can be a cruel one, but it is less so when authors help each other. It is my hope that this book guides you on your own personal journey, and perhaps gives you the push you have been waiting for to finally take your first step.

Dare to dream.

ACKNOWLEDGMENTS

The concept of a book exploring different publishing paths began with a presentation prepared for the New Tecumseth Public Library in early 2022. My thanks to the library, and especially Kim Burgess, the Adult Programming Director, for their ongoing support of local authors and creative content.

The concept was fleshed out further when Alexa Schlosser, Managing Editor of the Independent Book Publishers Association, commissioned an article on presentations for their member's magazine, the *IBPA Independent*, for the May/June 2022 issue. That article took me back to my journalistic routes and led to another connection: K.D. Sullivan, co-founder of Untreed Reads Publishing. K.D. liked the article, recognized my name from a story included in Untreed's *Flash and Bang: A Short Mystery Fiction Society Anthology*, and reached out. Before long, I was telling her about how I thought the presentation might work as a book, and as she helped me to brainstorm ideas, I knew it was something I wanted to pursue.

But wanting to do something and doing it are two different things. One thing I knew for certain was that I couldn't do it alone. Fortunately, fate had brought Emily Nakeff into my life. I'd met Emily a few years before while doing a NaNoWriMo talk at the Essa (Angus) Public Library, and she'd attended other presentations, including *Finding Your Path to Publication* and *Self-publishing: The Ins & Outs of Going Indie*, through the New Tecumseth Public Library. I knew that Emily was an aspiring author, working hard to hone her craft, and that she was also an editor. Hiring Emily to review and edit my weekly output (thereby keeping me accountable to the project) was the best decision I could have made. Her insights, gentle critiques, and suggestions were invaluable to the process and her assistance as a Research Assistant in the creation of the Additional Resources (Talking the Talk, Resources by Section and Category) cannot be overstated.

I also owe a tremendous debt of gratitude to my longtime editor, Ti Locke, for her review and edit of the final manuscript, beta readers Annie McQuaid, Elisabeth McGregor, and K.D. Sullivan, and my proofreader Nicky Hill. Writing a book may be a solitary process, but getting it to the finish line takes teamwork. I could not have come this far without you.

Last, but certainly not least, to the following individuals and organizations who gave permission to quote from their online resources and surveys:

The Alliance of Independent Authors (ALLi)
The Authors Guild
The Book Industry Study Group
The Independent Book Publishers Association
Jane Friedman
Sisters in Crime
WordsRated
WriterBeware

And finally, to the authors, whether aspiring or published and looking for a new path to explore. Thank you for trusting me with your vision.

Judy Penz Sheluk
May 2023

- A STEP-BY-STEP GUIDE -

SELF-PUBLISHING
THE *Ins & Outs* OF
GOING INDIE

JUDY PENZ SHELUK

BOOK 2: SELF-PUBLISHING

THE INS & OUTS OF GOING INDIE

INTRODUCTION

Ten years ago, when I sat down to write my first novel, the thought of self-publishing never crossed my mind. To be fair, times were different then. There was a greater stigma to self-publishing, and vanity presses had (deservedly) earned their reputation as the bottom feeders of the book publishing industry.

As an established freelance journalist and magazine editor, I was also no stranger to seeing my name in print, with bylines in dozens of North American newspapers and magazines. I assumed, wrongly as it turned out, that my good reputation would help pave the way to a traditional publishing deal.

It didn't, and in July 2014, after several (mostly nice) rejections and one offer from a New York City agent to ghost write a book in exchange for a small share of any royalties earned (I turned her down), I signed a contract for *The Hanged Man's Noose*, the first book in my Glass Dolphin mystery series.

I vetted the publisher, an independent press based in Oregon, as well as anyone can prior to submitting. I checked online reviews and ratings of the books in their catalogue, read a handful of titles to ensure they were well edited, then contacted three of their authors who, like me, belonged to Sisters in Crime. Feedback about the publisher was overwhelmingly positive. Quality editing, proofreading, and cover art were all handled in a collaborative manner with the author. Royalties were reported monthly and paid promptly. I was further assured by the publisher's Mystery Writers of America and International Thriller Writers approved standings.

Despite all that, when it came time to find a home for the first book in my Marketville mystery series, I decided to query elsewhere to make sure all my eggs weren't in one basket. I'd heard too many tales of authors whose series had been "orphaned" (an industry term meaning the premature cancellation of a contract due to the publisher shuttering its doors or discontinuing the genre). That wasn't going to happen to me.

Except, it did. Twice. It turned out having multiple baskets didn't offer the security I thought it might.

It didn't come as a huge shock; traditional print media had been declining for years, and my years in the magazine world taught me to read the signs of impending closure. One publisher had systematically begun to release every one of their authors from their contracts. The other had all but stopped communicating, including royalty reports and updates on books-in-progress. By July 2018, both of my series were officially orphaned.

Few "orphaned" authors find a new home for their existing series, even after months, sometimes years, of trying. Some start over. Some give up. I did neither. The knowledge both failed publishers had given me was knowledge of the industry. I understood what loomed on my horizon, and a few months prior to being officially orphaned, I'd set up my own imprint, Superior Shores Press. I was ready to take my destiny into my own hands.

I've learned a lot since 2018, made a few miscalculations along the way, overcomplicated some things, underestimated others. I've also guided a couple of traditionally published authors through their own indie journeys and, at the request of my then-local library, developed a presentation titled *Finding Your Path to Publication*, which led to a second presentation, *Self-Publishing: The Ins & Outs of Going Indie*, and an article in the Independent Book Publishers Association bimonthly magazine, the *IBPA Independent*.

If you've read *Finding Your Path the Publication*, you will spot some overlap between that book and this one. Here, though, I've adapted and delved further into that information expressly through the lens of self-publishing.

As with *Finding Your Path to Publication*, you won't find advice in these pages—it's not my place to tell you how or where to publish your novel. What you will find is information to understand this side of the publishing world and make your journey into self-publishing smoother and less daunting. Look for the (#AR) symbol as an indicator that a weblink to more information is included in the *Additional Resources* section at the back of this book. I've broken each of those resources down by section and sub-section, which allows for easy reference while reading, or later when you're getting ready to tackle your own project. You'll also find a glossary with common terms used in self-publishing, as well as a separate "Your Steps" page at the end of each section, with bullet points you can use to develop your own step-by-step guide.

When I first typed the words "*The Hanged Man's Noose*: Chapter One" a decade ago, I never envisioned that my journey would lead me to self-publishing through my own imprint, but it's turned out to be the right decision for me.

I've also accomplished far more in the past five years than I could have ever imagined. It is my hope that by sharing my knowledge and experience, you'll avoid some of the missteps that were part of my personal journey. That said, self-publishing is not for everyone, and once you've read this book, you may decide it isn't right for you.

Then again, you just may decide that you're ready to take the leap. Let's find out.

PREPPING FOR PUBLICATION

COVER ART & PRICING

As a self-published author, you have some decisions to make regarding retail distribution. Are you considering e-book only? Or will you be adding print version(s) now, or down the road? Will your books be accessible exclusively on Amazon? Or would you prefer to go "wide"—the industry term for uploading content to a variety of online storefronts in addition to Amazon?

Those are tough questions to answer, especially if you're not sure what each option entails. Not to worry. In this section, I'll go over the basics of digital (e-book) and Print on Demand (POD) distribution (your only viable option for publishing print copies). Later in the book, I'll review several online publishing and distribution options in "Publishing Platforms." But first, let's start with the one thing you're going to need, whether you decide to go wide or exclusive, e-book only, or print and digital.

Cover Art

I know, we're not supposed to judge a book by its cover, but let's face it—we all do it. and the truth of the matter is, good covers *can* help sell books.

One of the advantages to self-publishing is full control over the cover art design for your book (not so with traditional publishing paths). Ever seen a book cover and thought, "Please, not another... cozy mystery with a white picket fence and a cat...thriller with a woman in a red coat/dress running across a road or bridge... historical fiction with a cloaked woman and a suitcase."

Big name authors can get away with that—you can't. Which means your goal is to make sure your cover stands out from the already crowded shelves.

I'm not a graphic artist, but I always have a vision of what my book cover should look like. I do a rough sketch (and I do mean rough) with some notes on the vibe I'm looking for, and send those off to my designer extraordinaire, Hunter Martin. From those notes, he offers a few options for backgrounds, and we build the cover from there. I chronicled the steps involved in building the cover for my novel *Before There Were Skeletons* on my blog (#AR).

You have two options when it comes to creating cover art:

1) Hire a professional graphic artist who specializes in print and e-book covers. Some writing associations and publishing platforms offer discounts and/or recommendations for this service. Your agreement should outline the number of revisions included and timeline to complete the project. Above all, this should be a collaborative process.

2) Design it yourself using an online service, such as Canva or SelfPubBookCovers.com (#AR), or publisher, such as Draft2Digital or Kindle Direct Publishing. If you decide to choose a publisher's cover art options, check for restrictions in the terms and conditions, which could change. You'll want to have permission to use that cover at all other booksellers.

Pro Tip: Cover art, like any artistic pursuit, is subject to copyright. If you choose to hire a graphic artist, make sure this is a work-for-hire and that you (and not the artist) own the copyright to your book cover. If you choose to design your own, you must own the copyright or license for any image(s) or photograph(s) used, even if the image/photograph only takes up a small fraction of the cover.

Whether you choose to hire someone or do it yourself, always keep branding in mind. This is especially true when it comes to series, but you may have also noticed that your favorite authors have certain similarities from one cover to the next, regardless of whether the book is part of a series or a standalone. For books published under the Superior Shores Press imprint, for example, the key elements will always be in the same position (#AR):

- Subtitle (A Step-by-Step Guide)
- Title: Top quarter.
- My name: Bottom quarter.

Each series will also use the same font (typeface) for all text. Admittedly, not all book covers follow this structure, but it's advice I was given, and it has served me well. Whatever you decide, make sure your name stands out. This is no time to shy away from the limelight.

*Pro Tip: It's helpful to view your cover as a thumbnail (reduced image size) before you finalize it. This will give you a good idea of how it will appear on online retail sites.

Back Cover Copy/Jacket Copy/Book Blurb/Retail Copy

This goes by many names, depending on the publishing platform and/or book format (hardcover, paperback, e-book, etc.), but in a nutshell these are the terms used for the text on the back of your book, inside the book under "Praise for" (or other terms for advance reviews), as well as in the description box wherever your book is being sold. It's basically a sales pitch or a hook telling readers what the book is about and why they should want to read it. You'll need to enter this information when you upload your book for retail distribution. You'll also use this in your promotional efforts. In this section, I'll be referring to it as "retail copy." You can call it anything you'd like!

Ideally, your retail copy will run no more than two paragraphs and 150-200 words; shorter is always better. My copy for *Before There Were Skeletons* is 110 words, which allowed me to include four brief "praise for" blurbs on the trade paperback and large print versions (#AR).

You'll also want to write copy that is adaptable to an even shorter length. That's because some storefronts will allow two versions of your retail copy, a "long" version and "short" version. Some entry forms also limit the number of characters. Crime Writers of Canada, for example, sends out a monthly newsletter, *Cool Canadian Crime* (#AR), which announces new releases for their Professional Author Members (PAMs). It's up to the author to submit the title, along with a 125-character "teaser" and 300-character description.

Here's the thing about teasers. They don't usually quote from your retail copy, but rather act as a set up.

Let's look at *Before There Were Skeletons*:

Long version (110 words / 693 characters): The last time anyone saw Veronica Goodman was the night of February 14, 1995, the only clue to her disappearance a silver heart-shaped pendant, found in the parking lot behind the bar where she worked. Twenty-seven years later, Veronica's daughter, Kate, just a year old when her mother vanished, hires Past & Present Investigations to find out what happened that fateful night.
Calamity (Callie) Barnstable is drawn to the case, the similarities to her own mother's disappearance on Valentine's Day 1986 hauntingly familiar. A disappearance she thought she'd come to terms with. Until Veronica's case, and five high school yearbooks, take her back in time…a time before there were skeletons.

Short version (34 words / 190 characters): Callie's back, and this time she's been hired to find a woman who went missing on Valentine's Day, 1995. But that case leads to two others, and an unexpected connection to Callie's own past.

Teaser (6 words/40 characters): Valentine's Day isn't always about lovers.

Writing retail copy takes time, effort, and more than a few drafts. Before you get started, study and analyze the retail copy for books in your genre—and don't just concentrate on bestselling titles. Which ones grabbed your attention, and why? Which ones did you think fell flat? Look for similarities in style and structure that you can use as a guideline for your own book.

> **Pro Tip: Always run your teaser and your retail copy by your beta readers, as well as a few friends or family members who haven't read your book. This will ensure it reflects the essence of your story, and that it is also effective in capturing the attention of new readers. Always ask for (and accept) honest input—empty compliments won't help you sell books.*

TECHNICAL SPECIFICATIONS

E-books: The ideal dimensions for an e-book cover are 2,560 pixels in height x 1,600 pixels wide at 300 dpi (dots per inch) with an RGB (red, green, blue) color profile. Images can be JPEG (.jpeg) or TIFF (.tiff). (#AR). I always use JPEG, simply because it is adequate for this purpose, easier to share, and faster to upload.

Paperback or Hardcover: Print templates are available at no cost from POD distributors. Each POD publisher uses a different template and has different rules (I'll review these in greater detail in Publishing Platforms) but you will need to provide your ISBN, so have that ready.

Print templates are calculated using the following data:

- Trim size (e.g., 6" x 9")
- Paper type (cream, white, recycled).
- Interior type (black and white or color).

- Binding (paperback or hardcover).
- Cover finish (matte or glossy).
- Total page count.
- Optional: Retail price in USD and CAD. If provided, it will be included in the bar code (which also includes your ISBN) on the back cover.

If any of these variables change, you'll need a new template and a new cover. For example, you may think that adding four or five extra pages is no big deal, but it's the number of pages (as well as the thickness of the paper used) that determines the width of the spine.

It's important to note that there are no guarantees that a brick-and-mortar bookstore will stock your book, and the reality is, they probably won't unless there's proven customer demand. That said, most will list your book on their website as "not available in store" but "available online." If a customer purchases your title, the bookstore will immediately place an order to your POD distributor, who in turn will ship your book directly to the customer (who will be none the wiser that your book wasn't physically in the bookstore).

This non-stock issue isn't a knock against your book. The Big Five account for 80% of the books shelved in brick-and-mortar stores, leaving just 20% for independent publishers, hybrid/assisted, and self-published books. The bigger the independent publisher, the greater their odds increase...and yours decrease.

Pro Tip: While you can include the retail price on your cover, it's not a decision to be made lightly, as the cost to produce print copies continues to escalate (I'm sure you've noticed the dramatic increase in the cost of paperbacks over the past few years). I'll cover print charges a bit later in this chapter.

PICKING YOUR PRICE

E-BOOKS

Determining the price for an e-book depends on many factors, not least of which are estimated royalties, which are provided when you upload your book and enter the price information. But there's more to pricing than how much money you might make, emphasis on the *might*. Overprice your book and you'll limit sales. Underprice, and you risk giving the impression your book isn't very good. It's also worth noting that some vendors, (like Amazon), charge a significantly higher vendor fee for books priced below $2.99 or above $9.99. You may also want to put your e-book on sale at some point. A discount from $5.99 to $0.99 is much more appealing than $2.99 to $0.99.

To determine the right price for your e-book, start by doing a price comparison of books in your genre and sub-genre on Amazon and find a happy medium. The good news: with any platform, it's easy to change the price of your e-book temporarily or permanently, and changing the price doesn't require re-publishing—nor will you incur any revision fees. In most cases, the updated price will come into effect within a few hours, though if you're planning a paid promotion, you'll want to allow least 72 hours to make sure things run as planned, especially if you want it to align with your marketing plans for the sale (it's always better to err on the side of caution).

I've provided additional information on e-book pricing, including specific examples of royalty rates, under each individual publishing platform covered in this book. It's important to understand, however, that the royalty rates offered by each platform are non-negotiable: take it or leave it. The upside? The royalty rate paid to you, as a self-published author, will be the same as would be paid to any other publisher. In this case, at least, size doesn't matter. Even so, regardless of the cost of your e-book, you will only be paid a percentage of that price, because every publishing platform takes a cut. That's how they make money and stay in business. It's also the reason why setting up a vendor account is always free.

PRINT ON DEMAND (POD)

When determining how to price your paperback or hardcover book, you'll need to factor in two steps:

1) Print Charge: This is the actual cost the POD publisher charges to print the book, calculated by page count (cost per page) and type of ink (standard black and white or upgrade to color). The trim size (e.g., 6" x 9"), cover finish (matte or glossy), and choice of interior paper color (white or cream) do not impact the cost. The quality of the paper (regular, recycled, or premium, for example) will.

2) Wholesale Discount: The percentage off the suggested retail price, offered to the wholesale distributor. In turn, the wholesale distributor will make your book available for order by booksellers and libraries (after all, you can't expect booksellers to pay full retail AND make a profit, and libraries have limited budgets). The discount percentage varies by POD publisher and distribution options, but you're looking at a range between 40% (Amazon only) to 60%. I'll be providing more information, as well as specific examples, under the individual POD platforms.

Regardless of which POD publisher you select, your options to reduce the print cost are limited, but those you do have can have a substantial impact on your bottom line.

Let's look at the print costs (subject to change) for one 300-page 6" x 9" book using Ingram's Publisher Compensation Calculator (#AR).

Paperback

- Black & white on 50 lb. paper: $5.48
- Black & white on 70 lb. paper: $7.91
- Color on 50 lb. paper: $9.53
- Color on 70 lb. paper: $11.96

- Premium color on 70 lb. paper: $21.86

Hardcover (case laminate)

- Black & white on 50 lb. paper: $9.76
- Black & white on 70 lb. paper: $12.13
- Color on 50 lb. paper: $13.93
- Color on 70 lb. paper: $16.30
- Premium color on 70 lb. paper: $27.68

Hardcover (cloth cover)

- Black & white on 50 lb. paper: $11.55
- Black & white on 70 lb. paper: $13.92
- Color on 50 lb. paper: $15.88
- Color on 70 lb. paper: $18.25
- Premium color on 70 lb. paper: $29.50

Once you factor in the print charge and wholesale discount, you can understand why the cost of paperbacks and hardcovers has escalated over time, while earnings have reduced to marginal levels. It's a balancing act between selling books and trying to make money. Again, I'll give more specific examples under Publishing Platforms, but the bottom line is if you're making $2 on a book priced at $20, you're doing well. Be thankful. If you had a traditional publisher, you'd earn half that, and less than half if you also had an agent earning their commission.

*Pro tip: The industry standard for novels is trade paperback with black and white interior on 50 lb. paper. Premium options are generally geared towards books that rely heavily on color images, such as books on photography and cookbooks.

EPUBS & PDFS

PROPERLY FORMATTED OR NOT, no one's going to purchase your Word document. They'll be buying your e-book, or a printed paperback or hardcover copy. That's why you'll need to convert your manuscript into the correct format before uploading it for sale or distribution: EPUB (for e-books) or PDF (for print).

Note: EPUB is sometimes stylized as ePub. To keep things consistent, I've used EPUB throughout.

E-BOOK PUBLISHING

Short for electronic publication an .epub file is currently the only format recognized by e-readers, such as Kindle, Kobo, Nook, etc., and the most widely used.

Both Apple (Mac/Pages) and Scrivener offer document to EPUB conversion options, try them if you're a devotee of either platform. If not, the following options are available to convert your Word document (.doc or .docx) into an .epub file:

- Kindle Direct Publishing (KDP) and Kobo Writing Life (KWL) both offer tutorials on how to format a Word document to meet specific e-book conversion requirements (#AR). That said, the process can be time consuming and it's far from bulletproof. Files with complex formatting may not convert well (at the very least, it will probably limit your interior page design options), and you may not be able to use this "free" conversion on other publishing platforms.

- Draft2Digital, an aggregator that handles distribution services to multiple online retailers, subscription services, and libraries, also offers a free digital conversion service and unlike KDP and KWL, there's no restriction on using your file elsewhere. There are several templates to choose from.
- Hire a book formatter or purchase formatting software (#AR). I'll discuss both options in more detail later in this chapter).

PRINT ON DEMAND (POD) PUBLISHING

As a self-published author, your only viable option for publishing print copies, whether they are paperback or hardcover, is to use a Print on Demand (POD) distributor. I'll go into more detail about your POD options in Publishing Platforms, but the bottom line is you'll need a PDF file, and it's more complicated than simply selecting the "save as PDF" option. That's because you'll need to ensure the correct page size during setup, e.g., 6" x 9" (trade paperback), 6.14" x 9.21" (large print), etc. And because MS Word (and Pages) assume that every page has a front and a back, the programs often auto-inserts unwanted blank pages. There may be other design issues, as well. When it comes to converting to PDF, my recommendation is to either hire a book formatter or purchase book formatting software (#AR).

FORMATTING BASICS

As previously noted, there are two options when converting your manuscript into EPUB and/or PDF formats: hiring a third party or doing it yourself.

Hiring a Third Party

This is a good option if you're tech-averse. However, if you're planning to self-publish, you'll need to get over that aversion, since the cost can add up substantially over time, and more importantly, you'll lose an element of control.

Should you decide to go that route, you'll want to get references and a detailed quote outlining the turnaround time (after all, your book may not be the only one in their queue) and the cost per EPUB and PDF format (remember, you will need a different PDF for every print size). You may also want, or need, to revise your content down the road. As such, you'll need to know the cost and turnaround time per revision/file.

While fees vary, the cost to hire an outside service may be as much as, or more than, purchasing your own software, especially if you plan to publish additional books in the future. As previously noted, hiring an outside service may also mean relinquishing some control over the interior page layout and design elements. If you're like me and enjoy tinkering with a variety of fonts and finishing touches, purchasing software is probably a better fit for your needs.

Formatting Software

Should you choose to purchase software, select one that will allow you to format an unlimited number of books (always think ahead!) for *multiple* retailers, in EPUB and a variety of print sizes. There should be an option to upload sample material or a free trial period. Examples of formatting software include Atticus, Vellum (for Mac users only), Adobe InDesign, and Scrivener (#AR). I personally use Vellum, but that doesn't mean you have to.

ARCS, PRE-ORDERS & PUBLICATION DATE

TRADITIONAL PUBLISHERS CAN TAKE up to two years to get your book to market once the contract is signed, though most will do so within a year to eighteen months. As a self-published author, it will be up to you to establish a reasonable and achievable timeline, and while that will likely be quicker than any traditional path, the process should never be rushed.

To keep things simple, let's assume that your manuscript has already been professionally edited. That's great, but it's just the beginning. In this section, you'll learn about formatting your book for retail, Advance Reader Copies (ARCs), review blurbs, and how to set a realistic publication date.

ARCs (ADVANCE READER COPIES)

Advance Reader Copies, commonly referred to as ARCs, are sent to potential reviewers for "blurbs" on the back cover and/or inside as "praise for" (you see this a lot in e-books since they don't have a back cover). You may also choose to include a blurb on the front cover. The blurb itself should always be in quotation marks, with credit given to the blurber, as follows: "a cleverly plotted, intricately woven story."— *ALLISON DORE, HOST OF THE BREAKDOWN, SIRIUS XM*

> *Pro Tip: It's acceptable to take a snippet of a longer review and use it as a blurb. If you decide to do this, insert ellipses into the missing text.*

Here's an example of a review in *Kings River Life Magazine* for my novel, *Before There Were Skeletons*:

> "A daughter just looking for answers about her mother's disappearance sets Callie Barnstable on a journey uncovering curious connections and personal insights—an engaging mystery with more than just closure."—*KINGS RIVER LIFE MAGAZINE*

This review can be abbreviated as:

> "A daughter just looking for answers…a journey uncovering curious connections and personal insights…an engaging mystery."—*KINGS RIVER LIFE MAGAZINE*

Or, if space is an issue…

> "…an engaging mystery."—*KINGS RIVER LIFE MAGAZINE*

Sometimes less really is more. In all cases, whenever you use a blurb, you must always credit the source—no exceptions.

Unless you already have cover art and your book is uploaded for pre-order (more information on the technical nitty gritty to come), you won't be able to supply ARCs in paperback format. However, once you've converted your manuscript, you will have PDF and digital (EPUB) copies to send to potential reviewers. Services such as Book Funnel and Net Galley (#AR) will host your ARCs, track individual downloads, encrypt your files so they can't be copied, printed, or shared, and help readers load books onto their devices. You can also e-mail your EPUB directly to advance readers, but because the files you create won't be encrypted, you'll only want to go that route with trusted reviewers. Another option to encourage reader reviews at any time is to enroll your Kindle book into a Goodreads Giveaway (#AR).

While reader reviews are always welcome, they are never a sure thing and there's no guarantee they'll even be positive. Reader reviews can't be used inside your book, nor should they be used in social media posts unless you've obtained the reviewer's permission to do so. Since sites like Amazon and Goodreads strongly discourage any contact with reviewers (and may even boycott you for doing so), obtaining permission is unlikely. That said, you can always create a generic post with a link to your Goodreads, Amazon, or other storefront page with a message along the lines of "Whoot! Just received another 5-star review for *BOOK TITLE* on Amazon!"

You will, however, be able to use any "blurbs" solicited from other authors. I strongly recommend trying to line up "blurbers" well in advance of your release date. Start by making a wish list of your top five authors and contact them two to three months *before* you expect a completed ARC. These could be authors you've met networking through writing associations, conferences or conventions, or social media channels. Aim high. You never know who'll come through for you. Of course, asking for blurbs is difficult, though if it's any consolation, even bestselling, award-winning authors like mystery/suspense author and crime reporter Hank Phillippe Ryan face the same daunting task (#AR).

You can improve your odds by treating your request with the same deference you would with any other business communication. Your e-mail should include a brief introduction, a description of your book, the approximate date the ARC formats will be available, the tentative date of publication, and required turnaround time, something along the lines of:

Dear Name,

We met at the Writer's Conference in Toronto, where you mentioned you might be willing to provide a brief review of my book, TITLE, if time permitted. I'm happy to say that Digital ARCs (PDF, EPUB) will be available

by mid-March. Publication date is scheduled for July 15. I would request your
review by June 15 latest. Here's a bit about it:
 Retail blurb or brief summary.
 Thank you for your consideration.

You can also try your local paper, though the reality is fewer and fewer newspapers offer book reviews, and most won't even consider self-published novels. That said, sending a prepared press release might ease the way. You'll find more information on press releases in Marketing & Publicity.

There are also review sites which charge a fee, such as Kirkus Reviews and Midwest Book Reviews, though in the interest of their reputations, neither can guarantee a positive review. Reader's Favorite, which offers paid and free review options (the paid option fast tracks the process), is another option, however they will only post four- or five-star reviews. If your book falls short, you'll be sent a critique. Another free option is BookLife, the *Publisher's Weekly* review site for self-published authors, though the process can take 12 weeks or longer and only a small percentage of books submitted are considered for a review (#AR).

Because obtaining reviews can be a lengthy process, it's acceptable to send the ARC while it's still in the final editing/proofreading stage. Don't worry, minor mistakes are expected in an ARC. It's even okay if your cover is still a temporary placeholder. Just be sure the cover of your ARC is clearly marked as *ADVANCE READER COPY — Uncorrected Author Proof, Not for Resale* — and that the same wording is used on the inside title and copyright page (just don't forget to update both in the final version!).

Ideally, you'll have two or three blurbs, but worst-case scenario, you can always publish without any. Don't let a lack of reviews become an excuse to give up.

PRE-ORDERS

Allowing readers to advance order your book prior to its release, known in the industry as pre-orders, is optional, but if you choose to go this route, you will need to keep a couple things in mind:

1) You can't set up pre-orders without uploading some form of a finished book. You can, however, set up a pre-order using an ARC as a placeholder. That said, you will need to upload a final file at least 72 hours in advance of publication, and sooner is better than later. While you can always upload revised files at any time (more on that in "Publishing Platforms"), the last thing you want is an uncorrected advance reader copy going out on release day because you either missed a deadline or forgot.

2) Readers who pre-order your book do not receive (or pay for) your book in advance—in fact, they can cancel the pre-order at any time prior to publication. Because of that, pre-orders are not considered sales until your book's official release day. When that happens, print copies are mailed and e-books are automatically delivered to the purchaser's reading library, e.g., Kindle, Kobo, Nook, etc. At that point, pre-orders are considered sales, and you'll begin to earn royalties. (I'll be going into royalties and how they work in depth a bit later.)

Are pre-orders a good idea? That depends. They can be a good way to promote your book and rack up advance sales, but that's probably truer for well-known authors with a wide following than a debut or self-published author. Still, properly marketed, pre-orders can generate buzz, and the power of word-of-mouth advertising can't be understated.

One way to encourage sales is to discount your e-book for pre-orders. Let's say you've selected a retail price of $5.99. Offering a discounted (and promoted) "introductory" price might entice readers who are on the fence to give your book a try.

Print books can also be placed on pre-order by some (but not all) distribution channels. However, because of the fixed costs associated with print, they are never discounted on pre-order.

*Pro Tip: Unless you're planning to put your book on pre-order, pricing is a decision you don't have to make until you're ready to upload your book to the various publishing and distribution platforms. If you choose

to allow pre-orders, keep in simple: start with the e-book version, and hold off on print pre-orders until the final version of your manuscript, including cover art, is ready for upload.

SELECTING YOUR PUBLICATION DATE

Now that you know what's involved vis-à-vis ARCs, getting review blurbs, cover art, and pre-orders, you can determine a realistic date for the publication of your book. If you're still working on your novel, the good news is that now you can develop a working timeline. If you're like me, you may even have purchased a new notebook to track the process.

What if you've finished your manuscript and expected to upload it to Amazon and be done with it? Well, now you know better.

Ideally, you'll have three to four months from the day you send out ARCs before you officially publish, though you'll need to consider other factors. For example, if your book has a Christmas theme, you'll want to release it in November or December for the best results. If you haven't left yourself enough time to do that, you may have to forgo ARCs and blurbs and go straight to publishing.

Are there good and bad days of the week to publish? While there are no hard and fast rules, Kobo Writing Life recommends Tuesdays for new Kobo releases (#AR). I'd avoid weekends, holidays, election days, and big events like the Superbowl—you want your launch to get some fanfare on social media. Why compete with a known giant? Little about publishing is predictable, so it's important to use what you *can* predict to your advantage.

There's a lot to absorb in this section and you may have to read it more than once. That said, I really wish I'd had something like this when I decided to self-publish, which is why I'm sharing it now. I encourage you to check out the relevant weblinks for this section, as listed under Additional Resources (#AR), if anything seems unclear or ambiguous.

CATEGORIES & KEYWORDS

CATEGORIES AND KEYWORDS are an integral part of prepping your book for publication, with a long view to future sales. Get it right, and you're ahead of the game. Get it wrong and...well, the good news is, you can always change these down the road. That said, why not get it right the first time?

CATEGORIES

If you've ever paid attention to the Best Sellers Ranking on Amazon (found on the book page under Product Details)—and if you haven't, now is the time to start—you'll notice that in addition to an overall sales ranking there are three categories listed for each title. For example, when writing this section, Margaret Mitchell's *Gone with the Wind* was #9,933 overall in the Kindle Store, but within its listed categories it sat at #26 in Classic Literary Fiction, #77 in Action & Adventure Romance (Books), and #84 in Romance Literary Fiction.

Where do these categories come from, who assigns them, and how are they selected? I'm glad you asked.

The categories come from the Book Industry Standards and

Communications (BISAC) codes (#AR)—the U.S. categorization standard employed by online retailers, brick and mortar stores, and libraries. BISAC codes are the basis for the categories used by all publishing platforms.

Your job as a publisher will be to select the best primary subject heading and sub-categories to define your book. Understanding BISAC codes will go a long way in helping you do that and, ultimately, helping get your book in front of your target audience.

First, determine the primary heading. These are broad categories. For example, under FICTION, you'll find sub-categories ranging from Mystery & Detective to Fantasy, LGBTQ+, and Romance. Each of those sub-categories will be further defined, e.g., FICTION/Romance/Historical/Gilded Age. It's recommended that you choose no more than three sub-categories (even when more than three are allowed), though two is usually sufficient to adequately describe your book. What you don't want to do is pick a random category for the sake of selecting three, since that could misdirect readers.

Let's take my previous book, *Finding Your Path to Publication*, as an example. My inclination was to select RESEARCH, but nothing seemed to fit. To ensure accuracy, I went so far as to consult with the BISAC gurus (while also obtaining permission to reference their materials) and was advised that the primary subject heading should be LANGUAGE ARTS & DISCIPLINES, and the sub-categories Publishers & Publishing Industry and Writing Authorship. The other options available under the Language Arts & Disciplines heading did not apply to my manuscript.

Why not take a moment now to define your book's BISAC codes? You can always change them later (even after publication), but brainstorming can be a good way to get the ball rolling. Need more guidance? BISAC also offers advice on how to select codes (#AR).

KEYWORDS

At the same time you select categories, you'll be asked to choose up to seven keywords, which are just as important as categories. Keywords can be a single word, such as "horses," or a phrase, such as "horse racing mystery," or even a place or event, e.g., "Churchill Downs" or "Kentucky Derby." That said, your keyword should not be a repeat of your BISAC code. Keywords will help to *further* target your book to the right audience, and duplication of words won't cover any new ground. There's no point adding "publishing industry" for *Finding Your Path to Publication* when it's already been covered by BISAC. Rather, a better selection might be "how to get published," "self-publishing," "social publishing," "finding a publisher," and so forth.

Pro-tip: When selecting keywords, think of what word or words you might enter into a search engine when looking for a book similar to yours.

GETTING DOWN TO BUSINESS

I KNOW what you must be thinking. Are we ever going to stop prepping and start publishing? The good news is we're just about there, but before we get to publishing platforms, there's a bit more business to take care of.

ACCOUNT SETUP

One question I'm often asked during a webinar or presentation is how much it costs to set up individual accounts with the various publishing platforms. The answer is nothing, at least in terms of submitting your application to publish. That's because their compensation comes from a percentage of your royalties (monies earned from the sale of your books). I've provided specific examples of how royalties pay out for each of those platforms (also known as retailers or storefronts) in "Publishing Platforms."

Regardless of platform, all applications are completed online. As with any type of account application, you'll need to enter basic contact information. The information required varies by seller, but you should be prepared to share your first name, last name, e-mail, telephone, date of birth, mailing address, and your publisher name.

Once your account is verified (usually within 48 hours or less), you'll be allowed to upload your book(s) for sale. Before you do that, however, you'll want to make sure that you'll be paid for any royalties earned.

GETTING PAID

To receive payment, you need to provide all required bank and tax documentation. You'll also need to earn royalties that meet or exceed any minimum payment threshold as defined by the publishing platform.

BANKING

Each publishing platform has a preferred (or required) method of electronic payment (receiving payment by check is generally not an option). If you want to be paid, you'll need to be sure that you've set up the necessary financial accounts.

PayPal: Payments sent by PayPal are e-mail specific. If you have more than one e-mail address, be sure that the e-mail you provide in Account Setup matches your PayPal e-mail.

Electronic Fund Transfer (EFT): Also known as Direct Deposit. Most employers today use EFT/Direct Deposit to pay their employees, and when it comes to publishing platforms, this is the easiest way to be paid without incurring any fees. To set this up, you'll need to provide your checking account details, including:

- Location of bank (Country)
- Bank name
- Branch address
- Account number
- Routing number (more information below)
- Account currency (e.g., USD, CAD, Euros)

ABA (U.S.): Short for American Bankers Association, an ABA is a nine-digit routing number that identifies banks in the U.S. It can usually be found in the bottom left-hand corner of your personal check. It can also be found on your bank statement, which is usually accessible online. Many banks also put their routing number on their website.

Routing number (Canada): From left to right, the first set of numbers is the cheque (Canadian spelling intended) number, followed by a five-digit transit number and a three-digit institution number. Your routing number is the eight-digit combination of the bank institution number, followed by the transit number. For Electronic Funds Transfers, nine digits are required; enter a 0 at the beginning (in front of the bank institution number).

Wire Transfer: You'll need all the information required for EFT, as well as your bank's alphanumeric BIC (Business Identifier Code) or SWIFT (Society for Worldwide Interbank Financial Telecommunication) code. Both terms are used interchangeably and mean exactly the same thing. You can typically find the BIC/SWIFT code on a bank statement or on your bank's website. There are also numerous online resources that list all codes by country (#AR). The downside of payment by wire transfers is that there is typically a fee. For example, my financial institution charges a flat fee of $17.50 per wire transfer, regardless of the amount of the transfer.

ACH (Automated Clearing House): Similar to EFT, ACH is a type of electronic funds transfer that's used in the U.S. An ACH transfer links banks, creating a tally of credits and debits that are settled at the end of the business day. QuickBooks has a good article on the difference between EFT and ACH (#AR).

Tax Forms

You will have to report (and pay tax) on any royalty income

earned, though you may not receive a tax slip. I've included what you can expect to receive from each publishing platform under "Tax Information." The following information has been provided as a brief explanation of tax regulations for U.S. and Canadian residents and is in no way meant to replace professional advice, due diligence, and compliance with regards to income tax matters.

U.S. Publishers/Residents

A TIN (taxpayer identification number) is required by the IRS for the administration of tax laws. In most cases, your TIN is either an Employer Identification Number (EIN) or a Social Security Number (SSN). To process payments, you'll be asked to complete a tax interview and/or provide a Form W-9 (#AR). If you are a U.S. citizen, but residing in a country outside of the U.S., you must also submit a Form W-9. When valid tax information is provided, your royalty income will not be subject to tax withholding (taxes deducted from your payment). If the tax identity you provide does not match IRS records, you may be subject to payment holds or U.S. tax withholding of up to 30%.

Note: You are required to declare royalty income when filing your tax return. As a rule, W-9 forms do not expire.

Canadian Publishers/Residents

Because the United States and Canada have a reciprocal income tax agreement, each U.S.-based retailer will require Canadian authors to complete a tax interview and a W-8BEN form (#AR) to certify that your country of residence for tax purposes is in Canada, and that you agree to abide by Canadian tax laws for any royalties earned. In return, you won't have 30% of those royalties withheld to pay U.S. taxes, and you won't need to file a U.S. tax return. You will, however, need to file a Canadian tax return declaring all royalty income.

Note: W-8 BEN forms expire on December 31st three years after you submit to the publishing platform. Some platforms will remind you before (or when) that happens. Others won't. Set up a reminder system so your tax information doesn't lapse.

Pro Tip: As a self-published author, you're considered self-employed and/or a business owner. Maintaining accurate and meticulous records of expenses and income for reporting purposes is an important part of the process. You will also be required to complete a new W-9 or W-8 BEN if there are any changes to your name or address.

Metadata

Metadata is data about data. For publishing platforms, accurate metadata is critical for getting your book properly categorized and listed on their retail sites. Metadata includes:

- Title, subtitle
- Series name (if applicable)
- Author(s)
- Publisher name, and imprint (if applicable)
- ISBN
- Keywords and categories
- Retail blurb

For more information, an article on Kobo Writing Life does a good job of explaining the importance and significance of metadata fields for e-books (#AR).

Pro Tip: The title, subtitle, author name, and series information on your cover should always match the corresponding metadata fields. Even missing an "An" or "The" or changing the way you've capitalized words in the title or subtitle can mess things up. By paying attention to the details, you'll also ensure that every storefront has the exact same data.

DIGITAL RIGHTS MANAGEMENT

Because Digital Rights Management (DRM) encrypts your file, books where DRM is enabled (#AR) prevent cut/copy/paste/screenshot/screen grab functionality, as well the printing or sharing your e-book. I say "in theory" because professional hackers always find ways around these things, and while there are many advocates of DRM, it also has its downsides (#AR). I always select DRM when I am setting up an e-book for market, regardless of the digital format, e.g., Kindle, Kobo, Nook, etc. That doesn't mean you have to.

Many authors new to self-publishing start off by publishing in e-book format only, knowing the option for print version(s) will be available once they've gotten their feet wet. There's nothing wrong with that approach, and for reasons you'll understand by the end of this chapter, digital only will also be your easiest (and least expensive) foray into publishing. In fact, even the "Big 5" (Hachette Book Group, HarperCollins, Macmillan Publishers, Penguin Random House, and Simon & Schuster), have digital-first imprints, adopting a wait-and-see attitude when it comes to sales stats before selecting a title for print. One example of this is Carina Press, an imprint of Harlequin (owned by HarperCollins). In other words, don't feel pressured to release your book in print if you're not quite ready, whether that caveat is emotionally driven, financially driven, or both.

UPLOADING DIGITAL (E-BOOK) CONTENT

This is where you'll upload your formatted EPUB file. You will have an opportunity to review the file once the upload is complete. If you've formatted the file correctly, there should be no surprises with what the finished product looks like but take the time to make sure that nothing wonky has happened in the transfer.

UPLOADING PRINT ON DEMAND (POD) CONTENT

This is where you'll upload your formatted PDF file. As with the digital version, you'll have an opportunity to review the file after the upload is complete. Once again, you'll want to make sure nothing wonky has happened during the transfer, so take the time to check before approving the final file.

Pro Tip: Unlike e-books where revised uploads are free, there may be revision fees for POD—even if all you want to correct is a missing comma. Additionally, where e-book updates usually take effect in a matter of hours, new POD files can take up to two weeks.

RIGHTS

As the author of the work, you retain copyright of the material. What you are offering is the right to publish your work in accordance with the terms and conditions set forth by each platform. As such, you are asserting that the content of your book is not in the public domain, and that you own the rights to the content before putting your book on sale.

Rights and distribution area is also where you'll find the option to enable Digital Rights Management (DRM) for your e-book (DRM is not available for print). As noted earlier, files with DRM enabled are encrypted to prevent cut/copy/paste functionality from the file. It also blocks the ability to take screenshots, screen grabs, and printing or sharing your e-book.

It's important to note that DRM is title specific. Just because one of your books has DRM enabled doesn't mean you are obligated to enable DRM on all of your books.

Pro Tip: In most cases, the DRM selection you make is a one-time (final) option that cannot be changed after your book's publication.

DISTRIBUTION

Every publishing platform will provide options for where you want your book to be published. Since the point is to sell as many books as possible, your best option is to select distribution in all countries supported by the platform. This is referred to as "going global."

If you select global distribution, you will also need to set the retail price of your book for each individual marketplace, e.g. U.S., Canada, Australia. You can do this in one of three ways:

1) By entering a specific price for each individual country. If you choose this option, you'll want to review the prices on a regular basis, as currency exchange rates fluctuate based on market conditions.

2) By selecting the retail price based on the currency of the primary marketplace selected (e.g., USD for U.S., CAD for Canada).. This is the simpler option since the publishing platform will adjust the retail price in each market using the current currency exchange rate. Basically, this is set-it and forget-it. The primary marketplace is the country where you expect to sell the most books.

3) A combination of options 1 and 2. For example, I typically select the retail price using option 2, but override that for the Canadian market, reducing the amount that would otherwise be charged to either coincide with the USD price, or with a modest upcharge that would be substantially less than the auto-converted currency amount.

> **Pro Tip: The retail price you select should be the same across all publishing platforms, regardless of territory/country. Amazon in particular checks its competition regularly and does not take kindly to an e-book being sold for less than the Amazon market price (you'll be sent a stern warning to update the Kindle price). This is an important consideration when discounting a title for promotional purposes.*

Summary

There are several platforms (and more could be coming) that you can select from to publish your books. Below is a list of platforms in alphabetical order included in "Publishing Platforms," up next.

- Amazon (Kindle Direct Publishing)
- Apple Books
- Barnes & Noble Press
- Draft2Digital
- Google Play Books
- IngramSpark
- Kobo

As a self-published author, the publishing partners and the format(s) you choose are totally up to you. Select one, two, or more, mixing, nixing, and fully understanding that you will always have complete control and the option to change your choices.

You're in the driver's seat now. Rev up your engines! It's time to go to market.

YOUR STEPS

PREPPING FOR PUBLICATION

COVER ART & PRICING

- Hire a graphic artist or DIY.
- Retail copy: long, short, teaser.
- Technical specifications e-book/POD.
- Pick the price: e-book/POD.

EPUBS AND PDFS

- Review formatting software options.
- Convert your manuscript into EPUB and PDF formats.

ARCS, PRE-ORDERS & PUBLICATION DATE

- ARCs. Prepare 3-4 months in advance of publication date.
- Review blurbs: Request and establish before the ARC is available.
- Select a realistic publication date. Factor in the timeline you'll need for each step.

CATEGORIES & KEYWORDS

- Review and select best BISAC Codes.
- Select seven keywords or phrases.

GETTING DOWN TO BUSINESS

- Account setup.
- Banking and tax information.
- Digital Rights Management.
- Metadata.
- Upload content.
- Rights and distribution.

READY OR NOT?

STATS, STIGMAS & FIRST STEPS

THE SELF-PUBLISHING SPACE is filled with authors hoping to make a Top 10 list, and I do mean *filled*. According to WordsRated.com, a non-commercial, international research data and analytics group, the number of self-published books has increased by 264% in the last five years, with annual sales of $300 million and counting (#AR). Reminder: you'll see the (#AR) symbol when there is a weblink to more information in the Additional Resources section at the back of this book.

Three-hundred million dollars. That's an impressive number, though the same survey reports that the average self-published book sells 250 copies, and the average self-published author makes $1,000 per year from their books. Of course, there are exceptions. Andy Weir, best known for his self-published book, *The Martian*, has sold 5 million copies in North America alone. Which means it's possible to compete with the deep pockets of the "Big Five" publishers or get a movie deal. It's just not likely.

There are other factors to consider as well. Times may have changed since the early days of self-publishing, but in many circles the stigma remains. Some writing awards and grant programs, for example, exclude self-published work in their submission criteria.

Family members or friends may (whether outright or silently) wonder why your book didn't get "picked up," the assumption being you chose self-publishing out of desperation or lack of options rather than by choice. Or that your book simply isn't "good enough."

Whether you view these attitudes as snobby, antiquated, or just plain unfair, the fact remains that these perceptions, while lessening in recent years, do exist.

Perhaps part of the blame can be shouldered by past writers who equated the self-publishing journey with a cheap and easy, quick-to-market path for a mediocre manuscript. But you and I both know that you (and your book) are better than that.

Whether your dream is to publish your debut novel or set the foundation to build your own multi-author imprint, this step-by-step guide can help you get there. But first, let's get rid of a few things that might be standing in your way, starting with…

ARBITRARY & SELF-IMPOSED DEADLINES

One of the biggest mistakes writers make is sending their book out into the world before it's ready, and that's equally true for aspiring authors trying to land a literary agent and a Big Five deal as it is for those considering self-publishing.

Maybe you've given yourself a timeline to get your project done —a milestone birthday, a year after retirement. Whatever the reason, arbitrary deadlines are often unrealistic. Yes, it's good to have a date to work towards. It's also important to allow yourself, and your book, the flexibility to change and adapt. Which brings us to…

REQUESTING (AND ACCEPTING) FEEDBACK

Feedback comes in many forms and at various stages of the writing process. The most important thing to remember is that you are looking for an unbiased evaluation of your work. You don't have to agree with every comment or suggestion, but you should at least consider each one without becoming defensive. Think of it as thick skin training for the occasional 1- or 2-star reviews your book is bound to receive. After all, reading is subjective and not everyone is kind.

Carefully selected, advance readers can be an asset when it comes to identifying pitfalls and plot holes. And trust me, both will be there, even after multiple revisions, even if, like me, you're also an editor. We're simply too close to our own work. Where do you find advance readers? Here are a few options:

WRITING CRITIQUE GROUPS

A group of writers who meet regularly to workshop each other's work. I dabbled with a writing group early in my writing journey and knew it wasn't for me. But if you're the sort of writer who likes to connect with other writers on a regular basis, whether to exchange feedback, improve your craft, or remain accountable, this could be beneficial for you.

While there are no hard and fast rules, critique groups work best if the group is small—three to five people—allowing each member time to read and respond without becoming overwhelmed, while developing an ongoing and supportive relationship with one another.

Ideally, you'll also be working in the same genre. There's no point asking for feedback on your whodunit if your critique partner only reads historical romance and is therefore unfamiliar with the tropes of cozy mysteries.

It's also necessary to establish parameters from the get-go, like weekly word count limits and the type of feedback expected. Are you looking for big picture or line edits? Facebook, your local library, and writing associations can be great sources when searching for an established critique group online or in your area, or to connect with people to form your own.

While critique groups can be invaluable for some writers, they should never be the final step in the review process. You lose objectivity when immersed in your work for months on end. Those intimately familiar with your work will too.

Alpha Readers

Readers who provide detailed and constructive feedback, both positive and tactfully critical, about your book's premise, plot, characters, and other technical elements. Does the story flow, is it well paced, etc.? Whether you choose to hire a professional or ask a trusted friend or relative, they should be aware that they are commenting on an unpolished (first or early) draft. They should also be avid readers of your book's genre or sub-genre.

While a critique group focuses on workshopping with other writers, consider this the first test drive of your overall story from a reader's perspective. This will help pinpoint big picture problems within your story (and possibly your writing style) that need to be addressed.

Beta Readers

Unlike alpha readers who provide an early or first draft review, beta readers (or *betas*) critique finished manuscripts before they are published. As with alpha readers, it's advisable to have betas who are familiar with your genre/sub-genre.

Beta readers can be friends, family members, teachers, members of online writing groups, or other writers willing to do a manuscript swap—basically, anyone who will approach the book as a casual reader, pointing out things they liked and disliked. This will help you identify finer points of your manuscript that may need an adjustment.

You're no doubt familiar with the expression "too many cooks spoil the broth." The same holds true when it comes to betas. Ideally, you'll have no fewer than two and no more than five, allowing for a comparison of opinions without the risk of opinion overload. If one beta reader doesn't understand why the protagonist hates red, for example, it might just be their perspective (though you should still make a note of it). If two or more betas don't understand it, that's a must-fix.

While betas are an excellent way to obtain (usually free) feedback that allows you to tweak and polish your manuscript, they do not replace the role of a professional editor.

EDITING AND PROOFREADING (#AR)

If you plan to self-publish, hiring an independent editor is not a corner to cut. And yet, when I am teaching writing workshops, this is almost always the point where the budding writers in attendance balk. Oh, they'd have done at least one of the previous three steps (critique group, alpha reader, beta reader), but the thought of an editor dismantling their manuscript was terrifying. And *paying* for editing?

Why should they have to fork out cash when their Aunt Edna was a high school English teacher, willing to do the job for free? Besides, aren't editors expensive?

Here's the thing. Aunt Edna may be well versed in the rules and regs of grammar and spelling. She may even be an avid reader. But she's still your aunt, and she's probably not going to be the heartless assassin you need to kill the darlings in your manuscript that almost certainly exist. It's also unlikely she'll understand the Chicago Manual of Style (also known as CMoS), the editorial style guide/standard accepted in publishing (#AR).

"Okay," you might be thinking, "but if I'm going to be the publisher, can't I make up my own style?" Probably. In fact, most publishers have their own "house" style, tweaks on how they might display numbers or dates, for example. But the template? CMoS. As the adage goes, "you need to understand the rules before you can break them." That statement is as true for publishing styles as it is for the tropes of your genre.

But let's take it one step further. A good editor will provide an overview of your book, including comps (comparable titles to other books in your genre). You'll need this when it comes to promotion, and (in my case, anyway), they'll often come up with titles you haven't even heard of. Professionals are clever like that.

Still not convinced? I worked as a magazine editor for four different publications over the course of fifteen years, often concurrently. In those roles I've edited essays and articles by scholars, academics, amateur experts, and others in fields as diverse as antiques, art, home building, green energy, and historical sites and museums. In the fiction world, I've edited three critically and commercially acclaimed multi-author anthologies under the Superior Shores Press imprint. And yet, in addition to consulting with beta readers, I always hire a professional editor for the final stages of my work.

In the case of the step-by-step publishing books (this one and *Finding Your Path to Publication*), I hired two editors, one as I developed the work, section by section, and the other who critiqued and proofed the final pass. You'll find their names credited on the copyright page, as well as in the acknowledgments (which is exactly where you'll be crediting your independent hires).

On a personal level, I look at hiring the services of a professional editor as an investment in my personal publishing education. An editor will work with me to refine my manuscript; along the way I may discover that I overuse the passive voice, or that I have a favorite cliché.

Let's address the concerns and questions I hear the most:

Q: Will the editor steal my work or my idea?

A: No. These are trained professionals. They aren't about to keep getting hired if they're plagiarists and word in the writing community spreads fast when it comes to unethical behavior.

Q: Will they rewrite my book, changing it so much that it's no longer recognizable as mine?

A: No. They will offer comments, corrections (to grammar, spelling, etc.) and suggestions, usually using the Track Changes feature in

Word. It's up to you, as the author, to accept or ignore any suggestions. But understand this: the role of the editor is to improve your manuscript, to help you polish it until it shines. It's never to dismantle or revise. That's your job.

Q: Is hiring an editor expensive?

A: Editing rates vary widely based on the type of service provided, how "clean" your manuscript is, e.g., does it need a light touch or a complete overhaul, experience (a seasoned pro may charge more than someone building a portfolio), and the complexity of the manuscript, for instance, the amount of fact-checking involved. Most editors base their fee on word count, meaning a 50,000-word manuscript will cost you significantly less than one that clocks in at 85,000 words. Your contract should spell out the cost, as well as the timeline for return, so there are no surprises on either side. Unless you have a prior relationship, expect to pay a deposit of up to 50% on signing, with the balance due on completion.

Q: Where do I find an editor?

A: I've included links to editorial associations (#AR), but if you can get a referral from a fellow writer, that's the best place to start. Realize, however, that a good editor is like a good renovator. The best ones aren't usually sitting around waiting for a call, and you may have to wait a month or more. If you're still fine-tuning your work, start your search now, vs. later. If your book is ready and your editor of choice isn't, *resist the urge to keep tinkering with the manuscript* and take the time to get started on your self-publishing to-do list.

Types of Editing

There are differences in the types of service editors provide. Before you hire anyone, it's important to understand the nuances of each.

Developmental Editing

Also known as substantive or content editing, developmental editing is the first step of the editing process, focusing on big picture story elements. The developmental editor will also assess and shape draft material to improve flow and organization by revising or reordering content and clarifying arc of action, plot, characters, and/or thematic elements. This type of editing is especially invaluable for first-time authors who may be struggling with story structure, but it can be helpful to authors at any stage of their writing career.

Line Editing

Also known as stylistic editing, the line editor concentrates on coherence and flow, eliminating jargon, clichés, and euphemisms, while adjusting the length and structure of sentences and paragraphs, and establishing or maintaining the overall mood, style, or voice. While line editing is often used as a standalone, the narrower small picture focus can be very effective after a round of developmental editing. This "double duty" approach is the one I personally use for my works of mystery fiction.

Copy Editing

Ideally combined with line editing, the copy editor checks spelling, grammar, punctuation, and usage, and ensures consistency in character names, places, descriptions, and other details. Copy editing also covers fact checking and/or obtaining or listing permissions needed (e.g., use of song lyrics or trademarked products). If you can only afford one round of editing, this may be your best option.

Proofreading

Not to be underestimated, proofreading is the final step to catch errors (typos, punctuation, misplaced or missing modifiers, proper capitalization, consistency, and verb or tense usage) and ensure adherence to style. A proofreader will find glitches that made it past all your readers and the editors.

Note: This is *not* the time to revise or rewrite.

*Pro Tip: If you can't afford a proofreader (and even if you've hired one), print your manuscript and read it as you would in paperback format before publishing. You'll be amazed at the things that pop out at you that are missed when reading on a computer. Even better, order an author copy to read in actual paperback format. (More on author copies later.)

Still not sure which type of editing you should invest in? Most editors will provide a complimentary or modestly priced sample edit of a few pages, allowing both parties the opportunity to evaluate the relationship before signing a formal contract. I'd recommend taking this step before signing on the dotted line. And as with anyone you'd hire, it's wise to check references.

Social Media Platforms

It's never too early to start building your social media platform, but if you're about to publish your first book and haven't yet started, now's the time. You don't have to be on every platform, but you will need to do your research because social media options and optics are ever-changing. Do your books cater to teens and tweens, or older adults? What site is your target demographic most likely to follow? What are their expectations? Video clips or reels? Photo collages? Book reviews? Pictures of your dog? How often should you post? Find a lane (or lanes) where you feel comfortable sharing pieces of yourself—at least as it pertains to writing and books. The more you drill down into what works and what doesn't, the more successful you'll be at building your own following.

Social media isn't a one-way street. To be successful, you'll need to be a good member of the literary community. It's important to follow and tag writing associations you're affiliated with, as well as other authors—not just the big names or award winners, but those who, like you, may be just starting out. Share, comment, and like others' posts. Learn about hashtags (the best way to do this is by studying others).

I'll delve into social media platforms more in the "Publicity & Marketing" section. In the meantime, it's time to define (or redefine) your online presence. Which brings us to…

Building a Website (#AR)

Ideally, you'll have built a website, however rudimentary, before you're ready to self-publish your book. If you haven't, there's no time like the present.

You could hire a website developer or use one of the many do-it-yourself website builders. The fun part will be coming up with and registering your domain name. Ideally, a domain name will be your name (plus an extension like .com), but if you have a common first and last name, you'll have to get more creative. That's okay, but don't get so creative you lose your identity. JaneDoeCozyAuthor.com could work, whereas CozyAuthorJane.com could be anyone.

Now let's look at your options:

Hire a developer

Probably the easiest approach, it will also be the most expensive. If you do choose to hire a website developer, it's important to fully understand what the process will entail. Do you want to be able to add content yourself? If so, will you have complete or partial control of the website once it's built? Do you want to update and add content quickly and easily yourself? If not, will the developer be posting content for you? What will their responsibilities be? What's included in your web developer services will vary from one provider to the next. Some offer a set number of maintenance hours in your monthly or annual fee, with work over and above offered at an hourly rate, while others charge on a cost-per-change basis. Many web developers are open to negotiation and could be available in the future should you need additional guidance.

The fine print is important. Define your goals and get them in writing, whether you want to be completely hands-off, want to take complete charge once the basic structure is set up, and everything in between. Dates, deadlines, and dollars should be spelled out in the terms of your contract.

DIY Approach

The second, less expensive, but more time-consuming, option is to use a do-it-yourself website builder. (Don't worry, you won't need to turn into a techie). And while this is a DIY approach, the end result doesn't need to look amateurish.

Choosing the website builder best suited to you depends on your wants and needs. Start by visiting the websites of authors who write in the same genre as you, and of authors whose work you admire, but again, don't just go with the big names. Check out online bookstores for novels in your genre written by lesser-known authors, then check out their websites as well. Chances are, they've gone the DIY route for the same reasons you might.

Some websites will include a notation with the theme and builder, which is helpful if you like one particular look (every website builder offers a variety of themes—templates you can build on). For example, my website, www.judypenzsheluk.com, includes "Designed by Elegant Themes/Powered by WordPress" in the footer.

Next, make a wish list of the things you'd like to see on your own website. Not everything needs to be done the first day you go live—it's more than okay to start with a basic, functional website, just be sure that your selected theme and builder allow for future adaptions that align with your wish list.

One important consideration (since it's usually one or the other) is your website's landing page—the page readers are taken to when entering your URL. If you're planning to incorporate a blog, do you want a home (welcome) page separate from your blog? Or do you prefer that readers land directly on your most recent post? You should also decide whether you'll be using your website as an e-commerce site, selling books and any related merchandise direct to consumer.

The good news is that most website builders offer free trial accounts. Take advantage of that opportunity, and don't worry while you test out various options—your website won't be live until it's activated, so no one will be able to see it but you as you play with getting it right.

Another consideration is what the website builder offers in terms of registering your domain name and website hosting options. Prices vary for website hosting, so shop around. Keep in mind, there's usually a deal to be made if you're a new customer (including free domain name registration). Website hosting is typically billed on an annual basis. Regardless of the deal you make, *be sure to review the renewal rates, since these can escalate significantly over time.* You'll also want to select a host that offers 24/7 technical support via phone and chat. Trust me, when something goes wrong, you want to know that someone will be available to help you fix it quickly. The last thing you want is to lose sales or visitors because of technical difficulties.

Feeling daunted? The internet is your friend when it comes to researching what's out there, and trustworthy comparisons by industry professionals are a great way to understand the pros and cons of the various services.

Author Bio

Your author bio will be used in many ways. Inside your book. On your website. On promotional materials like press releases or blog posts. In conference catalogs or newspaper articles. It may also be requested when it's time to upload your book for retail or wholesale distribution. In other words, it's important.

Bios are *always* written in the third person, e.g., *A former journalist and magazine editor, Judy Penz Sheluk is…* vs. *I am a former journalist and magazine editor.* They should also be succinct (no more than two paragraphs) and relevant, including as much as possible of the following points:

- Recent writing-related publications and/or positions.
- Expertise in the field of your book (this is especially applicable to non-fiction).
- Memberships in any writing associations or organizations.
- A minor personal detail, e.g., *She lives in North Carolina with her husband and two children.* If your book is a memoir, you would expand on that by adding something along the lines of, *BOOK TITLE is based on her childhood life on the road with her father, an itinerant musician.*
- Website URL.

Of course, not everyone has writing-related publications, and that's okay. Here's an example of how to keep it simple:

Jane Doe is the author of BOOK TITLE and an avid reader of fantasy novels. A member of Science Fiction and Fantasy Writers Association, Jane lives in North Carolina with her husband and two children. Find out more about her at www.janedoe.com.

AUTHOR PHOTO

You'll use this for many things: your website, inside your book, guest blogs, newspaper articles, conference catalogs…the list goes on. A professional headshot or series of photos is a worthwhile investment, and while you want to put your best face forward, ask them to go easy on the filters and photoshopping. The idea is to be recognized from your author photo.

And there you have it—behind the scenes of self-publishing in a nutshell. You've dipped your toe. Are you ready to jump in with both feet?

BUSINESS BASICS

Self-publishing isn't just a way to get your book out in the world and, regardless of what you might have been led to believe, it's far from the easiest option. Sure, you may have developed a social media platform and a built a website, but that's the fun stuff—the rainbow sprinkles on top of your ice cream sundae. To be successful, you'll take on the tasks a traditional publisher should do for their authors. You'll don the hat of a small business owner, because by choosing to self-publish, that's exactly what you are. A small business owner. Maybe even…dare I say it…an entrepreneur.

Sounds a bit scary, doesn't it? But it doesn't have to be, at least not if you do it right.

Step 1: Define Your Publishing Identity

Do you plan to publish under your own full name, your initials and last name, or a pseudonym (pen name)? This is a personal decision. That said, if you've developed a reputation as an expert in the field of your book, let's say early childhood education (ECE), using your own name makes the most sense. If, as an expert in ECE, your novel falls under erotica, a pseudonym might be more appropriate. However, it's important to note that copyright is owned and registered under the name of the author, not your pen name or the name of your publishing imprint (aka publisher name). In other words, it's your legal name you'll be putting on the copyright page of your book. The exception would be if you were an incorporated business, e.g., the copyright listed on bestselling author Michael Connelly's books is Hieronymus, Inc.

While you can list yourself as the publisher of your book, I strongly encourage you to set up a publishing imprint (the term for your publisher name). Not only does it add a layer of professionalism to your product (and yes, if you are the small business owner, your book is the product), but it serves as a reminder that you're going to be self-employed as well as self-published. My publishing imprint, for example, is registered as Judy Penz Sheluk (sole proprietor) DBA (doing business as) Superior Shores Press, which is renewable for a fee every five years. On the copyright page of all my books, the publisher is listed as "Superior Shores Press, copyright © (year) Judy Penz Sheluk."

When selecting a name, you'll need to do a search to ensure the name isn't already registered, and it shouldn't be part (or all of) your name, e.g., Judy Penz Sheluk Press (since that would defeat the purpose—the idea is to establish credibility). Starting an online search will help narrow the possibilities; Google and Amazon are good entry points. You'll also need to search national trademark name databases to make sure the name you finally decide on isn't legally registered to someone else (#AR). Once you've registered your name, you may want to go the extra mile and have a logo developed, either by the same person you'll hire for your cover art, or a logo designer. (A quick online search will provide plenty of options.)

STEP 2: RESEARCH

As an author, you've undoubtedly honed your skill when it comes to researching information to include in your book. The good news is that skill is transferable when it comes to self-publishing.

Okay, you might be thinking, but what am I supposed to be researching? The business of publishing, including royalties, taxes, insurance, and recordkeeping. You will want to hire an accountant but before you do, you will want to do some research.

Pro Tip: Do not skip over this part in your haste to get your book "out there." Think about it. How long did it take you to write your book? Another few weeks won't make a difference in the long-term, and rushing things could cost you in more ways than one. Practice patience —your future self will thank you for it.

I've included a sample Q&A of the sort of questions you might want answered as a guide to get you started, including additional resources (#AR) where applicable. It in no way represents or takes the place of the advice of a qualified professional or government agency. Every author's circumstance will be different, so it's up to you to do your own due diligence. You may also want additional information on something I haven't covered.

SAMPLE Q&A

Q: How and where do I register my publishing imprint?

A: This varies depending on your location. Both the U.S. and Canada have business registration websites (#AR), but you'll also need to explore state or provincial legislation. Arizona tax laws, for example, will be different than those in Alaska or Alberta.

Q: Do I need a tax identification number?

A: All publishing platforms require that you answer a few basic personal questions, such as your legal name and address. Part of that process also involves providing your tax ID number (#AR). Without this information on file, you can't be paid for any royalties earned, and it's no different than what you'd need to provide to a traditional publisher or employer.

Q: How are taxes handled now that I'm self-employed?

A: Start with the federal (IRS – U.S., CRA – Canada) and state or provincial tax sites for more information (#AR). Once you know the right questions to ask, consult with an accountant.

Q: Do I need a business bank account?

A: You don't need a business account, per se, but you should have a dedicated checking account for expenses and writing-related deposits (most publishing platforms pay by Electronic Fund Transfer). To assist with your recordkeeping, you may also choose to have a credit card that you only use for business expenses, e.g., office supplies, business entertainment, travel, etc.

Q: Will tax be deducted from my writing income? Will I get a tax form or slip?

A: The short answer is no; taxes are not deducted from royalty payments. However, here may be exceptions based on country. For example, sales on Amazon.com.br are subject to Brazilian withholding taxation of 15% and royalty payments for sales on Amazon.in are subject to 10% Singaporean tax withholding.

As a rule, magazines, grants, government programs, and other sources of writing revenue are also not taxed at time of payment. Whether you receive a tax slip (or not) depends on the publishing platform. Kindle Direct Publishing (Amazon), for example, will issue a Form 1099-MISC (#AR) for U.S.-based publishers on or before January 31 each year (or the following business day if January 31 falls on a weekend or legal holiday). Non-U.S.-based publishers are issued a Form 1042-S (#AR) on or before March 15 each year (or the following business day if March 15 falls on a weekend or legal holiday). Kobo Writing Life, on the other hand, does not supply any tax forms beyond monthly sales reports. I've noted tax information for each specific platform in the "Publishing Platforms."

Even if you do not receive a tax slip, you will still be responsible to pay taxes on all income earned. Maintaining accurate records of your monthly sales by platform is essential.

> *Pro Tip: Set aside a percentage of your writing income (including sales tax, if applicable) and deposit that money into a savings account as soon as you are paid. The percentage should be equal to whatever the state/provincial and federal tax rate would be for your estimated annual earnings, e.g., 20%. Chances are you'll save more than you need, but that's a good problem to have!*

Q: What do I need to do to sell my books on my website?

A: You'll need a website that is transactional. That sounds fancy, but all it really means is a website where people can buy your product(s), also known as e-commerce. There are three main types of e-commerce websites: business-to-business, e.g., Shopify; business-to-consumer, e.g., Amazon; and consumer-to-consumer, e.g., eBay. Forbes Advisor has a good article on how to build an e-commerce website (#AR), and the Alliance of Independent Authors (ALLi) has a good article on the pros and cons of transactional websites (#AR).

Q: Do I need to collect retail sales tax?

A: You won't need to collect retail sales tax on royalty income earned from a publishing platform, e.g., Kindle Direct Publishing; any taxes that need to be collected and paid will be their responsibility. Your royalty income will be based on after tax earnings.

If you're selling your books at a market (farmer's market, book fair, etc.), you may be responsible for collecting state or provincial sales tax, depending on the dollar amount. Tax regulations vary widely by state/province, and in some cases, by municipality. For that reason, it's best to check with your accountant.

Q: I'm Canadian. Do I need a GST/HST (Goods & Services/Harmonized Sales Tax) number?

A: No, not until you earn $30,000 in four consecutive quarters (#AR), however there can be financial advantages to becoming a GST/HST registrant even if you're nowhere near that income level. BMO has an excellent article on understanding GST/HST and why you might want to apply at the same time you register your business (#AR).

Q: What expenses can I write off on my income tax?

A: Expenses typically include accounting, bookkeeping, and banking fees, as well as a percentage of business-use-of-home (heat, hydro/electricity, home insurance, property tax, condo fees, maintenance, etc.), internet and telephone, vehicle (mileage, maintenance, gas), postage and courier, business-related membership dues (including writing associations), conference costs (registration, hotel, travel, meals), etc. You may also be able to deduct some entertainment expenses, though what is allowed varies widely and doesn't always seem to make sense. For example, in Canada you can deduct a portion of your food, beverages, tickets, and entrance fees to entertainment or sporting events. You can also deduct tips, cover charges, room rentals to provide entertainment, such as hospitality suites, and the cost of private boxes at sports facilities. You can't, however, deduct any expenses relating to golf (and no, you can't get away with calling it a business meeting). If in doubt, your accountant will have a more definitive answer.

Q: What sort of records do I need to keep?

A: In one word: meticulous. You'll also need to keep your **original** receipts for everything you plan to write off. I personally keep an Excel spreadsheet with a separate tab for each type of expense, e.g., Professional Services (editing, proofreading, cover art, etc.), Advertising & Promotion (paid sales promos, website hosting, etc.),

Business Use-of-Home (heat, hydro/electricity, taxes, etc.), and so forth. You may prefer QuickBooks or another accounting package. It's more time consuming than throwing everything into a big box and paying a bookkeeper to do the recordkeeping and data entry for you, but your future self will thank you for it.

Q: What details do I need to record on my vehicle log?

A: You'll need to record your beginning and ending odometer readings. For example:

Beginning (January 1): 20,000 miles
Ending (December 31): 30,000 miles
Total annual mileage: 10,000 miles

You'll also need to record, by date, the mileage for any business-related reason, e.g., library for research, office supply store, meet accountant, etc., as well as any maintenance costs, loan or lease payments, gas, insurance, license fees, and automobile associations (CAA, AAA). Let's say your business mileage was 5,000 miles, or half of your total annual mileage. You would be eligible to write off 50% of those expenses. Your accountant can guide you through this process and prepare the necessary documents at income tax time.

Q: What about insurance?

A: That depends on the type of insurance. Some insurers, for example, require an endorsement or rider (condition) on your home insurance policy to cover your office equipment (printer, computer, reference materials, etc.). Other companies will include these items as part of your general household contents. There may also be restrictions on how you can use your vehicle for business purposes, e.g., does traveling to sell books at an outdoor market qualify as business use? There are also professional liability policies specifically designed for authors and freelance writers, however these can be expensive. As well, self-published authors are often excluded from eligibility. Consult with an insurance broker to learn about what options may be available to you.

Q: What happens if my business expenses exceed my earnings?

A: This is another question for your accountant.

Q: Now that I've done my due diligence, what's next?

A: Get a professional opinion (Step 3).

STEP 3: CONSULT WITH AN ACCOUNTANT

Do not skip this step in the hopes of saving a few dollars (the British adage "penny wise, pound foolish" comes to mind). An accountant's expertise is in accounting. Yours is in writing.

Some accountants will offer free or discounted initial consultations for new clients, but don't let that be your primary motivation for selecting an individual or firm. This is someone you'll want to build a long-term relationship with. The process is intimidating enough without feeling, well, intimidated. If you have a referral to a firm or individual from someone you trust, all the better.

> *Pro Tip: Accountants bill by the hour and their time is your money. Do as much advance research as you can (refer to Step 2) before any consultation. It's better (and less expensive) to have your findings confirmed than to go into the meeting unprepared. Plus, your accountant will appreciate your professionalism.*

STEP 4: FILING YOUR INCOME TAX RETURN

It's that old "penny wise, pound foolish" thing again. An accountant will fully understand the tax laws and implications of your business, as well as any other employment income, pensions, etc. Besides, their fees are income tax deductible. To cut costs, you'll want to have all your paperwork, receipts, and records in order (remember, avoid dumping everything into that cardboard box, however tempting).

Once your tax return is ready to file, you'll want to meet with your accountant to go over everything. After all, you should understand what it is you're declaring, and why.

STEP 5: UNDERSTANDING COPYRIGHT (AND WHY YOU NEED TO)

Copyright law provides protection for a variety of artistic pursuits, everything from literary to performance to musical works. This section deals exclusively with copyright as it applies to literary works, though I'd be remiss if I didn't mention that *you **cannot** use song lyrics in your work—not so much as a single line—without express written permission (unless it is in the public domain), and a lot of money. The same holds true for trademarked names.* If in doubt, leave it out.

You should be equally wary of quoting segments from any other copyrighted material, including other novels. The disclaimers included on the copyright page of a book are meant to be taken seriously. The Berne Convention for the Protection of Literary and Artistic Works, an international treaty ratified by 175 countries (including the U.S. and Canada) and administered by the World Intellectual Property Organization (WIPO) ensures that copyright is respected in those countries, regardless of where the copyright was filed (#AR).

So, what is copyright? Simply defined, it means just what it says — "the right to copy." Drilled down further, it means that the copyright holder (the author) owns the exclusive right to produce or reproduce their own original work, in whole or in substantial part. If the work is unpublished, copyright includes the right to publish or grant publishing rights for the work and/or any substantial part of it.

As the copyright holder, you are also automatically protected by copyright at the time of creation, with the following criteria:

- You are a citizen or resident of a treaty country.
- The work is first published in a treaty country even if, as the author, you were not a citizen or resident in one of the treaty countries.

Knowing this, you might wonder why you would apply and pay for copyright registration, and what you might receive back in return. Not a lot, to be honest, although you will receive a certificate of registration protecting your work, which can be used in court to prove ownership of your book, should the need arise. And yes, you can always frame the certificate to hang in your office.

Reminder: Copyright should always be filed under your legal name (unless you're incorporated), not your publishing imprint or pen name.

Whether you choose to pay to register your copyright is up to you, and if you were following a traditional publishing path, one that might not be entirely necessarily. As a self-published author? Personally, I'd err on the side of caution.

Like everything else in business, there are exceptions to copyright law. The biggie is that you cannot copyright a title. That's why you'll sometimes see books and movies with the exact same title. That said, titles are important, and the last thing you want is one too closely associated with a universally known classic.

How long does copyright last? In the U.S. and Canada, copyright protection for authors of an original work exists during your lifetime and for seventy years following your death. Different rules apply for anonymous works or works for hire.

That also brings up the question of who owns your copyrighted work(s) after you die. In general, as with other property you own, ownership of your copyrighted work will be transferred to the heir(s) of your estate, unless you specify another individual in your will. Once ownership has been passed on, the new owner may generally use and license your works in whatever way they wish, in the same way they can sell or dispose of any of your other belongings. And whether you choose to self-publish or follow a more traditional publishing path, it's best to discuss this with a lawyer specializing in estate law and should be part of the conversation when you're preparing your will.

After all, the only thing certain in life is death and taxes. And I've already covered taxes.

BOOK BASICS

THERE ARE a few steps you'll need to take before publishing your book. In this chapter, you'll learn about ISBNs, building your front and back matter (and everything in-between), as well as some quick and easy document formatting do's and don'ts.

ISBNs (INTERNATIONAL STANDARD BOOK NUMBER)

Every version of a book, e.g., trade paperback (typically between 5 x 8 to 6 x 9 inches), mass market paperback (4.25 x 6.87 inches), large print editions, hardcover, e-book, audiobook, etc., requires a unique product identification code known as an International Standard Book Number (ISBN) (#AR). In turn, the ISBN is used by publishers, booksellers, libraries, internet retailers, and others in the supply chain for inventory ordering and control, catalog or online book listings, and sales records.

ISBN(s) are included in a few places: on a book's copyright page, as a barcode at the back of a print book, and in the book details in catalogs and online listings. In Canada, ISBNs are free (#AR). In the United States, ISBNs must be purchased through the Bowker Agency (#AR), the only official source of ISBNs in the U.S. As the publisher of record, it will be your responsibility to assign a unique ISBN for every version of the book you plan to publish.

The structure of an ISBN is a 13-digit identifier broken down as follows:

- Prefix element: For books to conform with other barcoded products, the three-digit prefixes (either 978 or 979) were assigned to the fictitious country of "Bookland" for use by the publishing industry.
- Registration group element: 1-5 digits in length. This identifies the country, geographical region, or language area participating in the ISBN system. In the U.S. and Canada, this number is always 0 or 1.
- Registrant element: Up to 7 digits in length. This identifies the publisher or imprint. Because of this, the publisher of the book should always apply for the ISBN. As a self-published author, you (or, ideally, your imprint) are the publisher of record and *not* the publishing platform (e.g., Kindle Direct Publishing).
- Publication element: Up to 6 digits in length. This identifies the edition and format of the title.
- Check digit: The final single digit that mathematically validates the rest of the number.

Here's an example of the ISBNs assigned to *Finding Your Path to Publication*:

ISBN Trade Paperback: 978-1-989495-54-4
ISBN Hardcover: 978-1-989495-55-1
ISBN e-book: 978-1-989495-56-8
ISBN Large Print: 978-1-989495-57-5

Now let's break those numbers down:

978: Prefix element
1: English language country

989495: Superior Shores Press

54, 55, 56, 57: Edition and format. Note how the numbers are sequential. For example, the first book published by Superior Shores Press with the 978-1-989495 identifier was the trade paperback version of *The Best Laid Plans: 21 Stories of Mystery & Suspense* (ISBN 978-1-989495-00-1).

4, 1, 8, 5: The ISBN-assigned check digit.

When uploading your book for retail, you may be offered a "free" ISBN by the publishing platform, e.g., Barnes & Noble Press for Nook, Kobo Writing Life for Kobo, etc., but there's a catch. Because the ISBN's Registration Element is publisher-specific, you won't be able to use that ISBN with any other publisher. You'll also need to list the issuer of the free ISBN as the publisher, and not your publishing imprint. In the case of Kindle Direct Publishing, for example, the assigned ISBN is pre-registered under the imprint name "Independently published" rather than (in my case) "Superior Shores Press." Furthermore, once a book has been published, the ISBN cannot be changed. Not exactly sounding free anymore, is it?

Pro Tip: If you haven't set up your publishing imprint yet, do so before applying for ISBNs, otherwise the Registration Element will be in your name, vs. your business entity.

Building Your Book

Your final manuscript will need to include front and back matter, which includes (** denotes optional content), in this order:

Title page: Book title, series title, author(s), translator (if applicable).

**Praise for: Snippets of advance reviews/blurbs.

**Also by: A list of other novels and/or (selected) short stories which appear in an anthology. For the latter, include the title of the short story and the name of the collection e.g., Goulaigans (*The Whole She-Bang 3*). Do not include magazine articles.

Copyright page: This is vital if you want to protect your work from plagiarism or reproduction without permission (or compensation). Take the time to review a few copyright pages from different books, including fiction, non-fiction, memoir, and those in your genre. I've broken this section down further to identify all elements you'll need to cover.

Copyright notice, year, and the name of the copyright holder: This should be an individual, not your imprint, e.g., Copyright © 2023 Judy Penz Sheluk

Rights reserved notice: This varies by publisher (check out some books for an idea). Here are two examples:

- All rights reserved. No part of this publication may be reproduced or transmitted in any form or by any means, electronic or mechanical, including photocopying, recording, scanning or otherwise, or through any information browsing, storage or retrieval system, without permission in writing from the publisher.
- All rights reserved. No part of this book may be used or reproduced in any manner whatsoever without written permission from the publisher, except in the case of brief quotations embodied in critical articles and reviews.

ISBN: Enter the format of your book, followed by the ISBN, listed individually, e.g.,

- ISBN hardcover: 978-1-989495-55-1
- ISBN trade paperback: 978-1-989495-54-4
- ISBN e-book: 978-1-989495-56-8

Edition Number: The edition of the book. Examples include:

- First Edition Month/Year
- First paperback edition published Month/Year
- First Edition
- Subsequent editions (if republished with revisions to text or cover) would then be Second, Third, etc.

Legal disclaimer: This is included to protect against potential lawsuits. Wording varies by fiction, non-fiction, and memoir. Here are some examples:

- Fiction: This is a work of fiction. Names, places, and events described herein are products of the author's imagination or used fictitiously. Any resemblance to actual events, locations, organizations, or persons, living or dead, is entirely coincidental.
- Historical Fiction: The likeness of historical and/or famous figures have been used fictitiously; the author does not speak for or represent these people. All opinions expressed in this book are that of the author, or fictional.
- Non-fiction: If your book falls into this category, review examples similar to your work, e.g., true crime, health and wellness, self-help, finance, travel, how-to, etc. An example of the latter can be found on the copyright page of this book.
- Memoir: The events in this book are memories based on the author's perspective. In some cases, the names and/or places have been changed to protect the identity of those involved.

Permission Notice: If you are using an excerpt from a copyrighted work (literature, music lyrics, etc.) and have <u>obtained permission</u> to include it, you need to give credit on the copyright page. For example, in *Heartbreaks & Half-truths*, I've included the following: Excerpt from 'Hard Song' by Barry Dempster (Love Outlandish, Brick Books, 2009) used with permission.

Additional Credits: Editor, proofreader, illustrator, cover design, photographer, etc. You can choose to expand on the names in your acknowledgments, but they should at least be listed here as a matter of courtesy.

Publisher Information: The name of your publishing imprint and unique website URL (if applicable).

Author Website: By now you have one of these, right?

**Dedication

**Epigraph: A quotation included at the beginning of a book, e.g., in *Moonlight & Misadventure*, I include the following (public domain) quotation: "Don't tell me the moon is shining; show me the glint of light on broken glass."—Anton Chekhov

**Foreword: A short introductory essay preceding the main text of the book. For example, my novel, *Past & Present*, is dedicated to my late mother, Anneliese Penz. In the foreword, I share the reason behind that dedication. In collections, such as multi-author anthologies, this is often titled as an Introduction.

Table of Contents: You'll need to include a Table of Contents (TOC) for anything in an e-book format. For fiction and memoir, a TOC is not usually included in print versions, but that doesn't mean you can't do it. Choosing a TOC in non-fiction, self-help, and how-to books in print format is more common, but not essential. Formatting software (more on that to follow) will automatically build a TOC, regardless of format. Selecting inclusion in print will be optional.

**Prologue

Main text: Chapter 1 through to The End.

**Epilogue: A short passage added at the end of a literary work, basically a summation.

**Afterword: Also known as an Author's Note, this is meant to share information that is supplementary to the main text. For example, in my novel *Before There Were Skeletons*, which delves into five missing persons cases from the past, I include statistics and information on missing adults' databases.

Acknowledgments: Admit it, you've dreamed of writing your acknowledgements forever, right? Now's your chance to thank everyone who helped you get to this point (friends, family, experts in a certain field, etc.) as well as your beta readers, cover artist, editor, and proofreader. While you can still flex your creative muscles here to a certain extent, it shouldn't read like a grocery list.

About the author: Your third person bio. A headshot is optional, but if you choose to include one, no selfies. You want to come across as professional.

FORMATTING YOUR DOCUMENT

As an author, you've (hopefully) learned to properly format your manuscript, at least when it comes to sending it to literary agents or publishers. Even so, you might not worry unduly if you forget a page break or add a tab or two. But as a self-published author you won't have that luxury.

In the Prepping for Publication section (up next), you'll learn the ins and outs of converting your Word document into an EPUB (for e-book) and PDF (for Print on Demand, referred to in the industry as POD), the formats required for uploading your book to publishing platforms for online e-book sale or POD distribution. While it's true that Apple's Pages offers EPUB conversion, as does Scrivener (a writing program), with few exceptions (which I promise to reference), most EPUB formatting programs work exclusively with manuscripts in .doc or .docx format. That's also why you'll find that most literary agents and/or traditional publishers will only accept submissions in MS Word (.doc or .docx) format.

Here are a few manuscript formatting do's and don'ts:

Do: Double space.
Don't: Single space.

Do: Use hanging first line .3" or .5" (found under Paragraph settings in Word) rather than tabs.
Don't: Use the space bar to shift or indent your text.

Do: End each chapter with a page break.
Don't: Hit return until you get to the next page/chapter heading.

Do: Use only one space between punctuation and the beginning of the next sentence (one space has long been the new standard, and the extra space can really mess things up on layout). Always do a quick "find" for two spaces and "replace" with one space.
Don't: Use headers or footers or include page numbers (because these will be created during EPUB conversion).

Pro Tip: Click on the Show/Hide button to see if you've missed either of these:
—————————Page Break—————————
" *(two dots vs. one, indicating two spaces)*

Congratulations! You've just completed Ready or Not? and everything that entails. Are you eager to start prepping for publication?

I thought you might be.

YOUR STEPS

READY OR NOT?

Stats, Stigmas & First Steps

- No arbitrary deadlines.
- Feedback, editing, proofreading.
- Develop a social media platform.
- Build a website.
- Write a third person author bio.
- Get an author photo.

Business Basics

- Establish a publishing imprint.
- Prepare your questions.
- Look into insurance coverage.
- Create a recordkeeping system
- Consult with an accountant.
- File for copyright.

BOOK BASICS

- Apply for ISBNs.
- Build your book interior.
- Format Word document for EPUB and PDF conversion.

PUBLISHING PLATFORMS

AMAZON
KINDLE DIRECT PUBLISHING (KDP)

WEBSITE: https://kdp.amazon.com/

KDP IS Amazon's self-publishing platform for Kindle, hardcover, and paperback books. Website interface is available in Dutch, English, French, German, Italian, Spanish, and Portuguese. The Kindle app is available for iOS, Android, Mac, and PC globally in multiple languages and countries.

STORE: www.amazon.com: There are various domain extensions depending on country, e.g., Canadian store is .ca). You will be directed to the correct store for your country.

DISTRIBUTION

KDP distributes (at time of publication) to 13 Amazon marketplaces, accessible to readers around the world. You will need to select a Primary marketplace (the country where you believe you will sell the most books). The default is Amazon.com, and that is generally your best bet, regardless of the location where your book is set, e.g., a cozy mystery set in Canada. An exception would be if your book was in a language other than English. For example, Amazon.com.br (Brazil) would be a better selection for books written in Portuguese.

SERVICES & SUPPORT

KDP offers an extensive online help section, but if you can't find what you're looking for, there are also e-mail, live chat, ask the community, and phone support options. Based on your query, the preferred (best) option will be highlighted. I've personally found KDP support to be excellent and the live chat and phone support options actually connect you to a human being.

Recently, there has been an increase in the number of scams and scammers using Amazon's name and trademark to rip writers off. Writer Beware has written an excellent article on what to watch out for (#AR). If you are approached by Amazon either by phone or e-mail, there's a good chance it's fake. Any such requests can be verified with Amazon using KDP support. As well, you should always log into to the KDP link provided at the beginning of this section vs. doing a random search for "KDP publishing" which can lead you down a very dark and deceitful path.

ACCOUNT SETUP

If you already have an Amazon account, sign into the KDP site using your Amazon e-mail and password. If you don't have an Amazon account, you'll need to create a KDP account with your name, e-mail address, and password.

Once you've created your account (or logged in with an existing account), you'll need to complete your Author/Publisher profile, and provide your banking and tax information (#AR).

UPLOADING YOUR BOOK

All new books are created in the KDP Bookshelf. To start, click on "Create a Book" icon. This will take you to a page that asks what type of book you'd like to create. There is no charge to upload a book in any format to KDP. Even if you plan to produce a print book through KDP, your first step should be to create a Kindle e-book.

There are a couple of reasons for that; the first is that Amazon doesn't allow pre-orders for print books created through KDP, though they will usually list pre-order print books created through an outside wholesale distributor, such as IngramSpark or Draft2Digital (more on both POD distributors to follow).

The second reason is that the e-book version is the easiest to create, and when you're ready to use KDP for print post-publication, most of the metadata entry will already be done.

Creating Your Kindle e-book:

1) Enter e-book details (metadata), save and continue. This page is also where you'll enter your pre-order date, if applicable.

Note: Several book details cannot be changed after publishing. A complete list of what can and can't be changed can be found in the help section under Update Book Details (#AR).

2) Upload your Kindle e-book content (EPUB file and cover). ISBNs for Kindle are optional (even if entered, Amazon will replace it with an ASIN – Amazon Standard Identification Number on publication). However, you can (and I do) enter the same e-book ISBN that you plan to use for all e-book publishing platforms. This is also the ISBN that you've entered on the copyright page of your book. Remember, ISBN's are publisher-specific; if you use KDP's "free" ISBN, the publisher will be listed as "independently published" vs. the name of your publishing imprint.

After your EPUB has successfully uploaded, you will be notified of any spelling errors detected. You can choose to correct these (if so, you'll need to correct your EPUB for all platforms) or ignore (e.g., an unusual name might come up as an error). Upload your cover next. Once your book has passed the verification process (this can take several minutes), launch the online previewer. If all looks good, save and continue.

3) Select distribution (all sales territories or select specific ones), your primary marketplace (usually Amazon.com), and then enter pricing. The easiest way to do this is to enter the dollar amount under your primary marketplace and click "Base all marketplaces on this price." This means that any currency exchange will be handled at the point of sale, based on the current rates. You can choose to override this for one or more countries.

If your book is priced between $2.99 and $9.99 USD, it qualifies you to select the 70% royalty option. If it is priced below $2.99 or above $9.99 (in any marketplace), you'll need to select the 35% royalty option. This page will also show you what you can expect to earn, per copy. You will also be asked whether you'd like to enroll your e-book in KDP Select. More details on KDP's royalty structure, and KDP Select, follow a bit later in this chapter.

4) Click "publish your e-book." It can take up to 72 hours (but usually takes far less) for your Kindle e-book to be available for purchase or pre-order.

PRINT ON DEMAND

KDP offers POD publishing for paperbacks and case-laminated hardcover books, though there are differences in options available (#AR). KDP does not charge an upload fee or a fee for any file changes, including interior and cover art, post-publication.

1) Click on "Create Paperback" or "Create Hardcover" (under the Kindle e-book version of your book). Most of the metadata completed in Step 1 (e-book) will be filled in, though you will need to choose categories and select your publication date (the date you want your book to be published). While KDP now allows print books to be "scheduled" for future release, these are not pre-orders. In other words, the paperback version of scheduled books will not appear on your book's storefront detail page until the publication date.

2) Enter your print ISBN, paper choices, etc., and upload your print-ready PDF and book cover. You'll be given a chance to preview your book once the upload is complete.

3) Distribution & Pricing: Calculate your list price by using this simple formula: (royalty rate x list price) minus print costs. You can find the estimated cost to print your book using the KDP Printing Cost and Royalty Calculator (#AR). You will also be asked to select one of two distribution methods: Amazon Only (60% royalty rate) or Expanded Distribution (40% royalty rate).

Pro Tip: If you have made your book available for pre-order through another distributor, such as IngramSpark or Draft2Digital, save as a draft vs. scheduling for publication. Once the on-sale date has passed, you can select "publication date and release date are the same" and submit.

Amazon Only

With this option, your paperback or hardcover book will be sold on Amazon's global storefronts, but it will *not* be available for wholesale distribution to other markets or booksellers. That doesn't mean a library or another bookseller can't order a copy of your book, but to do so, they'd be ordering it in the same way as any other Amazon customer (an unlikely scenario from competing booksellers).

Expanded Distribution (paperback only)

With this option, Amazon will make your book available to an outside distributor, which in turn can distribute your book to other booksellers, libraries, etc., beyond Amazon's global exclusive (Amazon only) storefronts. Because there is a third party involved, the royalty rate is reduced from 60% to 40%. To enroll your paperback in Expanded Distribution, it must be available on Amazon.com or Amazon.co.uk and meet specific content and language requirements (#AR). Additionally, the ISBN used, whether "free" from KDP or your own, must not have been submitted to another POD distributor, such as IngramSpark or Draft2Digital.

Note: Because paperbacks sold through the Expanded Distribution channels might be manufactured by third parties, there may be minor manufacturing differences in paper thickness, color shade, etc.

It can take up to eight weeks for your paperback to become available for booksellers and libraries to order. There is no guarantee it will be accepted or ordered by any of those channels. Any changes to your book details, content, or pricing can also take up to eight weeks for the information be updated, though your book will still be available with the old information.

> *Pro Tip: To increase your odds, you may be tempted to list your POD book with IngramSpark and/or Draft2Digital, as well as through KDP's Expanded Distribution. Ignore the temptation. Duplication will only serve to create confusion in the distribution chain and may result it your book not being listed anywhere.*

At this point, you might be wondering why you'd take the extra step (after publication date) by opting for KDP's POD program if you've already decided to set up your book with another POD distributor, such as IngramSpark or Draft2Digital. The advantages are faster payment (60 days with KDP vs. 90+ days), the possibility of a higher royalty rate (KDP for Amazon only distribution is 60%), potentially lower print charges and faster POD service, up-to-date sales data, and the option to order Author Copies at print cost plus tax and shipping. If it's all seeming like one step too many, never fear: Amazon will still make your book available for sale. They'll simply purchase it from your POD distributor, vs. printing it themselves, and you won't be able to order Author Copies.

Print Proof (#AR)

Proof copies can only be ordered if your book is in "Draft" status. The cost per copy is based on print cost, applicable taxes, and shipping.

Note: The cover of these books will include a printed message that says: "Not for Resale," repeated several times. That's not necessarily a bad thing if you're looking to send out ARCs, or you're planning to review your book in another format before hitting "publish." You'll be surprised at the errors and glitches you'll find, no matter how many eyes have been upon it.

Author Copies (#AR)

If you've chosen KDP as a POD distributor, you'll be able to order author copies from your Bookshelf page to be printed and mailed to you for your personal use, such as your book launch. You can also order author copies to be mailed directly to friends, reviewers, etc. You'll be charged the base printing cost, applicable taxes, and shipping. Author copies may not be available for the first 24 hours after your book goes live.

*Pro Tip: Free shipping, e.g., orders over $35 or Amazon Prime membership, does not apply to proof or author copies.

OTHER OPTIONS & PROGRAMS

A+ Content

A free, optional add-on to add images, text, and comparison tables to your book page (#AR).

Author Central

Allows authors to create an author page with a bio on Amazon (#AR). Once your book is available, you can "claim it" on Author Central, then add editorial reviews. Author pages include a "Follow Author" button. Author Central provides authors with statistical sales information and the latest customer reviews. You can also recommend up to four of your books, recommend three books by other authors, and include your bio in several different languages.

*Pro Tip: Set up your Author Central account at the same time you set up your KDP account. That way it'll be ready when your book is.

KDP SELECT (#AR)

This option is available for Kindle e-books only. It does not include other versions of your book, e.g., print, audio, etc. To be eligible for enrollment you must own the exclusive digital publishing rights *and* your e-book must also be exclusive to the Kindle Store for the KDP Select enrollment period of 90 days. This means you cannot list or sell your e-book on any other publishing platform during the enrollment period (including listing for pre-order).

Note: You can sell print versions elsewhere—this is an e-book only program.

Books enrolled in KDP Select are automatically included in the Kindle Unlimited (#AR) program, a subscriber-based service exclusive to Amazon. There is no cost to enroll your book in KDP Select. Refer to Promotional Opportunities for books enrolled in the program, and to Royalty Structure for payment details later in this chapter.

*Pro Tip: Enrollment into KDP Select will automatically roll over unless you deselect the "automatically renew" option. Review your KDP Select revenues a few days before the expiry date of the enrollment period before deciding if you want to remove your title from KDP Select or renew for another 90-day period.

KINDLE VELLA

Available exclusively to KDP account holders, Kindle Vella was launched in July 2021 and is currently limited to U.S. authors and readers. Stories uploaded to Kindle Vella are meant to be released in a serialized format with 600 to 5,000 words per episode, with new episodes uploaded on a regular and frequent basis. Kindle Vella is a good alternative to social publishing platforms such as Wattpad or Inkitt.

While there is no requirement to do so, completed books can also be published via KDP as paperback, e-book, hardcover, and audiobook, with some restrictions. As terms and conditions can (and do) change, your best resource to do this, should you be interested, is to refer to KDP's help page on Kindle Vella (#AR) for current information.

KDP Promotional Opportunities

All KDP promotional opportunities can be found under the Marketing tab (#AR).

Amazon Ads

This is paid-by-you advertising based on your budget and ad clicks. Amazon offers an advertising webinar, as well as a free ad training course. You will need to set up an Amazon advertising account to register for either option (#AR), but I'd highly recommend investing the time to learn and understand Amazon ads before investing your cash. Refer to the "Advertising & Promotion" section for more information.

KDP Select

Kindle e-book titles enrolled in KDP Select for more than 30 days are eligible for one of two promotions in each 90-day enrollment term. There is no cost beyond royalty reduction for either option:

1) Kindle Countdown (#AR): Available for the U.S. and U.K. marketplaces only, you can select a (maximum) seven-day period to "count down" your Kindle e-book price in up to four increments, which will be evenly distributed throughout the campaign.

The term "countdown" is a bit confusing since the price actually increases by $1 with each increment. (The longer the wait, the less buyers save, so it's in their interest to act fast.) You may also select one discounted price, e.g., $0.99, for the entire length of the promotional period.

Whatever option you select, U.S. or U.K. customers will see the regular price, the promotional price, and the countdown clock, which shows how much time is left to purchase the Kindle e-book at the promotional price.

EXAMPLE A: Multiple Payment Increments

Start date: May 1, 12 a.m.
End date: May 8, 12 a.m.
Price increments: 4 (each increment is 42 hours)
Starting list price: $0.99
Increment 2: $1.99
Increment 3: $2.99
Increment 4: $3.99
End price May 8, 12 a.m.: $4.99 (original price of your e-book)

EXAMPLE B: 1 Price Increment

Start date: May 1, 12 a.m.
End date: May 8, 12 a.m.
Price increments: 1
Starting list price: $0.99
End price May 8, 12 a.m.: $4.99 (original price of your e-book)

Note: Your book price cannot be changed for 30 days before the countdown or for 14 days after.

Pro Tip: You will need to set up U.S. and U.K. promotions separately. They do not have to be scheduled at the same time.

2) Free (five days) book promotion (#AR): Books can be in the 35% or 70% royalty category. You can select five individual days, e.g., five Mondays, five consecutive days, or any combination thereof to offer your book at no charge. This free promotion will run in all Amazon marketplaces.

Pro Tip: Use it or lose it. Even if you choose to auto-renew, countdown and free book promos do not roll over into the next 90-day enrollment period.

Prime Reading

Amazon Prime (#AR) members are offered a rotating selection of free books. These books are selected by Amazon from books offered by authors who opt to enroll one e-book title in Prime Reading. Unless you check "automatically renew," each nomination expires after 90 days, at which time you'll be reminded that it's time to renew. If you only have one book, the auto renew option makes the most sense. There is no charge to submit, although there is no guarantee your book will be selected. Because books are being offered to readers at no cost, there is no monetary compensation for books downloaded or pages read, though it does afford the opportunity to gain additional customer reviews and/or followers.

Kindle Deals

You can submit your book title(s) for Kindle Deals promotional consideration, although nomination doesn't guarantee enrollment. Unless you check "automatically renew" each nomination expires after 90 days, at which time you'll be reminded that it's time to renew. There is no charge to submit, but your book must be enrolled at the 70% royalty option to qualify ($2.99 to $9.99). If accepted, your book will be discounted for a minimum of one day, up to several weeks. Royalties are paid on the discounted price.

SCHEDULING A SALE

Unlike other e-book publishing platforms, KDP does not offer the option to schedule a Kindle e-book sale in advance. However, if you reduce the sale price of your e-book on another platform, e.g., from $5.99 to $2.99, you must price match the sale price on KDP. The exception to this would be if the reduced price on the other platform was coupon-based (a promotional code entered at checkout to reduce the $5.99 retail sale price by a designated percentage).

Note: KDP does not offer a "free book" option for books outside of the KDP Select Program.

Because it can take up to 72 hours for any change to hit the purchase page, I recommend reducing the price of your Kindle e-book three days in advance of the scheduled sale. You'll also need to add a calendar reminder to adjust the price to "regular" pricing when the sale ends.

> *Pro Tip: If you are reducing the price to less than $2.99—even if it's only being reduced in one marketplace, e.g., U.S.—you will be required to change the royalty rate from 70% to 35%. When you readjust the price upwards, remember to change the royalty rate back to 70%. It's an easy box to miss.*

ROYALTY STRUCTURE

e-book sales

The e-book (Kindle) royalty rate is based on your sale price:

- Less than $2.99 or $10.00 and over: 35%
- $2.99 to $9.99: 70%

EXAMPLE A (<$2.99 or >$9.99)

Sale Price $2.99
KDP deducts 65% = $1.94
You earn @ 35% = $1.05

EXAMPLE B (>$2.99 to $9.99)

Sale Price $9.99
KDP deducts 30% = $3.00
You earn @ 70% = $6.99

Maybe you'd prefer to sell at a nice round number: $3.00 instead of $2.99 or $10.00 rather than $9.99. That penny difference can make a huge difference in what you earn. For example:

EXAMPLE C (<$2.99 to >$9.99)

Sale Price $3.00
KDP deducts 30% = $0.90
You earn @ 70% = $2.10

EXAMPLE D (<$2.99 to >$9.99)

Sale Price $10.00
KDP deducts 65% = $6.50
You earn @ 35% = $3.50

Note: Royalty rates depicted are based on the sale price in the U.S. and Canada, excluding taxes paid by the purchaser. Some currencies will have higher or lower payment thresholds.

Print on Demand

As mentioned earlier, regardless of POD distributor, profit margins are very thin for print and getting slimmer every year as print costs continue to rise. Play around with various price points using Amazon's print calculator (#AR), but be sure to leave yourself a buffer AND determine what sort of bottom line you're willing to live with.

Amazon Distribution

Currently 60% of list price, less printing cost, for both paperback and hardcover versions. Royalties are calculated in the currency of the country selected; print costs vary by location and are subject to change.

EXAMPLE (U.S.)

Based on 6" x 9" 300-page paperback, black and white ink. All prices in USD. Print charges subject to change.

Retail Price: $18.99
Royalty @ 60% = $11.39
Less Printing Cost: $4.60
Author Royalty: $6.79

EXAMPLE (Australia)

Based on 6" x 9" 300-page paperback, black and white ink. All prices in AUD.

Retail Price: $18.99
Royalty @ 60% = $11.39
Less Printing Cost: $9.02
Author Royalty: $2.37

EXAMPLE (Canada)

Based on 6" x 9" 300-page paperback, black and white ink. All prices in CAD.

Retail Price: $18.99
Royalty @ 60% = $11.39
Less Printing Cost: $6.06
Author Royalty: $5.33

EXPANDED DISTRIBUTION

Currently 40% of list price, less printing cost, available for paperback only. Royalties are calculated in the currency of the country where the sale occurred; print costs vary by location. Print costs are subject to change.

EXAMPLE (Expanded Distribution, U.S.)

Based on 6" x 9" 300-page paperback, black and white ink.

Retail Price: $18.99
Royalty @ 40% = $7.60
Less Printing Cost: $4.60
Author Royalty: $3.00

EXAMPLE (Australia)

Based on 6" x 9" 300-page paperback, black and white ink. All prices in AUD.

Retail Price: $18.99
Royalty @ 40% = $7.60
Less Printing Cost: $9.02
Author Royalty: ($1.42)

Note: A negative royalty is not allowed; to sell your paperback book in Australia, you would need to increase your retail price.

EXAMPLE (Canada)

Based on 6" x 9" 300-page paperback, black and white ink. All prices in CAD.

Retail Price: $18.99
Royalty @ 40% = $7.60
Less Printing Cost: $6.06
Author Royalty: $1.54

KDP Select

Kindle Unlimited

In addition to royalties earned through sales of your Kindle e-book, titles enrolled in KDP Select will be paid based on the number of Kindle Edition Normalized Pages (KENP) read by unique Kindle Unlimited subscribers in a month. In other words, you will only be paid the first time someone reads your book, even if they read it a dozen times. On the other hand, you'll be paid for any pages read even if someone doesn't finish your book. The KENP Start Reading Location (SRL) is generally set at Chapter 1, regardless of front matter, meaning you won't be paid for pages prior to the SRL.

The amount paid per page read is based on a program called the KDP Select Global Fund. While the Fund varies each month, based on several factors, on average authors can expect to earn about $.040 to $.050 per 100 pages read. Based on that average, a 300-page book would earn between $1.20 and $1.50 per complete customer read. More detailed examples can be found on the "Royalties in Kindle Unlimited" help page (#AR).

There is no payment for the number of pages read for e-books not enrolled in the KDP Select program. However, once a book has been borrowed by a KU subscriber, you will continue to be compensated for any pages read, even if your title's enrollment period has expired and you chose not to re-enroll.

Note: Amazon does not permit (and is vigilant in preventing) market manipulation (marketing that incentivizes Kindle Unlimited customers to read your Kindle e-book in exchange for compensation of any kind, such as contest entries, gift certificates, giveaways, etc.).

Kindle Countdown

As covered earlier in this chapter, there are two options:

1) Free book promotion: Maximum five days. No royalties are earned on free books downloaded during this period.

2) Price reduction countdown: Royalties are based on your regular e-book royalty rate and are not reduced to the lower rate during the promotion.

EXAMPLE

Regular price: $5.99 (70% royalty/ $4.19)
Countdown price: $0.99 (70% royalty / $0.69)
End of promotion: Resume regular price of $5.99 (70% royalty / $4.19)

Kindle Vella

The first three episodes of all Kindle Vella books are free, after which time readers purchase tokens to access the rest of your Kindle Vella content. Compensation on Kindle Vella (#AR) is royalty-based (50% of what readers spend on tokens to unlock your story), as well as bonus-based (based on customer engagement and activity).

Reports & Payments

The Reports tab on your KDP dashboard offers several data-point options. You can customize further by defining one or all books by marketplace or book format. It is a very comprehensive reporting system with graphics and easy-to-understand information, including:

- Orders: Units ordered.
- KENP Read: Pages read for books enrolled in KDP Select.
- Month-to-Date: Information about your unit sales transactions and KENP.
- Promotions: Results of Kindle Countdown promotions.
- Pre-orders: Number of books pre-ordered.
- Royalty Estimator: A handy calculator of what you can expect to earn. Be sure to view the calculator in the

currency you will be paid in.
- Kindle Vella: Takes you to the Kindle Vella dashboard, when applicable.
- Prior Months' Royalties: Broken down by currency and country; includes KENP.
- Payments: Current and past sales periods by month/year and marketplace. Includes foreign exchange rate and adjusted amount where applicable.

Royalties are paid monthly as per your stated payment preference approximately 60 days after the end of the month the sale was recorded. For example, a book sold between January 1 to January 31 would be paid by the end of March, provided you meet the minimum threshold. A minimum threshold is applicable to wire transfers and checks only; there is no minimum threshold for direct deposit.

Tax Information

All publishers must complete a tax interview. Tax interview links and downloadable tax forms can be found on Amazon Tax Central (#AR). You can also request the option of paper (mailed) vs. paperless (e-mailed) tax forms.

U.S. Publishers

A Form 1099-MISC will be issued on or before January 31 each year (or the following business day if January 31 falls on a weekend or legal holiday).

Non-U.S. publishers

A Form 1042-S will be issued on or before March 15 each year (or the following business day if March 15 falls on a weekend or legal holiday).

APPLE BOOKS
ITUNES CONNECT

WEBSITE: https://itunesconnect.apple.com/

THINK of iTunes Connect as the home base for managing your account and content. It houses the tools, guides, and reports you'll need while working with Apple Books. Apple is a digital only platform and does not offer a POD option, nor do they sell paperback or hardcover books.

STORE: http://books.apple.com/us/book/

DISTRIBUTION

Apple Books are available in more than 50 countries and regions, of which you can select one, some, or all as part of your book distribution. The Apple Books app is available for Mac, iPad, iPhone, and Apple Watch.

SERVICES & SUPPORT

Apple Books Partner Support is available by phone in English only during set hours each day, seven days a week in several countries (including U.S. and Canada). Support in English, Japanese, and Chinese is also available by e-mail. You'll get a ticket for any new request for support and can check the status on the dashboard.

ACCOUNT SETUP

You will need to create an iTunes Connect account for Apple Books using an Apple ID. If you're already an Apple user, you will already have an Apple ID. If not, you will need to create one. The easiest way to do this is to go to the online Apple store (#AR).

Note: Creating an Apple ID requires two-step identification and a valid credit card on file.

Once you have an Apple ID, you'll be able to set up an Apple Books account in iTunes Connect (#AR). As part of the account setup, you will be asked to choose your publisher type. Select Individual if you are representing yourself or if you are a sole proprietor.

UPLOADING YOUR BOOK

There are three ways of uploading your EPUB file to iTunes Connect: iTunes Producer, the Pages application, or the Web using the Apple Publishing Portal (#AR).

1) iTunes Producer: You'll need to download the iTunes Producer app first but this method is restricted to users with a Mac with OS X 10.10 or later, at least 20GB of available hard disk space, and a broadband internet connection with an upload speed of 1 megabit per second (Mbps) or faster (these specifications are subject to change).

If you meet these requirements, the advantage of using iTunes Producer is that you can submit your book details, pricing, cover art, and EPUB book files (known as assets in Apple lingo) for immediate release or pre-order. You can also use iTunes Producer to update the book's metadata, pricing, or assets after your book has been submitted.

2) Pages: You can handle a lot of the process using this application, but not everything. You'll be able to publish your book directly from Pages to Apple Books on your iPad, iPhone, Mac, or online at iCloud.com, however you will still need to use iTunes Producer to set rights, pricing, and sales territories.

3) Apple Publishing Portal: The Apple Publishing Portal allows you to set up a new book, update a previously submitted book, and set up pre-orders. When uploading a new book, you will be asked to:

- Upload your EPUB file.
- Upload a sample file for online previews (e.g., the first 3 chapters).
- Upload your e-book cover.
- Enter your book's metadata.

Pro Tip: If you don't want your book to be published immediately be sure to select "Set up a pre-order" before you complete the process.

After you've submitted your book, you will need to set rights, pricing, and sales territories using iTunes Producer.

Apple Books Promotional Opportunities

Each book with an "On Store" or "Ready for Store" status in Apple Books is assigned 250 unique promo codes to generate book buzz and early reviews, both of which help with overall long-term sales. When the code is entered at checkout, the book's retail price is reduced to $0.00, giving readers a free copy.

As the publisher, you have the option of requesting as few or as many of these promo codes as you wish at any time while your book is live on Apple Books, up to the maximum of 250. For example, you might try a weekly draw, or offer the first ten to comment on a social media post a free copy of your book, requesting an honest review in exchange. The marketing possibilities are endless. And because this is a coupon-based promotion, you don't need to worry about price matching with other retailers.

Note: Promo codes can only be redeemed in countries or regions where your Apple e-book is available for sale.

Pro Tip: Apple Books promo codes expire four weeks from the date you request them, and will not be replaced, so do not request more than you can distribute for redemption within that time frame. The balance of your promo codes will be available for future use when you're ready to use them.

P.S. Don't forget to advise promo code "winners" of the deadline to redeem.

SCHEDULING A SALE

For third party sales promotions, schedule promotional pricing by selecting your book in My Books, then setting price intervals (start and end dates) on the Rights & Pricing page. Start by clicking on Edit Countries/Regions and Pricing. Select one or more, or all countries/regions, as well as the base currency, e.g., USD, and price. Be aware, this process can be labor-intensive if your sale is offered in more than one currency. For example, if you wanted to price your book at $0.99 in all markets, e.g., $0.99 CAD in Canada, $0.99 USD in the U.S., $0.99 GBP in the UK, $0.99 NZD in New Zealand, and $0.99 AUD in Australia, you will need to manually enter each one. If you enter USD as your base currency, any country outside of the U.S. will have prices based on the current U.S. exchange rate, which may be higher or lower than the $0.99 USD price.

ROYALTY STRUCTURE

Apple Books distribution costs are 30% regardless of the price of your e-book, leaving you, the author/publisher with a 70% royalty. Exclusivity on Apple Books is not required.

EXAMPLE A (<$2.99)

Sale Price $1.99
Apple Books deducts 30% = $0.60
You earn @ 70% = $1.39

EXAMPLE B (>$2.99)

Sale Price $12.99
Apple Books deducts 30% = $3.90
You earn @ 70% = $9.09

REPORTS & PAYMENTS

The Sales and Trends Reports page provides a Summary Sales Report by title(s), retail price, royalty price, and sales territory for aggregated sales, minus refunds. You can choose to get this report daily or weekly. Payment is made no later than 45 days following the end of each month by Electronic Funds Transfer (EFT) directly to your bank account in your local currency, e.g., USD for U.S. residents, CAD for Canadian residents. Canadian residents will have GST deducted from all Canadian sales. An online, downloadable, payment report is summarized by country, units sold, royalty earned, tax and returns, and total owed. A detailed report is available for download.

TAX INFORMATION

All forms are completed online and can be found in the Agreements, Tax, and Banking section (#AR).

U.S. Publishers

You will need to complete a W-9 form. Apple does not send a Form 1099-MISC for royalty income earned. A Form 1099-K

(#AR) will be mailed by January 31 if you meet the following requirements:

- At least $20,000 in unadjusted gross sales (the total amount of your sales, not adjusted for Apple's commissions, fees, refunds, etc.).
- More than 200 transactions in a calendar year.

Canadian Publishers

In order to sell on Apple books, you must register for a Goods and Services Tax/Harmonized Sales Tax (GST/HST) number. You will also need to submit a Canadian GST/HST Form 506. This form gives Apple permission to deduct GST on your behalf for any sales made to Canadian end users. Because you'll also want to sell books in the United States without U.S. withholding tax, you'll be required to complete a W-8BEN.

BARNES & NOBLE PRESS

BARNES & NOBLE PRESS (B&N PRESS)

WEBSITE: https://press.barnesandnoble.com

FORMERLY NOOK PRESS, B&N Press is a free self-publishing service created by Barnes & Noble, an American bookseller with the largest number of brick-and-mortar bookstores in the United States. Just as Amazon has the Kindle e-reader, B&N has the Nook (also stylized as nook).

In addition to Nook e-books, B&N Press offers a POD option for sale in Barnes & Noble stores. This doesn't mean your book will be stocked in Barnes & Noble stores, but rather that it will be available for friends and fans to order online. That said, some B&N stores may be willing to hold a consignment event for you and your books (#AR). I'll go into bookstore consignment opportunities in more detail in "Author, Author," the final section of this book.

Note: You don't need to use B&N's POD service to have your print books available at Barnes & Noble, though you will need to use a distributor like IngramSpark or Draft2Digital to make it happen.

STORE: www.barnesandnoble.com (can also be accessed at BN.com) and NOOK.com.

DISTRIBUTION

E-books uploaded to the B&N Press platform are available for purchase through Barnes & Noble's digital storefronts and are available on the Nook app and/or e-reader device. While the Digital Rights Management (DRM) protection that Kindle e-books use prevents books from being loaded to devices not sold by Amazon, e-books purchased for Nook can be read on other platforms once the Nook app (#AR) has been downloaded. There are several online articles on how to read your Nook book on Kindle and other devices.

At time of publication, supported languages include Afrikaans, Basque, Catalan, Danish, Dutch, English, Finnish, French, German, Hungarian, Icelandic, Indonesian, Italian, Norwegian, Portuguese, Romanian, Spanish, Swedish, and Turkish.

SERVICES & SUPPORT

E-mail support is available BNPressSupport@bn.com. My personal experience is that response time can be slow.

Pro Tip: You must use the e-mail address associated with your vendor account when contacting B&N Press for support, otherwise you'll receive an e-mail advising you to do so before assistance can be provided. To avoid delays, include all relevant data, e.g., ISBN, title, nature of request, and screenshots if applicable.

ACCOUNT SETUP

There is no charge to set up an account on Barnes & Noble Press, though you will need to also sign up as a vendor to submit and sell your book(s). To become a vendor, you must submit banking and tax information.

UPLOADING YOUR BOOK

There is no charge to upload your book material. B&N Press is completed as follows:

E-book

This is where you'll upload and approve your EPUB (digital) file and e-book cover.

Print

Skip this step if you're using another POD distributer like IngramSpark or Draft2Digital.

If you elect to use B&N's POD option, you'll need to upload a formatted PDF file, and use B&N's cover template (#AR) to create your cover. Your options are:

- Interior print color: Black & white, standard color, or full premium color. Black and white is the standard for novels. Paperbacks printed in standard color have a matte finish, with less richness and definition than premium color. Premium color is ideal for image/photograph-heavy color interiors, such as cookbooks or children's books.
- Cover format: Paperback, case laminate (hardcover with printed case), hardcover with dust jacket.
- Cover finish: Gloss or matte.
- Paper color: Cream (50 lb.), white (50 lb.), or white (70 lb.).

Pro Tip: The price to produce your book will depend on the options you choose. For example, the least expensive would be paperback, black & white ink, and 50 lb. paper. The color of the paper and cover finish does not impact the price.

The following steps apply to both e-book and print:

Default sample: You will be offered choices for the reading excerpt on your book's detail page. The default sample automatically includes the first 5% of your book. You can also upload a custom sample or select any number of consecutive chapters. The option to customize your reading excerpt is a nice feature not offered on most other platforms.

- Book details: This is broken down into six sub-sections as follows:

1) Title, subtitle, publisher, edition, publication date, and book description. The default description (aka cover copy or book blurb) allows 2,000 characters (includes spaces), which is quite generous. An optional long description allows 5,000 characters (approximately 770 to 1,000 words). I have personally never written or posted a long description, don't remember reading one, and can't begin to imagine why you'd want to—or how such a detailed description would grab a reader's attention. Nonetheless, the option is there.

2) Author and up to five contributors: Contributing authors in an anthology, co-author, or an author who has written the foreword. Contributors do not include editors, proofreaders, cover artists, etc. This is also where you'll post your author bio.

3) Categories: B&N allows up to five primary categories and sub-categories. You will also enter your keywords on this page.

4) Pricing: Enter the price in U.S. dollars (USD). This page will also depict the author royalty per book sold, as well as the retail and distribution share, a nice visual feature.

5) Rights & other information: Digital Rights Management (DRM), copyright, ISBN.

6) Editorial reviews: You can enter up to five editorial reviews. These will be included on your book's product page. Another nice feature. These "nice" features are one reason you might want to set up a direct account with B&N vs. going through an aggregator (like Draft2Digital) where they would not be made available.

- Review and publish: You will be notified by e-mail when your book is live.

Changes to metadata (excluding ISBN, which cannot be changed), content, distribution, and pricing can be made at no cost following the same steps during the pre-order period or after publication. Updates can take up to 24 hours to appear on BN.com.

B&N Promotional Opportunities

Go to the Promotions tab in the Book Details section and click on the "create a promotion" link. Note that B&N promotions only work with published titles. Pre-orders are not eligible.

You will be taken to a page with two options:

X% Off with Coupon Code

- Select the start and end date of the promotion.
- Book title.
- Enter a discount amount, e.g., 25%, 75%, etc.

Creating your coupon code: This will always start with BNP and will be 7 to 10 alphanumeric characters. Each promotion must have a unique coupon code and should also serve as a quick reminder of what you're offering. For example, if I was creating a 50% off coupon for this book, it might read as follows: BNP50SP. If I decide to rerun the same promotion in the future, it might be BNP50SP2.

*Pro Tip: There is nothing in the B & N system to prevent you from duplicating a code, but failure to update a coupon code will result in the coupon not being recognized or accepted at checkout. Take it from one who has been there and done that.

Buy One Get One X% Off (BOGO)

This only works if you have two or more e-book titles with B&N.

If you do, follow the same steps as outlined in "X% Off." The discount will automatically be applied at checkout after the coupon code is entered.

Whichever option you choose, royalties will be calculated at 70% of the discounted sale price.

EXAMPLE

Original Price: $5.99
Discount: 50%
Sale Price: $2.99
B&N deducts 30% = $0.90
You earn @ 70% = $2.09

Because these promotions are coupon-based, you don't have to worry about price matching with other retailers. While this may sound exciting (after all, free promo opportunities are always welcome), it's important to note that B&N does not promote or endorse these discounts in any way; 100% of the promotion falls on you. Despite social media posts and website/newsletter blasts, I've never had much success with B&N promos, but that doesn't mean you won't.

Scheduling a Sale

For third party sales promotions go to the Book Details/Pricing page. Enter the sale price, as well as the start and end dates.

Pre-orders

Nook allows pre-orders. Enter the pre-order date at the same time you are setting up your book.

Royalty Structure: e-books

B&N distribution costs are 30% regardless of the price of your e-book, leaving you, the author/publisher with a 70% royalty. Exclusivity is not required.

EXAMPLE A (<$2.99)

Sale Price $1.99
B&N deducts 30% = $0.60
You earn @ 70% = $1.39

EXAMPLE B (>$2.99)

Sale Price $12.99
B&N deducts 30% = $3.90
You earn @ 70% = $9.09

ROYALTY STRUCTURE: POD

B&N Press pays a 55% royalty (minus the per book printing cost) on books created through their POD program and sold in Barnes & Noble stores or through the B&N online storefront.

EXAMPLE

Suggested Retail Price: $18.99
Retail & Distribution Cost @ 45%: $8.55
Author Royalty @ 55%: $10.44
Less Printing Cost: $5.46
Net Author Royalty: $4.98

REPORTS & PAYMENTS

Orders are tracked by units sold and royalties earned in an easy-to-navigate Sales Reports page, with daily at-a-glance and in-depth unit sales and royalties earned reports. Royalties are paid at the end of each month for sales the prior month if a threshold of $10 USD is reached, or bi-annually regardless of amount earned, e.g., if

October sales exceed $10, you will be paid at the end of November, with an accompanying report by title. If October sales are less than $10, royalties will be held on account until the threshold is reached, or six months has passed. Payment is made by Electronic Funds Transfer (EFT) directly to your bank account in USD.

TAX INFORMATION

U.S. Publishers

You are required to submit a W-9 form (#AR). Royalties paid in the prior tax year will be reported on Form 1099-MISC, issued on or before January 31, and filed with the IRS. B&N Press does not deduct taxes.

Canadian Publishers

You are required to submit a Form W-8BEN in order to be paid and to avoid paying U.S. withholding tax.

Pro Tip: Keep a record of when you submit your W-8BEN, which will expire on December 31st, three years after you submit. B&N will not advise you that your form has expired; they'll just stop paying you until you submit a new form.

DRAFT2DIGITAL

DRAFT2DIGITAL (D2D)

WEBSITE: https://draft2digital.com/

DRAFT2DIGITAL (#AR) is what's known in the industry as an aggregator—a distributor of books to multiple sales platforms ("storefronts" in D2D lingo). Established in 2012, D2D acquired Smashwords in 2022, a long-time and significant player in the aggregator marketplace, making Draft2Digital one of the world's largest distributors serving self-published authors and independent presses. They acquired SelfPubBookCovers.com in 2023.

D2D's reach continues to expand and acquire new distribution outlets. When such an acquisition happens, publishers (that's you) will have the choice to opt in or opt out. In addition to digital distribution, D2D offers a Print on Demand (POD) option.

STORES & DISTRIBUTION

D2D distributes to several e-book sales channels and subscription services (#AR) including (at time of publication) Amazon, Apple Books, Barnes & Noble, Gardners, Kobo/Kobo Plus, Tolino, Everand (formerly Scribd), Vivlio, and Smashwords (which retains an online catalogue). Digital-only library distribution platforms, which would be largely inaccessible to self-published authors on a "go direct" basis, include Baker & Taylor, OverDrive, Bibilotheca, Hoopla, BorrowBox, Odilo, and Palace Marketplace.

Note: this doesn't mean that D2D is the only game in town when it comes to library sales. Kobo, for example, offers OverDrive distribution, while IngramSpark is the primary distribution service for print. But insofar as the other named players, D2D is your best (and possibly, only) option.

For authors who want to self-publish, but really don't want to set up several separate retail accounts, D2D is a good one-stop option, though I would strongly recommend using KDP for Amazon.

If you've already published your e-book through one or more platforms, for example, Kobo or Barnes & Noble's Nook, you can still use Draft2Digital to expand into other markets, including library and subscription services—but no double dipping. By that I mean if you've set up an account and uploaded your book to Kobo, don't also select Kobo on D2D. The same is true for Print on Demand publishers. If you've set up your title on IngramSpark or Amazon's Expanded Distribution, do not use D2D. All three target the same distributors and double (or worse, triple) dipping will only create chaos and the very real possibility that your book won't be picked up anywhere.

Note: You can always delist a title on D2D (with one, more, or all vendors), but because each publishing partner operates on their own timeline, you'll need to allow a couple of weeks for the process to complete.

SERVICES & SUPPORT

D2D's extensive Knowledge Base (#AR) is a good place to start, but there's also telephone and e-mail support (recommended). Queries are handled during business hours (Monday to Friday, 8 a.m. to 5 p.m. CST).

ACCOUNT SETUP

There's no cost to set up an account with D2D. You'll be asked the usual questions, and you'll be required to complete payment and tax information.

UPLOADING YOUR BOOK

Even if you plan to produce a print book through D2D, your first step should be to create an e-book. There is no charge to upload a book to D2D.

E-books

Start by clicking on "My Books" and then "Create New eBook."

1) Upload your book cover and enter your metadata, including ISBN. D2D will provide an ISBN, but you can only use it for books distributed on D2D. That means if you decide to open an account later with one or more of D2D's sales channels, you'll need to get another ISBN for that platform. As always, I recommend using your own ISBN.

2) Upload your EPUB.

Note: D2D offers the option of uploading a Word document, and they will build your EPUB, including the title and copyright page, and back matter. Unlike other publishing platforms, D2D allows you to use their EPUB on other sales channels outside of those you've selected through D2D.

3) Choose your vendors. (Remember, no double dipping!)

4) Enter your e-book list price in USD and any territorial prices. Territorial pricing, either higher or lower, is only required if you do not want automatic currency conversion for a specific country. Your e-book list price can be changed at any time, and you'll be able to view your projected royalties for each sales channel. (I'll cover library distribution shortly.)

5) Review and publish your book. Pre-orders are allowed and can be set up before your content is finalized (but don't forget to

update at least three days before the publication date). There is no charge to upload revised interior or cover files after publication, but these changes will not be instantaneous. Best to get it right the first time!

Print on Demand

D2D currently offers POD for standard-size paperbacks only (5" x 8"/5.25" x 8.5"/5.5" x 8.5"/6" x 9"/7.5" x 9.25"/8.5" x 11") though at press time for this book they were working on hardcover and large print options for a future rollout. D2D does not charge a fee for the initial setup of your paperback book, but there may be charges for revisions. Refer to Step 3: Terms & Conditions for more information.

To get started, click on "My Books" and then select one of two options:

1) Create a New Book Project and Start Print Book.

Choose this option if you did not create an e-book. You'll need to complete steps 1-5 in e-books above, replacing the EPUB file with a print ready PDF, and your e-book cover with a print cover. You will be notified of POD terms and conditions before you hit Publish.

Go to your existing e-book title and click on the Print tab, then Start your Print Book. A pop-up message of POD terms and conditions will appear for your review and approval. You'll then be taken to the metadata page, where you'll follow the same five steps outlined in Uploading Your E-book. Note that you can have D2D format your paperback from your e-book file, and you'll be offered formatting choices, e.g., page numbers and headers, trim size, etc.

2) Upload your previously formatted PDF.

Your other option is to upload your previously formatted PDF (D2D will autodetect the trim size and page count). Select page color (white or cream), review your file, then click on save and continue. D2D will generate a wraparound print cover from your e-book cover with text fields for you to complete. You can also upload your own custom PDF cover using the D2D blank template automatically generated at this step. (They really do make it easy.)

Terms and Conditions: I've included the link (#AR), but the gist of it is that unlike e-books where free changes are unlimited (uploading of new interior or cover art files), any POD changes that impact the physical product of your book are limited to one free revision upload every 90 days. After your one freebie, you will need to purchase something D2D calls a Print Change Token (currently $25 USD) for any additional change(s). The bottom line? Don't submit incomplete, placeholder, or non-finalized files to be published. Of course, you can always complete all the steps and save as a draft, but why not wait until you've got everything finalized to begin?

Note: A Print Change Token is *not* required to revise your book price or other online metadata. You will receive one free Print Change Token every 90 days. These do not roll over (in other words, you can't save them up for later use).

Publishing Time: Print books can take two or more weeks to go live, so factor that in when planning your publication date.

Pre-orders: POD pre-orders are allowed but the interior file (PDF) and cover art must be final. If you need to make a change before your publication date, you're back to the Print Change Token situation again.

Distribution: Your D2D POD book will be made available to Amazon and all distributions channels served by IngramSpark (the best-known POD distributor for self-published authors), including Barnes & Noble and most independent bookstores in the U.S. However, just as with IngramSpark, there is no guarantee a bookstore will order your book, and chances are they won't unless there's customer demand. That said, it is likely they'll list it as part of their online catalog. This non-stock issue isn't a knock against your book, D2D, or IngramSpark. Remember, the Big Five account for 80% of the books shelved in brick-and-mortar stores. That leaves 20% of shelf space for books published by independent presses, assisted/hybrid publishers, and self-published authors.

Pricing: D2D's print book price calculator (#AR) is a handy tool to estimate your bottom line. I've included an example below under Royalty Structure: POD, but I encourage you to tinker with the calculator and test out different retail prices. Remember, though, that if you overprice your book in the hope of earning higher royalties, you may discourage sales. Big name authors can get away with charging $20 or more for a paperback. Chances are, you can't, at least not when you're first starting out. You can always change your retail price later (at no cost to you).

Reminder: You might be tempted to list your POD book with IngramSpark and Amazon's Expanded Distribution. Because D2D's distribution reaches the same markets, this will only create confusion among vendors and may result it your book not being listed by any of them.

Note: Opting to go direct on Amazon using Kindle Direct Publishing's Amazon-only distribution platform will not create a problem. To refresh your memory on the differences between KDP's Amazon-only vs. Expanded Distribution, revisit the chapter on Amazon.

Proof Copies: You'll be able to order a single print proof copy of your title before finalizing publication. The charge will be the print cost, applicable taxes, and shipping. Once you have received and reviewed your proof copy, you can amend any errors and upload a new version of the manuscript file to your print book. A print token will not be required unless you've already gone live.

Author Copies: These are copies printed and mailed to you for your personal use, e.g., your book launch event. You'll be charged the base printing cost, applicable taxes, and shipping.

LIBRARY DISTRIBUTION

For e-book library distribution, Draft2Digital offers two payment types (#AR). While both payment types are turned on for your account by default, not every library system supports both. You will be able to view your estimated royalties next to the selected library service, which are:

One Copy, One User (OCOU)

The library purchases a copy and lends it out in the same way physical books are handled, e.g., once the book is checked out, it is no longer available until it has been returned. When a library purchases your book, you will earn a royalty on that sale. There will be no further payment, regardless of how many times the book is checked out. For this reason, D2D recommends a higher retail list price for libraries. If you decide to opt out of library distribution or delist your book, any OCOU copies already acquired by a library will still be available for their patrons to check out, however it will no longer be available for purchase.

Cost Per Checkout (CPC)

Also known as Price Per Unit or PPU, CPC allows multiple copies and multiple users to borrow your book at the same time without the library purchasing a copy. The library is charged per copy checked out (usually about 1/10 of the library list price). If you decide to opt out of library distribution or delist your book, it will no longer be available for library patrons to find and check out.

PROMOTIONAL OPPORTUNITIES

Opt-in promotions: D2D occasionally offers limited time opt-in promotional opportunities. A recent example is the "Smashwords 2023 Read an Ebook Week," where authors could select to discount their title(s) for books in the Smashwords catalog (#AR).

Refer a friend program (#AR): If you refer a friend, D2D will pay you 10% of its share of your friend's royalties for two years (it won't cost your friend a cent). There is no special code to enter; the link itself is the referral link (using the referral link to create an account triggers the refer-a-friend system). My D2D refer a friend link is: https://www.draft2digital.com/Path

Universal Book Link: Under the Books2Read umbrella, authors can create one buy link for multiple sales channels, including direct accounts not with D2D (#AR). This is a very handy sales tool and it's free to use. Here's an example of my customized Universal Book Link for *Finding Your Path to Publication: A Step-by-Step Guide*: https://books2read.com/FindingYourPathtoPublication.

SCHEDULING A SALE

You can schedule a sale using D2D's promotional pricing tool (the green tab on your book's page labeled "Promotion"). Simply enter your start and end dates and the promo price and you're good to go.

Note: Promo pricing does not apply to library partners.

ROYALTY STRUCTURE: E-BOOKS

Royalty rates vary widely based on sales channel.

Note: The following data was provided by D2D in February 2023 and may be subject to change.

D2D Retail Sites

Most retail sites keep 30% of your list price, and the remaining 70% is paid to D2D, who in turn deduct 15% of the net amount received, or roughly 10% of your list price. The royalty rate shown is what you can expect to earn for books sold from that retailer.

- Amazon (for e-books prices between $2.99 and $9.99): 60%
- Amazon (for e-books priced below $2.99 or above $9.99): 30%
- Apple Books: 60%
- Gardners: 60%
- Nook (Barnes and Noble): 60%
- Kobo (and several affiliate sites): 60%
- Tolino (a conglomerate of stores located in Germany and Eastern Europe): 60%

- Vivlio (a conglomerate of stores in France): 55.25%

EXAMPLE A (60%)

Sale Price $5.99
You earn royalty @ 60% – $3.59

EXAMPLE B (55.25%)

Sale Price $5.99
You earn royalty @ 55.25% = $3.31

Subscription Sites

Everand (formerly Scribd): Everand shows a 20% preview of your file. Once the reader borrows the book and reads past the preview you would receive a full royalty payment of 60% of your listing price. See Example A above.

Kobo Plus (only an option if you opt for distribution to Kobo): Kobo Plus has a complex algorithm that calculates the royalty on the book by taking into account the number of books listed in the service, the number of subscribers enrolled in the service, and the amount of time spent reading your book through this subscription model.

Library Sites

In all cases, D2D's fee is 15% of the net amount they are paid by the library site.

One Copy, One User (OCOU)

- Bibliotheca (OCOU only): 46.25% of listing price less D2D fee.
- Baker & Taylor (OCOU only): 46.25% of listing price less D2D fee.

- BorrowBox (OCOU only): 46.25% of listing price less D2D fee (15% of net).
- Odilo (OCOU): 46.25% of listing price less D2D fee.
- OverDrive (OCOU): 46.25% of listing price less D2D fee.
- Palace Marketplace (OCOU only): 59.5% of listing price less D2D fee (15% of net).

EXAMPLE

Library List Price $14.99
D2D deducts 15% = $2.25
You earn @ 46.25% on $12.74 = $5.89

Cost Per Checkout (CPC)

- Odilo (CPC): 46.75% on 1/10 of your listing price less D2D fee.
- OverDrive (CPC): 46.75% on 1/10 of your listing price less D2D fee.
- Hoopla (CPC): Tiered pricing model, with an average of 5-7% of the digital list price, from $0.99 to $1.49. New releases will be priced at the top tier level ($1.49), while backlist titles will be priced at the $0.99 level to align with library pricing expectations. Authors receive 45% royalty rate based on these prices, less D2D's fee.

EXAMPLE A (OverDrive)

Library List Price $14.99 / 10% = $1.49
D2D deducts 15% = $0.22
You earn @ 46.75% on $1.27 = $0.59

EXAMPLE B (Hoopla)

CPC @ $0.99
D2D deducts 15% = $0.15
You earn @ 45% on $.084 = $ 0.38

Royalty Structure: POD

D2D's POD royalty rate is 45%.

EXAMPLE (POD)

Based on 6" x 9" 300-page paperback, black and white ink.
Suggested Retail Price: $18.99
Retail & Distribution Cost @ 55%: $10.44
Author Royalty @ 45%: $8.55
Less Printing Cost: $5.21
Net Author Royalty: $3.34

Test drive your own title using D2D's POD calculator (#AR).

Reports & Payments

The Reports tab takes you to a page that shows current month and previous month sales and estimated royalties. There are also options to download statements, view your account ledger (royalties earned by month and payments), access charts, raw sales data by sales channel, and more. In short, if you're curious about any aspect of your D2D sales, you'll find it under Reports.

Most D2D partners pay 60-90 days following the month of sale. Once funds are received, D2D will pay you in their next monthly payment. You have several options for payment:

- Check: $100 USD minimum payment threshold.
- Direct Deposit US: No minimum payment threshold.

- Direct Deposit International: $10 USD minimum payment threshold.
- PayPal: $0.00 for US; $5 USD minimum payment threshold for Canada.
- Payoneer: $20 USD.

One unique aspect of D2D is that they allow royalty splitting between collaborators (#AR), e.g., between author and translator, two or more authors, author and illustrator, etc. No other publishing platform, including those referenced in this book, allow this. However, the collaboration organizer (usually the primary author) and all collaborators must have a Draft2Digital account, a payment method, and a completed tax interview to get paid.

TAX INFORMATION

Based on the tax interview completed on account setup, tax forms are available for download as a drop-down option on your Reports page. All forms (listed below) are filed with the IRS.

- 1099-MISC: For earnings paid to US residents and US citizens.
- 1099-NEC: For earnings paid for money earned by referrals to US residents and US citizens (#AR).
- 1042-S: For earnings paid to non-US citizens living outside of the U.S.

GOOGLE PLAY BOOKS
GOOGLE PLAY BOOKS PARTNER CENTER

WEBSITE: https://play.google.com/books/publish/

GOOGLE PLAY BOOKS is the e-book digital distribution service of the Google Play product line, accessible via computer through the Google Play Library (#AR) or for e-readers by downloading the Google Play Books app, available in iOS and Android. Google Play does not offer a POD option.

STORE: https://play.google.com/store/books/

DISTRIBUTION

Google Play distributes to 75 countries and more than 3 billion users.

SERVICES & SUPPORT

Google Play offers an extensive online help section as well as e-mail and live chat options. I've experienced prompt and knowledgeable service with the live chat option on more than one occasion.

ACCOUNT SETUP

Sign in using your existing Google account or create a new account, free of charge. Provide account details and contact information, then review and approve the terms and conditions. Once you press continue, you'll be taken to the Partner Center home page. This is where you'll upload books, set up promotions, find your sales stats, view or update your account information, and provide your banking and tax information in the Payment center.

UPLOADING YOUR BOOK

There is no charge to upload a book. There are five steps:

1) From your Partner home page, select Book Catalog, then Add Book. Select "Sell e-book on Google Play," add your ISBN, and hit enter. This will take you to the About Your Book (metadata) section. Complete and select enter.

2) In Settings, you'll be asked if you want DRM, what you want your preview limit (select 20%, which is the minimum) as well as the copy and paste limit (select 0% to help protect your work from potential copyright infringement and lost sales), and territories. Complete and select enter.

3) In Content and Cover, you'll upload your EPUB file and book cover. There are six verification steps for the content; this can take quite a long time, and I've experienced a "timed out" situation at one of the six steps, without any "issue" being listed. If that happens to you, you'll need to re-upload the file and try again. Patience is your friend at this step. That said, you won't need to stay logged in during the processing for the upload to work. Keep your fingers crossed.

4) Enter book price and countries. The easiest option is to select USD and World (which covers all countries where Google Play is active) and Google Play will take care of the currency exchange

based on the USD price. However, you can select individual territories and pricing if you'd like to increase or decrease your retail price in a specific market. If you choose to do this, you will need to deselect the country or countries from the "World" setting.

5) Select Publish. Your book should be live within 24 hours after processing is complete. You will *not* be notified when your book is live, so remember to check back.

SCHEDULING A SALE

There are two ways to enter sale prices:

1) Under the Pricing tab on your book page by clicking "show additional settings" under the country/countries you wish to include. In addition to the price, you must enter a start and end date, and whether sales tax is included in the price. If tax is not included, but is applicable, your royalty will be based on the net (after tax) sale.

2) Under the Promotions tab on your main dashboard. This is helpful if you'd like to name your promotion, e.g., "September newsletter." You'll need to enter a start date, end date (optional), countries, and price.

ROYALTY STRUCTURE

The Google Play royalty rate in more than 60 countries (including the U.S. and Canada) is 70% regardless of the sale price of your e-book. The royalty rate for Hong Kong, India, Indonesia, Japan, Malaysia, Philippines, Singapore, South Korea, Taiwan, Thailand, and Vietnam is 52%.

EXAMPLE A (70%)

Sale Price $5.99
Google Play deducts 30% = $1.80
You earn @ 70% = $4.19

EXAMPLE B (52%)

Sale Price $5.99
Google Play deducts 48% = $2.88
You earn @ 52% = $3.11

GOOGLE PLAY PROMOTIONAL OPPORTUNITIES

Promo codes can be generated on request via the Promotions tab. Select the Promo Codes option, then enter your promotion name, start and end dates, title, countries, and type of promotion (free, fixed price, or percentage off).

You can select One Code (the same code for all customers) or Multiple Codes (unique codes per customer). You can request up to 5,000 codes per promotion. You can also pause, resume, or end your promotion early by clicking on "Manage promotion." Statistics for promotions are available to download.

There is also a "series bundle" option where customers must purchase two or more (you specify) books in a series to receive the discount.

Note: You must accept terms and conditions. If, after doing so, the "create a promo code" or "series bundle" page doesn't come up, refresh your screen and it should appear.

Pro Tip: To avoid price matching concerns with other platforms, select the percentage off option and enter the discount amount (1% to 99%).

REPORTS & PAYMENTS

The Partner Center on your home page includes a Reports tab and an Analytics tab. Payment reports are downloadable in a .csv format. You can also customize reports by month, country, and title. Analytics is also where you'll find your month-to-date sales stats, which can also be sorted into other categories, e.g., last 30 days, year-to-date, or custom.

Payments are made on the 15th day of each month, or on the

next business day (which varies by region) by Electronic Fund Transfer (EFT) or Wire Transfer. Because the minimum payment threshold for Wire Transfer is $100, I recommend EFT, which has a $1 USD threshold.

TAX INFORMATION

All publishers must complete a tax interview in the Payment center. This information must be updated if you change your address.

U.S. Publishers are issued Form 1099-MISC (#AR) if earnings exceed $10 and a W-9 Form is on file.

Non-U.S. publishers are issued Form 1042-S if a W-8BEN is on file, but only for the portion of royalty income earned in the U.S.

INGRAMSPARK

A DIVISION OF INGRAM CONTENT GROUP

WEBSITE: https://myaccount.ingramspark.com/Account/Signup

A DIVISION of Ingram Content Group, IngramSpark was launched in 2013 to offer professional Print on Demand (POD) publishing services to independent publishers and self-published authors. In addition to POD, IngramSpark also provides global distribution of print and e-books.

STORE: IngramSpark is a wholesale distributor. They do not sell directly to consumers.

DISTRIBUTION

After your book has been approved for distribution, a metadata feed (information and pricing for your book) will be sent to more than 40,000 bookstores, libraries, and retail outlets around the world (#AR). This information (known as an insertion) is also available to stores and other account holders on Ingram Book Company's iPage website (#AR). You can view your insertions under the Marketing tab (found on your account's home page).

It can take up to six weeks before your book will be displayed on a retailer's online store or website, or on a distributor or retailer's internal ordering system, and (depending on the retail partner), it's possible that the cover may never be displayed. There is also no guarantee that stores or libraries will order your book, and 100% of all book marketing and promotion is the sole responsibility of the publisher (that's you).

SERVICES & SUPPORT

Ingram's Help Center (#AR) page covers account information, title setup, file help (book building tools), ordering, distribution, marketing, e-books, reporting, and to how-to videos. Each sub-section includes links to additional information, FAQs, and videos. A Tools & Resources tab on the home page will take you to file creation tools (guidelines, cover templates, etc.), a pricing and services guide, and calculators to determine compensation and print and shipping costs. There's also a User Guide in downloadable PDF format (#AR).

Additional questions? Click on the Support tab, which offers two options: IngramSpark Connect (a paid service for one-on-one support) or e-mail (response time varies though it is generally within seven days). You will receive an automated message confirming receipt. There is no live chat or telephone support.

ACCOUNT SETUP

Limited to one account per publisher. To set up an account, you'll require:

- A valid e-mail address.
- A credit card (kept on file and can be changed at any time).

- A Tax ID number. The Tax Information section will generate a W-9 based on the information provided. Once completed, the W-9 will be available in the "Paperwork" area (dropdown menu, top right-hand corner).
- Banking or PayPal information.

Complete information can be found on the website (#AR).

Pro Tip: The currency you select to be paid in <u>cannot</u> be changed at a later date.

UPLOADING YOUR BOOK

Global distribution is free. Until May 1, 2023, IngramSpark charged a setup fee to process your print or e-book. This has since been waived.

Pro Tip: If you use IngramSpark's free ISBN (available to U.S. publishers only), the publishing imprint will be listed as "Indy Pub" and cannot be used elsewhere. But you already know not to use a free ISBN, right?

Global Print and E-book Agreement: You'll need to read and approve this to upload and distribute books through IngramSpark. When terms and conditions change or additional agreements are added, you'll see a "New Opportunity Available" button on your home page (#AR). Completed agreements can be found in your Paperwork section (dropdown menu on the top righthand side of your home page).

Complete title setup instructions for print and e-book (#AR) can be found on the IngramSpark website, though you'll need the usual metadata and PDF (print) or EPUB (e-book) files. You can also download the IngramSpark's File Creation Guide (#AR).

Print Proof: You'll be able to download the print "eProof," which will include your cover art, to view online before approving it.

If you spot any errors, you can make those changes without charge. However, once you've approved the eProof and your book is in production, any revisions made after 60 days will be subject to a revision fee (currently $25 USD). Some writing associations offer members a limited number of coupon codes to offset the cost of revisions. Refer to the Associations section in "Author, Author" for more information.

Note: You cannot order a print proof copy until your eproof has been approved and the book is listed as "available for printing."

Author Copies (#AR): After you've approved your book, it will be made available for printing. You can then place an order for printed copies of your book(s) through your IngramSpark account at print cost plus a small shipping & handling fee (currently $1.99 USD per order) and sales tax, if applicable. You can do this even if your book is on pre-order.

Personalized Copies (#AR): This is a nice feature that allows you to add a personal message when placing an order, currently not offered by other POD publishers. IngramSpark will add a page to each book in that order (don't worry, you won't need a new cover and it can be applied to a single copy or small batch only). For example, you could personalize copies for your book launch or to donate copies to your local library as a book club set (just make sure you don't overorder). Simply add a message such as "Thank you for attending my book launch" or "Donated by the author."

Note: You'll need to contact your local library to determine their policy as regards both donations and book club sets. Even if the library doesn't have the space to accommodate your books, the gesture can serve to aid in developing a relationship with them, which can lead to other opportunities. I've personally visited library book clubs (virtually and in-person), which in turn led to other opportunities and connections. Case in point: I met Emily Nakeff, my research assistant and front-line editor for both Step-by-Step guides, when presenting at a NaNoWriMo library event.

E-book Conversion

Using a cost-per-page calculation, IngramSpark can create a reflowable EPUB file once you have uploaded a print PDF file. The total conversion cost will be displayed for your approval, and the amount due will be charged to the credit card on file. The conversion process typically takes 15 business days.

POD Wholesale Discount

There's a short video on the IngramSpark site that explains wholesale discount (#AR) and why you need to offer one. In a nutshell, the wholesale price is the amount that Ingram Book Company (IngramSpark's wholesale distributor) pays for each copy of your book ordered by a retailer, library, etc. Because they are in the business of making money, they keep a percentage (about 15%) of the wholesale discount. The remaining discount is known in the industry as a trade discount. The trade discount industry standard is 40% off the retail price, meaning a book selling for $18.99 with a 55% wholesale discount would be purchased by the retailer for 60% of retail, or $11.39.

As the publisher, you have the option to decide what discount to offer (though the minimum allowed for the North America market is 40%), as well as if you want to allow returns. I've included more information on returns, as well as some compensation examples under Publisher Compensation later in this chapter.

Setting the POD Price

To establish your retail price, you'll need to factor in the wholesale discount as well as the print charge. As noted in earlier chapters, the print cost is based on page count, ink color (e.g., black & white), interior paper, (e.g., 50 lb.), and binding, e.g., case laminate or paperback. The type of cover finish (matte or gloss), color of paper (white or cream), and trim size don't affect the cost. Use

IngramSpark's Publisher Compensation Calculator (#AR) to determine the print charge.

OTHER OPTIONS & PROGRAMS

iPage Listing: Separate from the free metadata feed (mentioned in Distribution earlier as iPage insertions), an iPage listing (#AR) is a paid advertisement in Ingram's monthly online catalog. At the time of this book's publication, the cost was $150 USD. The ad includes a thumbnail image of your title, publication date, author name, and price. Ads run for one month only and must be purchased by the 20th of the month to run in the following month, e.g., June 20 for July insertion.

Target.com: Because the Target.com program (#AR) is different from the other distribution services offered through IngramSpark, a separate agreement must be signed to participate. Note that Target is very selective and completing the agreement in no way guarantees that your title will be selected.

PROMOTIONAL OPPORTUNITIES

IngramSpark makes no false promises when it comes to book promotion. The bottom line? It's up to the publisher or author to market and promote their book to bookstores and retailers in Ingram's Global Distribution network, though they do provide a partial listing of some of those sales outlets (#AR). However, the reality is that, as an independent publisher, big name purchasers such as Costco or Walmart aren't likely to take your call or respond to a written query. That said, some may offer consignment opportunities. I'll talk about that more in the section titled "Author, Author."

PUBLISHER COMPENSATION: PRINT ON DEMAND

IngramSpark refers to royalties as "publisher compensation." Publisher compensation is calculated using the Retail/List price less wholesale discount and print cost. As noted earlier, the wholesale discount can be adjusted (minimum 40% in North America, recommended 53-55%). Playing around with this in Ingram's Publisher Compensation Calculator can help you land on a retail sales price that makes sense for both you and the market.

EXAMPLE A (53% Wholesale Discount)

Based on 6" x 9" 300-page paperback, black and white ink.
Suggested Retail Price: $18.99
Less Wholesale Discount @ 53%: $10.06
Less Printing Cost: $5.48
Net Author Royalty: $3.45

EXAMPLE B (40% Wholesale Discount)

Based on 6" x 9" 300-page paperback, black and white ink.
Suggested Retail Price: $18.99
Less Wholesale Discount @ 40%: $7.60
Less Printing Cost: $5.48
Net Author Royalty: $5.91

POD RETURNS

Many booksellers will not purchase non-returnable books to stock or display on their shelves. For example, Chapters Indigo, Canada's largest bookstore chain, will only consider books that are fully returnable, and have a Canadian Price on the back cover or book jacket.

Even retailers who are open to self-published authors are, at the end of the day, a business, and shelf space is a valuable commodity. With unknown and self-published authors, selling your book increases the risk of sluggish, or worse, no sales. Many retailers aren't willing to take that risk without the option to return or destroy unsold copies. That said, if you elect to allow returns, you must also be prepared for the negative financial impact book returns have on your net publisher compensation.

As noted earlier, there are two methods of returns: Yes, deliver and Yes, destroy. Each one is handled differently:

Yes, deliver: You will be charged back the wholesale price of any returned books plus a shipping and handling fee. At the time of this writing, the S&H fee was $3 USD per book, for books shipped to U.S. addresses, and $20 USD per book for returns to non-US (Canadian/International) addresses.

Yes, destroy: You will be charged back the wholesale price of each book. The unsold books are not returned to you.

*Pro Tip: Ingram uses the current wholesale price when calculating the return, and not the price paid on the date of sale. This only factors into the equation if you've changed the list price, the wholesale discount, or both.

EXAMPLE A (Yes, deliver)

All prices are per book, in USD.
Suggested Retail Price: $18.99
Wholesale Discount @ 53%: $10.06
Wholesale Price: $8.93
[Original publisher compensation: $3.45]
S&H: U.S. $3.00 / Canada/International $20.00
Return chargeback: US $11.93 / Canada $28.93
Net loss U.S. [$3.45 - $11. 93] = ($8.48)
Net loss Canada/International [$3.45 - $28.93] = ($25.48)

EXAMPLE B (Yes, destroy)

Suggested Retail Price: $18.99
Wholesale Discount @ 53%: $10.06
Wholesale Price: $8.93
[Original publisher compensation: $3.45]
S&H: $3.00
Return chargeback: $8.93
Net loss U.S., Canada/International [$3.45 - $8.93] = ($5.48)

Pro Tip: It's not as easy as changing the status from "No" to "Yes-Deliver" or "Yes-Destroy," if you decide it's not for you. That's because booksellers are allowed to immediately return books from the date of notice. If a returnable title is removed from distribution altogether, booksellers have 180 days to return any unsold copies. In both cases, the publisher is responsible for the cost of returns.

PUBLISHER COMPENSATION: E-BOOKS

Publisher compensation is 85% of net revenue, which is based on several e-book sales models, partnerships, and discount structures, further defined as Retail Models, Library Models, or Institutional Sales Models (#AR). I've included some examples to provide a general idea, but there are several variables.

EXAMPLE A (Retail Model, One Book, One Sale)

Partners include B&N, De Marque, ebooks.com, fable, Gardners, Medium, Hummingbird, ITSI, Libreka, Libri.de, Perusall, Publica, RedShelf, SpoonRead, VitalSource, WOOK, Chegg, and Legible.

Sale Price $5.99
Retail Discount @ 50% = 3.00
Net Revenue = $2.99
Publisher Compensation @ 85% = $2.54

EXAMPLE B (Library Model, Single User)

The library purchases a copy and lends it out in the same way physical books are handled, e.g., once the book is checked out, it is no longer available until it has been returned.

Sale Price $5.99
Library Discount @ 30% = $1.79
Net Revenue = $4.20
Publisher Compensation @ 85% = $3.57

EXAMPLE C (Library Model, Pay-per-Use)

The library is charged per copy, per checkout. They do not own the book, but can accommodate several patrons at the same time by purchasing multiple pay-per-use copies.

Sale Price $5.99
Library Discount @ 90% = $5.39
Net Revenue = $0.60
Publisher Compensation @ 85% = $0.51

REPORTS & PAYMENTS

Ingram's online Compensation Earnings and Payment Report details earnings and payments for print books sold through Ingram's Global Distribution network and for e-books sold through Ingram's CoreSource distribution platform and includes paid and unpaid compensation earnings, as well as returns (#AR).

Monthly compensation reports (generated only when there are sales to report) are e-mailed in the first week of each month for the month prior, e.g., a March report will include February sales.

Reports are two-part, the first page an overview of net units sold and net compensation by the current period and year to date. The second page details net sales (including returns), print charge, any distribution fee, and net publisher compensation. You will receive a separate Compensation Report for each IngramSpark operating unit, e.g., Unites States, Australia, and currency, e.g., USD, AU.

Print book sales are recorded once shipped from Ingram's print facility. Payment is sent 90 days from the end of the month in which the book was shipped, e.g., books sold in January will be paid the first week of May. E-book compensation is paid 90 days after the end of the month in which the sale was reported to Ingram.

Payments are issued by Lightning Source, an Ingram Content Group Company, and are made in the currency you selected during account setup (remember, once selected, you cannot change the currency selection). Payment options include:

- USD PayPal: No minimum.
- USD ACH direct deposit (must be U.S.-based bank): No minimum.
- CAD ACH direct deposit (must be Canadian-based bank): $25.00 minimum.

Additional currencies and payment information can be found on the IngramSpark site (#AR).

Tax Information

IngramSpark/Lightning Source LLC does not provide publishers tax forms, e.g., IRS Form 1099-MISC (U.S.) or 1042-S (outside U.S.) for publisher compensation.

KOBO
KOBO WRITING LIFE (KWL)

WEBSITE: http://www.kobo.com/writinglife

A CANADIAN E-BOOK, audiobook, and e-reader retailer headquartered in Toronto, Rakuten Kobo (known more simply as Kobo) is a subsidiary of the Japanese ecommerce conglomerate Rakuten. The name Kobo is an anagram of "book." Kobo does not offer a POD option.

Website interface is available in English, Dutch, French, German, Italian, and Spanish. The Kobo app and each e-Reader device supports 68 languages, with global distribution to more than 200 countries.

STORE: https://www.kobo.com

DISTRIBUTION

KWL does not offer or require exclusive distribution, instead encouraging self-published authors to "go wide." Non-exclusivity also applies to any book enrolled in Kobo Plus, a monthly subscription service that allows subscribers access to Kobo books on an all-you-can-read basis for a flat rate.

The KWL Rights & Distribution page also offers publishers the option to enroll books on a title-by-title basis in OverDrive, a global distributor of digital content for schools and libraries. Libby, OverDrive's library reading app, is used by 90% of North American libraries (#AR). To enroll, simply check the box and enter a unique USD library price. Because you will only be paid for each individual e-book sale (regardless how many times your book is checked out), it is recommended that the price be set a few dollars higher than USD retail. Additional information on OverDrive and other library distribution services can be found under Draft2Digital.

SERVICES & SUPPORT

KWL works with outside partners to provide author services for ISBNs (U.S. only), reviews, cover design, editing, and foreign translation. The Author Services tab can be found on the main page.

The KWL Helpdesk includes a comprehensive series of articles covering everything from account set-up to understanding payments, monthly reports, and promotions (#AR). There are also several Kobo Writing Life how-to tutorials on You Tube.

Personalized support is available by clicking on "contact us" and completing an online submission form outlining your question or concern. All submissions are acknowledged by e-mail. Response time varies but is typically within 2 business days. There is no live chat or telephone option.

ACCOUNT SETUP

There is no charge to open an account on Kobo Writing Life. You will be able to upload your material once your account has been verified, however your title will not be published until the payment information section is complete.

UPLOADING YOUR BOOK

There is no charge to upload your book material. Publishing your book to Kobo is completed in five easy-to-follow steps:

1) Describe your e-book: This is where you'll enter your book's metadata.

Note: KWL refers to your cover copy/retail blurb as a synopsis. You can enhance the content of your synopsis by underlining, bolding, or italicizing text.

2) Add e-book content: This is where you'll upload your cover art and formatted EPUB file.

3) Rights & distribution: This is where you'll find the boxes for Digital Rights Management, Kobo Plus (more on this in a bit), and OverDrive options.

Note: You will be required to assert that you own the geographic distribution rights (confirming that you are the copyright holder) for all territories.

4) Set the price: Enter the retail price in your default currency. KWL will automatically convert this dollar amount to all other available currencies using recent default exchange rates stored in its system. You may, however, override any of the converted prices by country/currency, e.g., rounding up $4.87 to $4.99. You may also change the price at any time by clicking on the "schedule a price change" link on this page.

5) Publish your e-book: Enter the publication date. If you are making pre-order available, enter a date in the future and select "allow pre-orders." Then click "Publish Your Book." Allow 48 hours for KWL review. You will receive an e-mail notification when your book is available in the Kobo store, generally within 72 hours of submission.

Changes to metadata (excluding ISBN), content, distribution, and pricing can be made at no cost by following the same steps during the pre-order period or after publication. Updates will be published within 24 to 72 hours. If you selected the option "notify on publication or update" during account setup, you will be notified by e-mail when updates are live.

Scheduling a Sale

You can discount the sale price of your book(s) for a limited period by going to the "Set the Price" page and selecting "Schedule a sale." I'd suggest doing this as soon as you have your promotional period nailed down (so you won't forget!), and no later than five days before to allow for processing time.

After entering the start and end date, select the currencies/countries you wish to include, e.g., U.S. Dollars (USD) only, all currencies, or any combination.

Note: This is only for sales promotions created with independent book promotion sites outside of KWL. Examples of book promotion sites are included in "Advertising and Promotion."

> *Pro tip: Add an extra day or two to the start and end date of a sale, e.g., if the paid promotion runs from March 1 to March 15, select February 27 to March 16. This way you can double check that your sale price is in effect on March 1 and gives last minute procrastinators an extra day to get the deal.*

Royalty Structure

e-book sales
$2.99 and over (no upper limit): 70%
Less than $2.99: 45%

EXAMPLE A (<$2.99)

Sale Price $1.99
KWL deducts 55% = $1.09
You earn @ 45% = $ 0.90

EXAMPLE B (>$2.99)

Sale Price $12.99
KWL deducts 30% = $3.90
You earn @ 70% = $9.09

Note: Royalty rates depicted are based on the sale price in the U.S. and Canada, excluding taxes paid by the purchaser. Some currencies will have higher or lower payment thresholds.

Kobo Plus

Originally launched in 2017 in the Netherlands and Belgium, KWL has continued to add other countries, currently Australia, Canada, France, Italy, Portugal, Norway, Sweden, Finland, Denmark, and New Zealand. While enrollment in Kobo Plus is optional, there is no downside to doing so. In my experience, earnings from Kobo Plus frequently match or exceed royalties earned from e-book sales. In other words, don't be afraid to check the box that states, "Include everywhere Kobo Plus is available *includes future territories." By doing so, your book will automatically be included whenever a new sales territory is added.

Kobo Plus royalties are based on the following formula:

Total **Monthly Revenue** earned from all Kobo Plus subscriptions divided by the **Total Minutes** that all subscribers spent reading in that month equals **Value per Minute Consumed** (VPC).

The VPC will fluctuate month to month based on subscriber number and total reading time. Authors are paid 60% of the VPC multiplied by the number of minutes subscribers spent reading your book.

EXAMPLE

For demonstration purposes, let's assume the following:

- There are 100 subscribers paying $9.99 each = $999.00.
- The average reading time per subscriber is 2 hours (120 minutes) per day.
- 120 minutes x 30 days = 3,600 minutes per subscriber.
- 3,600 minutes x 100 subscribers = 360,000 minutes.
- $999.00 / 360,000 = $ 0.0027 (VPC)

Now let's assume that your book was read for a total of three hours (180 minutes). Your payment would be calculated as follows:

180 (minutes) x $0.0027 (VPC)= $0.486 (total earned)
60% (royalty) x $0.486 = $0.2916 (amount paid)

OverDrive

Payment is 50% of the USD library price for any sale made to an OverDrive-enabled library.

KWL Promotional Opportunities

Open exclusively to KWL publishers, the Promotions tab lists all promotions currently accepting submissions and will be clearly defined by details, money matters, and applicable countries.

Often themed and/or country specific, e.g., Holiday (Halloween, Valentine's Day, Christmas), Summer "Down Under" (Australia and New Zealand), Mother's Day, Father's Day, etc., and usually further defined by genre (Romance, Mystery & Thrillers, Sci-fi & Fantasy), KWL promotions fall under one of two broad categories:

1) Publisher discounted price: Enter the sale price, e.g., $0.99, on application. Typically, higher priced books are more likely to get a spot; a book that sells for $8.99, discounted to $0.99, is more of a bargain than a book that regularly sells at $2.99. The cost of these promotions is usually a 10% reduction of the royalty rate applicable to the price submitted.

Note: If accepted, you *must* discount (price match) the Kindle version (KDP/Amazon) for the duration of the KWL promotion.

Price matching on other retailers, while optional, can be an effective strategy if you develop a coordinated marketing plan.

2) Discount applied at checkout: Examples include VIP sales, BOGO (Buy One, Get One), Daily Deals, etc. The cost for these ranges from a 10% reduction of royalties (e.g, 60% vs. 70%) to $100 per placement. Because the discount is applied at checkout, there is no requirement (or easy way) to price match.

Shortly after the promotion application deadline closes, books are either selected or rejected, and the publisher is notified of the result. Don't get discouraged if your title gets rejected. There are far more submissions than there will be availability. My personal rate of acceptance is about 35% but, in each case, there was a decided uptick in both the number of books sold, and overall revenue earned.

In summary, it pays to review the KWL Promotions page on a regular basis and apply for any opportunities that are a good fit, and include your reason(s) for submitting in the comments section.

If accepted, KWL will do all the work for discounting on the Kobo store. However, it will be up to you to promote the details on your website, social media, and/or newsletter, e.g., My Title is 25% off on #Kobo from March 1 to March 15. Enter 25MARCH at checkout.

> *Pro Tip: Check your sales dashboard daily during a promotional period. If there's a nice bump in sales in one or more countries, check out the Kobo store(s) for those territories. The default will always be your home country, but you can choose a different country by clicking on the flag at the top of the Kobo Store page (#AR). A screenshot showing your book in the Top 10 (or better yet, #1) in one or more categories is worth a thousand words.*

OverDrive

Occasionally, KWL will offer an OverDrive promotional opportunity. If you've opted for e-mails from KWL (and you should), they will e-mail you with instructions on how to participate.

Reports & Payments

Data provided on the KWL dashboard is meant to provide a live *estimate* of the dollar amount and total number of sales for all (or individual) books, broken down by day, week, this month, and last month. There's also a tab for actual Kobo Plus (prior months) earnings.

Detailed sales reports are provided in a .xlsx (Excel) format at the end of each month for the previous month's sales, e.g., your January sales reports will be uploaded by the end of February. You can find your reports on the dashboard under the "My Account" dropdown menu. Reports are split into one for all Kobo e-book sales (including OverDrive), and a separate report for Kobo Plus.

Combined royalties (Kobo and Kobo Plus) are paid approximately 45 days after the end of each monthly period (e.g., January sales are paid mid-March) provided you have met a minimum threshold of $50 USD (regardless of your local currency). If the $50 USD threshold is not met, royalties are held on account until the threshold is reached.

Payment is made by Electronic Funds Transfer (EFT) directly to your bank account in your local currency, e.g., USD for U.S. residents, CAD for Canadian residents. If your local currency is not supported, payment will be made in USD. To receive payment, a bank account in one of these currencies is required.

Tax Information

KWL does not send out any reports for tax purposes other than the monthly sales reports posted under My Account - Payment Information.

COMPENSATION COMPARISON

ROYALTY RATES DEPICTED ARE BASED on the sale price in most countries, including the U.S. and Canada, excluding taxes paid by the purchaser. Some countries and/or territories will have higher or lower price thresholds.

In all cases, payment terms are paid based on sales per calendar month, e.g., January = January 1 to January 31; payments made in 90 days would be paid at the end of April; in 60 days at the end of March; in 45 days in mid-March.

Electronic Funds Transfer (EFT) may also be referred to as Direct Deposit. The term is interchangeable. Unlike wire transfers, there is no bank fee for receiving payment by EFT.

Note: All terms and conditions are subject to change.

AMAZON (KINDLE DIRECT PUBLISHING)

Title setup fee: None

Royalty Rates
e-book: $2.99 to $9.99: 70%
e-book: <$2.99 to >$9.99: 35%

Print—Amazon Only: 60%
Print—Expanded Distribution: 40%

Payment Terms: Approximately 60 days.

Payment Methods:
EFT: No minimum payment threshold.
Check: $100 USD minimum payment threshold.
Wire transfer: $100 USD minimum threshold.

APPLE BOOKS (ITUNES CONNECT)

Title setup fee: None

Royalty Rate: e-book only—70% (no minimum or maximum retail price)

Payment Terms: No later than 45 days.

Payment Method: EFT: $0.02 USD minimum payment threshold.

BARNES & NOBLE PRESS

Title setup fee: None

Royalty Rate: e-book only—70% (no minimum or maximum retail price)

Payment Terms: End of month for prior month, e.g., June 30 for May sales.

Payment Method: EFT: $10 USD payment threshold or bi-annually if threshold not met.

Draft2Digital (D2D)

Title setup fee: None; 1 free revision every 90 days for POD (e-book revisions are always free). Additional POD revisions within 90 days will incur a charge per revised file upload.

Royalty Rates:
e-book: varies by D2D partner, though the average is 30%. D2D deducts approximately 10%, leaving you with about 60%.
Print: 45%

Payment Terms: Most D2D partners pay 60-90 days following the month of sale. Once funds are received, D2D will pay you in their next monthly payment.

Payment Methods:
Check: $100 USD minimum payment threshold.
Direct Deposit US: No minimum payment threshold.
Direct Deposit International: $20 USD minimum payment threshold.
PayPal: $0.00 for U.S.; $5 USD minimum payment threshold for Canada.
Payoneer: $20 USD.

Google Play (Google Play Partner Center)

Title setup fee: None

Royalty Rate: e-book only—70% (no minimum or maximum retail price)

Payment Terms: The 15th day of each month, or on the next business day (varies by region).

Payment Methods:
EFT (recommended): $1 USD.
Wire Transfer: $100 USD.

INGRAM SPARK

Title setup fee: None. $25USD fee for revisions after 60 days.

Royalty Rates:
e-book: 85% of net revenue.
Print: Determined by wholesale discount entered (minimum 40%, recommended 53-55%).

Payment Terms: 90 days after the end of the month in which the sale occurred.

Payment Methods
USD PayPal: No minimum
USD ACH direct deposit (must be U.S.-based bank): No minimum.
CAD ACH direct deposit (must be Canadian-based bank): $25.00 minimum.

KOBO WRITING LIFE (KOBO)

Title setup fee: None

Royalty Rates: e-book only
$2.99 and over (no upper limit): 70%
Less than $2.99: 45%

Payment Terms: Approximately 45 days.

Payment Method: EFT: $50 USD minimum payment threshold.

YOUR STEPS

PUBLISHING PLATFORMS

- Familiarize yourself with the royalty and reporting structure of each platform.
- Set up publisher accounts.
- Enter metadata.
- Upload your book (EPUB and/or PDF) and cover art.
- Set the publication date (pre-order or immediate).
- Publish your book!

AUDIOBOOKS

AUDIOBOOK BASICS

ONCE YOU'VE NAVIGATED the self-publishing waters of print and digital, consider test driving the audiobook market. According to a 2023 article on WordsRated, audiobooks are the fastest growing segment of the publishing industry, with reported U.S. sales of 1.6 billion in 2021, and a global market of more than $5.3 billion (#AR).

That data is backed by the Audio Publishers Association's (APA) tenth annual audiobooks sales survey. The survey, released in 2022, reported 2021 revenue gains of 25% (up from 12% in 2020) across its 28 member companies (#AR). APA's Consumer Survey, which polled Americans 18 and older, reported that 41% of U.S. listeners subscribe to one or more audiobook services. Interestingly, only 1% of Canadians listen to an audiobook through a subscription service (ReviewMoose.ca/#AR).

THE BASICS

As the rights holder, when it comes to audiobook narration, you have three options:

1) Do it yourself: Unless you have access to a studio, you'll need

to set one up in your home or another accessible location (#AR). You'll also need to learn the tips and tricks to narrating like a pro (for instance, breath control and voice modulation).(#AR).

Unless you're in the "business," e.g., a radio announcer, voiceover artist, actor, etc., this may not be your best option, but it's certainly possible.

2) Auto-narration: Also known as AI narration, digital narration, or synthesized voice narration, audiobook content is generated using text-to-speech technology. The audiobook's metadata should include a disclaimer. For example, Apple Books requires the following statement: "This is an Apple Books audiobook narrated by a digital voice based on a human narrator," whereas audiobooks generated for Google Play will include something along the lines of: "This audiobook is narrated by Mary, who is not a real person. She is one of Google's auto-narrators."

Though there are auto-narrated books in the fiction genre, AI narration tends to work best for books with limited dialogue and emotional content, e.g., nonfiction, including self-help, health, history, etc. Avoid using auto-narration for books that rely heavily on images, such as cookbooks.

3) Hire a narrator: Places to search for professional narrators include audiobook creation platforms, such as Findaway Voices and ACX, as well as talent websites like Voices.com and Fiverr. Book Riot's "The Best Places to Find Audiobook Narrator Jobs for Beginners" (#AR) includes several options.

The industry standard for calculating payment for audiobook narration, voice acting, and voiceover work is known as PFH (Per Finished Hour). While a beginning audiobook narrator may charge as little as $50 PFH, the union rate is $250 PFH and experienced narrators may charge as much as $400 or more. As a rule of thumb, 9,000 words of text equals one finished hour of audio. Using $250 PFH as the rate, hiring a narrator for a 54,000-word audiobook will take 6 finished hours (54,000 / 9) and cost the rights holder $1,500 (6 x $250).

In short, it can be an expensive proposition and as with all books, regardless of format, margins tend to be thin. If you're thinking of audio as a way to get rich quick, you might want to invest your $1,500 in another scheme. That said, it's nice to have an audiobook component and there are less expensive alternatives beyond straight PFH compensation. ACX, Amazon's audiobook publishing platform, for example, also offers two royalty share options. Refer to ACX in "The Players," up next.

As with any publishing and/or distribution platform, there will be a contract to sign. The terms and length of those contracts vary by platform and are subject to change. As with any contract, you'll want to carefully read and review the conditions before proceeding.

Pro Tip: Audiobook covers are square, so you'll need to have your cover art resized to 2400 x 2400 pixels, minimum 72 dpi. That's not as simple as taking your e-book cover and changing the size from 1600 x 2500 pixels, since all that will do is distort the overall image. As well, some distributors, like ACX, will also add a diagonal banner on the bottom right side, so you'll need to make sure that any pertinent text (title, author name, etc.) doesn't get hidden. For example, the font used for my name in the audiobook versions of my titles has been reduced to accommodate the banner, while maintaining the overall appearance of the e-book and print cover.

THE PLAYERS

THE PAST and projected growth of the audiobook industry has led to fierce competition and ongoing changes. The following serves as a sampling of available production and distribution platforms for self-published authors. You'll need to do your own research when the time feels right.

ACX (#AR)

Amazon's audiobook production and distribution platform, ACX refers to the author as the "rights holder" and the narrator as the "producer." As the Rights Holder, you may choose to narrate the book yourself or hire a producer.

If you choose to hire a producer, you'll need to post your book and basic information (word count, genre, male/female narrator, preferred accent, e.g., Southern, New England, Canadian, etc.) along with any comments and a small sample (two or three pages) of the text. You'll want to ensure that your sample includes a section for each main character. For example, how your female narrator will voice a male character (or vice versa) or how they might handle a Southern drawl.

All audiobooks produced by ACX are currently distributed to Audible, Amazon, and iTunes. The royalty structure is 40% rights holder / 60% ACX. This is referred to as exclusive distribution. If you choose non-exclusive distribution, in addition to ACX's distribution to Audible, Amazon, and iTunes, you may also upload your audiobook directly to other distribution channels. The non-exclusive royalty structure is 25% rights holder / 75% ACX.

As noted earlier, in addition to hiring a narrator on a PFH basis (referred to by ACX as Pay for Production), ACX offers two other options:

1) Royalty Share: The rights holder splits their royalties with the producer, meaning each party will receive 20% of the sales directly from ACX. There is no PFH payment, however, since there is no guarantee an audiobook will sell, this option is usually only selected by narrators trying to build a portfolio. Royalty share is only available for exclusive distribution to Audible, Amazon, and iTunes.

2) Royalty Share Plus: The rights holder pays the producer a flat fee, negotiated up front, and share the 40% royalties earned 50/50 (20% each) with the producer. This ensures that the narrator will be compensated for at least some of their time, but at a reduced rate, e.g., $150 PFH vs. $400. This option is meant to encourage experienced narrators to audition. Royalty Share Plus is only available for exclusive distribution to Audible, Amazon, and iTunes.

Once the audiobook process is complete and the book is available for sale, the rights holder and producer will each receive 50 promo codes for the U.K. Audible market and 50 promo codes for the U.S. Audible market. U.S. codes can be redeemed in Canada, though the audiobook will be in the audible.com library. Promo codes are meant to garner reviews on Audible and are provided at no charge by ACX. As such, there is no payment when redeemed.

ACX also offers a Bounty (bonus referral program) by providing URL/book-specific codes, though the terms and conditions of what constitutes a "qualified purchase" are somewhat onerous (#AR). To earn the bonus ($75 to the rights holder for Pay for Production; $100 split equally for Royalty Share), the purchase must be made by a first-time customer of Audible who purchases your audiobook using the code, becomes a member of Audible, and remains a member in good standing for at least 61 consecutive days.

> *Pro Tip: Audiobooks published through ACX will not be published by libraries, who purchase exclusively through digital distributors like OverDrive or Hoopla.*

APPLE (#AR)

Apple Books has partnered with Draft2Digital (#AR) to produce digitally narrated audiobooks using Apple's text-to-speech technology. To be eligible, you must own the audiobook rights, your e-book must be in English, in flowable EPUB format, and available for sale on Apple Books through D2D. The audiobook description must include, "This is an Apple Books audiobook narrated by a digital voice based on a human narrator." You may choose one voice type, soprano or baritone. The selection cannot be changed once your book is submitted. The narration process takes one to two months.

Apple Books also accepts audiobook uploads through selected aggregator partners (#AR). These aggregators use human narration to generate audiobook content.

Royalties from all sales are paid directly to the aggregator, who in turn will pay you based on the terms and agreement signed with them.

BARNES & NOBLE PRESS (B&N) (#AR)

B&N has partnered with Findaway Voices for audiobooks, which means if you use Findaway Voices to create and distribute your audiobook, it will be listed for sale under Audiobooks on the Barnes & Noble online store. If you've used another distribution platform, your audiobook won't be listed on B&N Audiobooks.

Draft2Digital (D2D) (#AR)

You'll find a tab for Audiobook on your book's home page. Click on that and you'll be prompted to Start a Findaway Audiobook. Click on that link and you'll be directed to Findaway Voices (see next subhead). From that point on, all audiobook creation and any royalty payments will be handled by Findaway Voices.

If your title is published on Apple Books through D2D, you also have the option of creating a digitally narrated book through Apple (refer to the earlier Apple subhead).

Findaway Voices (#AR)

You can access Findaway Voices via Draft2Digital or set up an account directly with Findaway.

Note that unlike ACX, Findaway Voices does not offer royalty share options, offering instead a selection of narrators that you may approach to audition for your audiobook project. The narrators' rates and bios are included, with sample auditions and preferred genres.

One big plus in Findaway Voices' favor is that they distribute to multiple retailers and library services. You also have the option of selecting some or all distribution partners (going wide). Your selections can be changed, though changes can take up to 30 days, so it's best to make a decision and stick with it.

As a rule, going wide is your best bet, since it provides the most opportunity for sales. You can also use Findaway Voices to distribute an audiobook you've created through another source, such as Google Play.

Google Play (#AR)

Audiobooks created through Google Play are auto-narrated, using Google's text-to-speech technology to read your EPUB file. This digital disclaimer is included at the beginning of all Google Play audiobooks. In addition to owning the audiobook rights, you'll need to have your book active (listed for sale) in the Google Play catalog.

The Google Play audiobook platform offers more than 35 narrator options, e.g., accent, age, and gender, as well as a suite of editing tools to fine-tune pronunciation and correct content.

Once an auto-narrated title is complete and available for sale in the Google Play store, publishers can download the file for distribution to any online retailer that accepts them.

While publishers can "recommend" a list price for their audiobook, the final sale price will be at the discretion of Google Play. The current royalty structure is 52% publisher/48% Google Play. There is currently no charge to produce an audiobook through Google Play.

KOBO WRITING LIFE (KWL) (#AR)

While Kobo Writing Life doesn't produce audiobooks, it does provide a distribution platform that allows rights holders to upload their completed audiobook file (in either .mp3 or .mp4 format) directly for online distribution to Indigo (Canada), Walmart (U.S.), BOL (Netherlands), and Booktopia (Australia). Uploading direct to KWL also allows participation in Kobo's exclusive audiobook promotional opportunities.

KWL accepts auto-narrated audiobooks with the proviso that the audiobook is read by a computer-generated synthesized voice.

Pro Tip: If you're not familiar with audiobooks, do so before taking the audiobook plunge. Join a service, like Audible (they usually have discounted trials for new members) and/or borrow audiobooks from your local library. Listen to a dozen or more in your genre and make a note of what you like and don't like. Be sure to listen to AI and human-narrated books, as well as books narrated by the author.

YOUR STEPS
AUDIOBOOKS

Audiobook Basics

- Weigh pros and cons of narration options: Do it yourself, auto-narration, or hire a narrator (PFH).
- Square cover art (2400 x 2400 pixels).

The Players

- Weigh pros and cons of each publishing platform.
- Listen to a variety of audiobooks and make notes.

GETTING THE WORD OUT

ADVERTISING & PROMOTION

As a self-published author, 100% of advertising and promotion (A&P) will fall on your shoulders. Don't be intimidated, this is a role taken on by most authors these days. Unless you're a big name, traditional publishers, regardless of size, will expect you to plan, promote (and pay for) all or most of the A&P for you and your title, while still taking their full share of royalties for any increased sales. The smaller the press, the more you'll be doing (and paying for). As for hybrid publishers, they'll certainly offer plenty of A&P options, but each one will come with a cost, and without guarantee of success.

Of course, there are no guarantees, no matter who's doing the funding. But as a self-published author, you'll be able to select the paths and partners that appeal to you. Most importantly, since you'll have up-to-date access to sales on your retail partner dashboards (statistics you wouldn't otherwise have), you'll also be able to assess what's working—and what's not—in real time. That's a tangible benefit.

Because money is hard-earned and easily spent, I've started this chapter with a few freebie ideas, listed alphabetically, to help you build your brand. That said, just because it's free doesn't mean you have to take these ideas and run with them, or that you can't find a few of your own. This is your publishing imprint, after all. *You* call the shots.

Freebies

Author Central

Author Central (#AR) allows authors to create an author page with a bio on Amazon. In addition to English, bios can be added in several other languages, including French, Spanish, and German. Once your book is available, you can "claim it" on Author Central, then add editorial reviews. Author pages include a "Follow Author" button which readers can click on for news of your latest release. Author Central also provides statistical sales information and the latest customer reviews.

Blogs

A personal blog can be the first step in building a following. Even if you don't have a blog or website yet, follow one or more writing/genre-related blogs that interest you. This will allow you to gradually cultivate a relationship with other bloggers by sharing their posts on social media and/or leaving insightful comments on posts that resonate with you. When the time comes to celebrate your own book news, you can legitimately approach that blogger for a spot or tag them in a social post, which they will (hopefully) share.

BookBub

BookBub (#AR) is an e-book marketing site where selected titles, submitted for consideration by authors and publishers, are deeply discounted for a limited time. I'll include more information on BookBub advertising a bit later, but the good news is you can claim your free author profile on BookBub's partner dashboard and add your book(s), including publication date, without any financial commitment.

If your book is available for pre-order, BookBub will send an e-mail to all your followers on release day. Of course, initially you won't have many followers, but you can build your list by reviewing and recommending other books, following other authors, and by getting the word out on social media or through your writing groups.

> *Pro Tip: When you set up an account, you'll be asked for your reading preferences. This setting allows BookBub to send you daily and weekly deals specific to your country. At this time, only those with a U.S. reading preference can rate, review, and recommend books. If you're outside the U.S. and want to leave reviews, temporarily update your reading preference to United States, then switch it back when done (#AR).*

GOODREADS

Many readers (including me) use Goodreads to rate and review books (#AR). Setting up an author profile is free, as is adding your book to be included on Goodreads' searchable listings by author name or book title. If you have a blog, you can link that directly to your Goodreads author profile page. There's also an area on your profile for questions from readers (or make up a couple of your own) that you can answer, as well as reader groups you can join (typically defined by genre of interest, e.g., cozy mystery). If you aren't reviewing books there already, now's the time to start. It's an easy way to be a good and active member of the literary community. Besides, you can't expect to get reviews if you're not willing to give them.

LIBRARYTHING (#AR)

Similar to Goodreads, LibraryThing is a free online service to help people catalog and review books they've read, join reading groups, and more. Adding your author page and your book(s) is simple and free. There is also a good place to put in a plug for your local library when setting up your author profile.

PINTEREST (#AR)

Have fun with it. Post pix of the actors you'd cast if you were making a movie, or places your book takes place. Add Boards of your favorite (comparable) books or blog posts that resonate.

SHEPHERD.COM (#AR)

The vision of Ben Fox, Shepherd was launched in April 2021. Since that time, more than 10,000 authors (and counting) have been asked to pick their five favorite books around a topic, theme, or mood they are passionate about, along with why they recommend each of those books. In turn, readers can find these lists by searching for an author by name, or by a topic of interest, for example, cozy mysteries, WWII history, or ocean liners.

Once approved and posted to the site, Shepherd promotes the author, their book, and their book list throughout its website and marketing channels at no charge to the author. Select "Join Author Program" to be sent the Word template to guide you through the process, but before you submit an idea, be sure to check out what's already on the site.

Initially, Shepherd was completely bootstrapped by Fox's savings, though he's now set up a membership and donation program (#AR) with exclusive perks for authors who sign up as Founding Members (which I did in January 2023). You can find my "the best cold case mysteries with a twist…or three" list (posted October 2022) on the website (#AR), as well as my favorite reads of 2023 (#AR).

PAY TO PLAY

Advertising. Do it right and you might break even, gain a following, and possibly come out ahead. Do it wrong and advertising can be the proverbial money pit. Before you invest your hard-earned cash, invest the time to learn the ins and outs of selling books on your selected platform.

ADVERTISING COURSES & TUTORIALS

Amazon

While Amazon has a dedicated advertising info page (#AR), if you're interested in advertising with Amazon, you'll want to check out Bryan Cohen. Cohen has created several free and paid courses about marketing that are informative and easy to follow, and will allow you to test drive your marketing strategy. Check his events calendar for the next available course (#AR).

BookBub

Offers several free tutorials on creating BookBub ad campaigns and design, understanding audience targeting, as well as examples of winning ads and mistakes to avoid.

Meta Blueprint

Online self-guided marketing courses for Facebook, Messenger, Instagram, and WhatsApp.

SOCIAL MEDIA

Never underestimate the power of social media, or the effort you'll have to put in to understand your target demographic and keep up with the changing times (there's always something newer and shinier…anyone remember MySpace?).

While regular social media posts are free, there are always options to pay for advertising or boost a post beyond your existing followers. Targeting criteria makes it easy to get your content in front of individuals with specific interests that line up with your book to find new readers. Targeting can also be defined by a specific geographic area, which can be helpful when promoting in-person events. Before you head down this path, you'll need to understand the difference between clicks, impressions, and clickthrough rates, and the cost of each. Here's a quick primer:

- Clicks: The number of people who click on your ad.
- Impressions: The number of people who saw your ad.
- Clickthrough Rate (CTR): Clicks divided by impressions.

Example: CTR = 50 (Clicks) ÷ 1,000 (Impressions) = 0.05 x 100 (percentage) = 5% CTR.

While there is no hard and fast rule, a CTR of 4 to 5% is generally considered good, and 3% or less means something is lacking. In the above scenario of 1,000 impressions at 5%, it also means that 950 people who saw your ad did not click on it.

A few pennies per click can also add up quickly, and it's important to remember that not all clicks equal sales. How often have you inadvertently clicked on an ad? Or clicked on it and then thought, "no, I don't think so." And you really don't want to pay per impression.

While some authors have success (meaning they'll recoup their investment and make a few dollars), advertising on social media is a bit like going to a casino. At the end of the day, the house usually wins.

There are ways, however, to increase your odds. Creativity (whether a static post or a clever video), not salesmanship, is essential. Repeated "enough about my book, here's more about my book" campaigns will turn off readers. Consider collaborating with other authors to promote each other's work. I'm more inclined to purchase a book recommended by a friend, or fellow author whose books I enjoy, than when the author is pitching their own book. My guess is, you're much the same.

BOOK PROMOTION SERVICES

You've already learned how to discount your book and set up limited time promotion periods on various retailers. But where do you set up those promotions and what do they cost? The answer is, a lot of places and with price points starting at $5 to $1,000 and up. Reedsy has done a great job of rating and reviewing multiple book promotion services (#AR).

*Pro Tip: You'll be sent all manner of offers promising the moon and stars. In my experience, promo sites worth their salt don't solicit for business because they don't have to.

MARKETING & PUBLICITY

Product (your book), Price, Place (where folks can find it), and Promotion—those four "P's" have long served as a basic framework for marketing strategy. We've already covered promotion and advertising. Now it's time to figure out how to market and publicize both you *and* your book. Ready?

Marketing Materials aka Swag

There are any number of marketing materials (#AR) you might consider purchasing if you plan to attend a conference or other events. Business cards, while not nearly as popular as they once were, are portable and inexpensive, though I've found bookmarks, which are equally as easy to put on a display table or take with you (I always have some in my purse), offer a better bang for your buck. It's also a nice touch to have bookmarks to include with your autographed books. The bookmark should have a facsimile of your book cover, your social media links, contact information, and website. I'd avoid including your phone number. After all, you are handing these out to strangers.

Printed handouts don't have to stop at business cards and

bookmarks. When I was part of the author "speed dating" event at Left Coast Crime Vancouver, I had postcards made up with all my book covers on one side. On the blank side, I added a peel-on label which included my panel topics and times, and the times I'd be manning the Crime Writers of Canada booth. It was validating to see attendees amble up the table or into the panel room, my postcard in hand.

Promotional pens are another easy-to-travel option, with a variety of price points, but don't go too cheap or it'll just look cheesy. You want your pen to stand out among the crowd in a good way. That said, the one thing I've learned from attending conferences (where the swag tables sag with handouts) is that tabletop space is limited. Use it wisely.

The bottom line? Set a strict swag budget and stick to it. Would it be nice to hand out t-shirts, golf balls, or coffee mugs? Sure. But the reality is, swag isn't going to buy you a reader because readers can't be bought. When it comes to promotional materials, creativity, not cash, is king.

Pro Tip: When designing a one-sided bookmark or postcard, keep the blank side matte vs. glossy. Ink on matte paper is less likely to smear, and you may want to jot down your private e-mail, mobile phone number, or other information to a potential reader or connection.

Blog Tours & Blitzes

Technically, these fall under advertising and promotion, but in my experience, and based on feedback from many other authors, blog tours and blitzes are more about exposure (aka publicity) than sales. In other words, you may recoup your financial investment, but it's unlikely. Manage your expectations going in to avoid disappointment.

What are blog tours? Basically, they are an online version of a traditional book tour, designed to promote books that have already been, or are about to be, published. Blitzes feature several blogs posting the same content at the same time. Both blitz and tours can be arranged by a blog tour company, of which there are many, but do your due diligence to find the right fit. There's no point hiring a blog tour company that accepts tour hosts featuring erotica if you write Christian-based fiction.

Pro Tip: Blog companies list links to their current and upcoming tours and blitzes. Vet them using your own specific criteria, e.g., were the blog hosts a good fit for the novel being promoted, or were they just trying to fill up available slots, regardless of the genre or sub-genre?

Newsletters

In addition to, or instead of, a personal blog, you can also send out a weekly, monthly, or bi-monthly newsletter, but if you're a new author starting out, gaining a following can be a challenge. A blog, after all, is static and, unless removed, always available for future reference, whereas a newsletter only reaches those who are signed up to receive it (anti-spam and privacy legislation prohibits you from signing someone up without their permission, so don't even think about purchasing a mailing list). Mailchimp, an e-mail marketing service, has a good article on what's allowed, what isn't, and what you need to do to comply with regulations (#AR). There are ways of building a list—contests on social media, getting folks to sign up at events, including a link on your website, etc.—but it will take some time.

While a blog is free (beyond the cost to keep your website up and running), e-mail marketing platforms do charge a service fee, though that's sometimes waived until you reach a certain number of followers. Mailchimp, for example, is free until you reach the 2,000-audience member threshold (dare to dream!), but there are some features, such as targeted scheduling, that aren't available with unpaid versions.

One nice thing about newsletters is the ability to view statistics (clicks, the name of the individuals who opened and read it, percentage performance by campaign, etc.), as well as e-mail bounces and unsubscribes (including reason, if provided), and notification when new subscribers sign up.

Check out Kindlepreneur for a comparison of four e-mail marketing services for authors (Mailchimp, MailerLite, Mad Mimi, and ConvertKit) (#AR), though there are many others. This is also a great topic to discuss with other authors. My guess is you'll get almost as many options as answers.

GOODREADS GIVEAWAYS (#AR)

Goodreads offers two giveaway options, print and Kindle. You might wonder why you'd want to give your book away and the answer is simple: reviews. Here's how it works:

Kindle: Your book must have been published through KDP and be available on Kindle. Beyond that, you can schedule the length of time entries are accepted and give away up to 100 copies of your Kindle e-book. Goodreads randomly selects the winners and notifies the winners as soon as the giveaway period has ended. At present, Kindle giveaways are only available to U.S. readers, but Canadian and U.S. authors/publishers can list their book. The cost is $119 USD for the "Standard" package and $599 USD for the "Premium" package (#AR), whether you opt to give away 1 book or 100 (the fee covers the cost of the Kindle e-books). You will not be provided with a list of the winners' names and the giveaway will not impact your overall Amazon ranking. Further, since these books are giveaways, you won't be paid any royalties for those copies.

Print: This option is available to all publishers and authors. In addition to paying the Goodreads fee of $199 USD or $599 USD, you are responsible for shipping print copies to the winners, which means it can get expensive, however you can elect to have winners in the U.S., Canada, or both.

Are you guaranteed reviews if you try a Goodreads giveaway? Unfortunately, no. Not everyone who wins a copy will take the time to read your book, let alone review it, though in my experience those who do will leave an honest review. And if the review isn't five-star? That's okay too. After all, no one trusts a book with only five-star reviews. Would you?

PODCASTS

Podcasts have become increasingly popular, and many hosts are looking for new voices and content to share. If you're a podcast listener, there's a good chance you follow those you find relatable. Maybe you write true crime, and the podcaster features cold cases. Or perhaps your book is a how-to renovate a century home and the podcast focuses on energy efficient building practices. If they invite guests, there's no reason to think they won't consider you. Of course, you'll need to be familiar with past podcasts before approaching the host, and you should make a list of what you've determined to be their hot buttons (because there are bound to be some). Then give it your best shot. Worst case, you'll get a no. But hey, you're a writer. You're used to rejection.

PRINT MEDIA

In our ever-increasing digital world, newspapers don't carry the weight they used to. Few still do book reviews at all (and those that do generally won't consider self-published work). Nonetheless, newspapers can still be a viable resource, especially at the local level.

Getting the attention of the usually overworked and underpaid editor is the first step. When I worked as a magazine editor, I appreciated a professionally written press release, but that didn't mean the magazine used every last one that landed in my mailbox, whether it came from a PR professional or an individual. In fact, regardless of the magazine, press releases were considered "filler," a way to fill in a blank spot that had been left open in the hope a last-minute ad might be booked. As such, relatively few were used (unless, of course, our sales team could talk the PR pro or individual into a paid ad as well). My personal experience is that local media will usually include a press release I've written if I direct it to the correct individual and personalize the request as coming from a local author.

Niche magazines might also be a good fit. For example, my Glass Dolphin mysteries (and to a lesser extent, the Marketville series) have an antiques angle, and so I approached two antiques publications for a spot in their magazine. Both agreed (though I did have to write the content, and in one case, place a small, inexpensive ad, which they designed for me). The point is that you need to think outside of the traditional book box, and sometimes it means a bit of "I'll give you this, if you'll give me that."

You can also look at paid advertising in newspapers and magazines. If you aren't a graphic designer, most outlets offer creative work at an hourly fee in addition to the cost of the ad space. And with so many newspapers moving to digital platforms, there are plenty of options for reasonably priced digital ads on their websites and newsletters that are more affordable than their print ads. These can also be hyperlinked directly to your online store or website to help close the sale. Digital ads also often have a longer shelf life than print ads in a weekly or daily paper, giving you more bang for your buck.

While press releases have no guarantee of getting published, advertorials do. Often overlooked, but a commonly used tactic in marketing, these are paid articles that appear in a newspaper as regular content but give you more control over the messaging of the story. Ever notice the words "sponsored content" at the top of an article? It's this cleverly disguised form of advertising. The cost varies by publication, and by length, but you may decide this tactic is money well spent. Explore every option, assessing the pros, cons, and costs, before making any commitment.

*Pro Tip: If you do get coverage in a newspaper or magazine, ask for a sharable PDF of the article. Most will be more than willing to supply one free of charge. Then start sharing!

Radio & TV

Television stations, especially those run by a cable network, are often willing to feature local talent. The same holds true for radio programs, though here you can also try to expand your reach. For example, I've been a guest on Sirius XM Canada's *The Breakdown with Allison Dore* on a few occasions, and I've been interviewed on *House of Mystery Radio on NBC* with Alan Warren as well (#AR). In the case of Allison, my "in" was Crime Writers of Canada—she's a big supporter of Canadian mystery fiction. In the case of Alan, I'd listened to the show and just went for it, though I'd had a few books under my belt by then.

YouTube

YouTube can provide some variety to your creative outlets and be an effective way to put a face to your author brand. Here you can explore the same variety of content as on a blog—book trailers, writing tips, and day-in-the-life videos are just a few examples of how viewers can get to know you and your book, and they're easy to share on social media. Some associations also have YouTube channels you might be able to tap into (or be interviewed for) as a member benefit. It never hurts to inquire.

Shameless Self-promotion

There's no point going to all the trouble of lining up interviews if you don't make the effort to capitalize on them. That's where shameless self-promotion comes in, but once you've shared on your newsletter, social media, or blog, what's next? I solved the dilemma by including links to my past programs (along with the episode length and information), on my website's About page. Underneath my third person bio, I've included a section called "Enough about me, here's more about me…" (#AR).

KICKSTARTER (#AR)

A crowdfunding platform that may work best for authors who already have a following, or at least more to offer than a free book once published. Kickstarter takes a 5% cut of the funds you raise, but only if you reach your funding goal. In addition to the 5% cut, Kickstarter will charge a processing fee of 3-5%, depending on your country. Check out campaigns by other authors and/or take a course before attempting. You don't want to alienate potential readers or make your friends and family feel obligated to support you.

THIRD PARTY MARKETING

You can always hire a book publicist to take care of the vetting and promoting for you (and maybe even write some, or all, of the content for an added fee). Because this involves the most hands-on involvement by a third party, it should also be the most personalized and, as such, it will be your most expensive option. In my opinion, there are better ways to spend your indie-author nest egg, but hey, it's your money!

YOUR STEPS

GETTING THE WORD OUT

ADVERTISING & PROMOTION

- Set up author profiles.
- Blogs and other freebies.
- Advertising courses/tutorials.
- Book promotion services.

MARKETING & PUBLICITY

- Marketing materials (swag).
- Blog tours and blitzes.
- Newsletter.
- Goodreads Giveaways.
- Podcasts.
- Print media.
- Radio & TV.
- YouTube.
- Shameless self-promotion.
- Third Party Marketing.

AUTHOR, AUTHOR

NO ONE WANTS YOU TO FAIL

Congratulations! You've made it this far in the book and by now you may have already decided that self-publishing is (or isn't) for you. Either answer is okay, it is your journey after all. But whatever path you choose, you'll need two personas post-publication: the private, at-home face that only you and your best friends and family see, and your public "author" face. This section will address the "Author, Author" stuff that invigorates, terrifies, or tantalizes you (sometimes all on the same day, and occasionally, even in the same hour). And once again, there are no right or wrong experiences.

I'll be honest. When I signed my first book deal in 2014—and even after I started my own publishing imprint four years later—I wasn't entirely comfortable in the role of "Author Judy." By nature, I'm what can best be described as an introverted extrovert. In other words, I *can* be an extrovert when it's absolutely required, but I'm happiest when I'm alone in my office making up stuff on my computer or eating chocolate mint ice cream in my pj's while binge-watching TV with my dog lying at my feet.

Notice I said, "I *can* be an extrovert." While that's true today, it wasn't always. At the December 2014 *World Enough and Crime* (Carrick Publishing) book launch at Toronto's Sleuth of Baker Street bookstore, I was too afraid to read an excerpt from 'Live Free or Die,' my short story in the anthology. Instead, I pleaded with co-owner and publisher Alex Carrick to read it for me. Poor Alex, how uncomfortable he must have been, reading a story about a young woman and the older man who had taken unfair advantage of her. To his credit, he did a commendable job, but I knew it should have been *me* reading *my* words. I expect everyone else there felt much the same.

You'd think I would have learned from that experience, but in the fall of 2015, shortly after my debut cozy mystery, *The Hanged Man's Noose*, was published, I was invited to join local author Timothy Weatherall at the Wasaga Beach Public Library. I couldn't believe it. A library (and not even my local library), asking me to take part in an author event! I enthusiastically agreed.

When the day arrived, I was a wreck. Thankfully, Tim was gracious (and a fabulous speaker), and the audience was small (as I recall, there were about six people in attendance, one of whom was Tim's wife and another the librarian who'd invited us). But when it came time for me to read an excerpt from my book, memories of tongue-tied high school speeches (a project on Sir Isaac Newton still triggers nightmares) flooded my mind. I begged the librarian to read for me.

She did, but as I listened to her recite my words (not quite capturing the Arabella and Emily in my mind) I remember thinking, "If I ever want to truly become 'Author Judy,' I need to conquer my fear of public speaking." Which was all fine and good, except I'd registered to attend the 2015 Bouchercon mystery convention in Raleigh (an idea that had seemed inspired in 2014) and the organizers had slotted me on a panel with Tom Franklin, the American Guest of Honor. Me, a debut author no one had ever heard of. With Tom Franklin, author of the multi-award-winning *Crooked Letter, Crooked Letter*, a book I'd devoured in a few short hours.

I remember nervously pacing the halls of the hotel before the panel, wearing what has become my official Author Judy "look" (a black jersey-knit camisole, black pants or skirt, and a black-and-some-other-color "flouncy" overtop), when Nancy G. West, author of the Aggie Mundeen Mysteries, came out of her room. I must have looked green or some other shade of violently ill because she stopped, concerned, and asked me what was wrong. When I told her that this was my first panel *ever*, that I'd be on with Tom Franklin, and that I was afraid I'd make a fool of myself (or worse), she said the six words that changed my life.

"No one wants you to fail."

I thought about that. About watching other scared school kids, or the convention panelists who hadn't yet honed their public speaking skills, how I had silently rooted for them. And in that moment, I knew Nancy was right. No one wanted me to fail, least of all me.

Was I flawless on that Bouchercon panel? No. But I held my own, and even managed to elicit a laugh or two from the crowd. Since then, I've been both a panelist and a moderator at other conferences and conventions, spoke at PROBUS clubs in front of more than 100 members, and led seminars, workshops, and webinars on writing online and in person to groups of all sizes. Do I still get nervous? Sure, sometimes. But then I remind myself that no one wants me to fail.

Here's the thing. No one wants *you* to fail either.

I've got a few other tidbits I've learned along the way, tips that I'm sharing in this "Author, Author" section. Hopefully you'll pick up a few tricks of the trade, though the reality is you're probably going to stumble a few times as you find your own way. Don't worry —that's okay, too.

And now it's time to put on your own author hat. Hey, this is what you've been waiting for, right? Savor it, if only for a moment. You can always eat ice cream later.

ASSOCIATIONS, ARTS COUNCILS & AWARDS

I JOINED my first writing association in 2012 after attending Bloody Words, a now defunct mystery conference once held biannually in Toronto. I went as a fan of the genre. By the time the conference ended three days later, I was inspired to try writing my own mystery novel.

The conference was, in part, sponsored by Crime Writers of Canada (CWC), which offered (and still does) two levels of membership: Associate (readers, publishers, librarians, unpublished, etc.) and Professional Author Member (PAM). At the time CWC had a mentorship program, which suited my immediate needs, but my long-range goal was to become a PAM. When that day came in 2015, it felt a bit like winning the lottery. Just three years earlier, I'd been wide-eyed at the chance to meet and mingle with mystery authors I'd long read and admired. Now, I was officially one of them. Validation at its finest.

In early 2018, bestselling author Vicki Delany, then Chair of CWC, invited me to join the Board of Directors as a Regional Representative for Toronto/Southwestern Ontario. I'd met her at Bloody Words 2014, but until that moment I hadn't considered that such a role could even be a possibility.

I ended up spending five years on the Board (the maximum term), advancing to Director Toronto/Southwestern Ontario, Vice Chair under Mike Martin, author of the award-winning Sgt. Windflower series, and serving the last two as Chair. Yes, it was a lot of work, all of it unpaid, but the knowledge gained, and the professional opportunities it afforded me, far outweighed any time and effort invested.

The moral of my story? Volunteer! Most associations depend heavily on volunteers and are actively seeking members to work on committees and special projects. Some, like CWC, offer positions on their Board of Directors. Don't be afraid to ask if you're interested in getting involved. Volunteering can be an invaluable experience for networking and understanding the behind-the-scenes world of book publishing.

FINDING YOUR FIT

After joining CWC, I explored other writing associations. My first was the Short Mystery Fiction Society, followed by Sisters in Crime, International Thriller Writers, and the International Book Publishers Association. As a self-published mystery author who occasionally dabbles in writing short crime fiction, each of these associations offers me tangible benefits, such as promotional opportunities and discussion forums, workshops and webinars, and discounts or free access to specialized goods and services.

So, how will *you* decide which association(s) are right for you? After all, there are a lot of writing associations (#AR) to choose from, and membership benefits and resources vary widely. What sort of outreach are you looking for? National or regional? Big or small? Remember, too, that many associations charge an annual membership fee, and while those fees are considered a tax-deductible business expense, tax-deductible doesn't mean free.

You might start by making a wish list of what you're looking for in an association. I've included a sampling of benefits that might prove beneficial to a self-published author, but your list might include something I've missed.

•Access to liability and/or health insurance.
•Author bio page.
•Blog page.
•Book promotion.
•Codes for free IngramSpark revisions.
•Directory of additional resources.
•Discounts on paid book promotions.
•Discounts on professional services (editing, design, etc.).
•Discounts on ISBNs (U.S. only).
•Discounts on writing-related magazine subscriptions.
•Educational courses.
•Forums (in-person or virtual) to meet other members.
•Genre-related reports.
•Grants for professional development.
•Lending library for writing-related reference books.
•Member meetings (in-person or virtual).
•Marketing memos.
•Member magazines or newsletters.
•Membership badge (for website use).
•Members' directory.
•Members-only website access.
•Networking with other members.
•Online members-only discussion forum.
•Reciprocal association membership discounts.
•Regional and/or local chapters.
•Reports and/or surveys on publishing.
•Social media promotion.
•Sponsorship of events, conferences, and conventions.
•Volunteer opportunities.
•Webinars and workshops.
•Writing awards.

*Pro Tip: Although some associations offer lifetime memberships, joining one doesn't have to be a lifelong commitment. Associations most valuable to you as a debut author may hold less value after you've gained

a following. The reverse is also true. Start with a trial membership, if
offered, and an annual membership if one is not.

Arts Councils

If you're fortunate enough to live in a location where an arts
council exists, don't discount it as an exclusive forum for visual
artists, such as painters, potters, and the like. Many also support
local authors, and some offer a brick-and-mortar and/or online
store where you can sell books on consignment. There's usually a
modest annual membership fee and some volunteer commitment
involved, but it's a great way to actively participate and get known in
your community.

Awards

I've included awards in this section because many are sponsored
or endorsed by associations. Awards examples include the Crime
Writers of Canada Awards of Excellence, the Mystery Writers of
America Edgar Awards, and the Independent Book Publishers
Association's Benjamin Franklin Award.

Of course, there are far more awards than there are associations.
For the indie author, *Writer's Digest*'s annual Self-Published Book
Awards (#AR) offers awards in multiple categories. Many conferences
or conventions also have an awards component. Bouchercon's
Anthony, Malice Domestic's Agatha, Left Coast Crime's Lefty, and
Killer Nashville's Silver Falchion are examples for the mystery genre.
Some awards, like the Agatha, Anthony, and Lefty, are selected by
ballots distributed to conference attendees. Others, like CWC's
Awards of Excellence, Killer Nashville's Silver Falchion, and IBPA's
Benjamin Franklin, are submitted for consideration by the author or
publisher in exchange for an entry fee, the shortlist and winner
determined by an independent panel of judges. It's also important to
note that not all award competitions accept self-published books.

Are awards worth entering? They can be. Winning, being short-

or long-listed, even getting an honorable mention, can serve as validation while making a nice addition to your bio. Here are a few points to consider:

- Application process: Rigorous and time-consuming? Or simple and straightforward?
- Entry fee: If not free, does the reward, financial or otherwise, justify the cost? Do you need to mail physical copies of your books (an added expense), or do they accept e-books or PDFs?
- Judging process: Judges' names are often anonymous, but the process should be clearly defined and transparent.
- Past winners: Legitimate competitions list the names of past winners, and often the names of those who were shortlisted.
- Who, what & how long?: Who is sponsoring the award? What's their reason for supporting it? How long have they been doing it?
- Fine print: The part where you usually just scroll down and click "I agree" without reading it. Read it. Then treat it like a contract—because it is.

If the idea of entering your book for an award is something that appeals to you, a good place to start your search is the *Poets & Writers* website. Not only does it showcase a fairly comprehensive list of both grants (to be covered next) and awards, *Poets & Writers* (#AR) reviews the practices and policies of each entry before including it, which is helpful (be aware, there are many fake awards competitions and not everything that's advertised is legit). As with any undertaking, doing your due diligence cannot be overstated.

*Pro Tip: Make a list of possible Awards that your book might qualify for, then add costs and criteria.

GRANTS & PROGRAMS

GRANTS

WRITING-RELATED grants typically come in two forms: project-based or professional development. Project-based grants are meant to fund your time and research while working on a new literary work, whereas professional development focuses on skills training, such as a course in screenwriting or mastering the art of public speaking.

Whether backed by local, regional, or federal government initiatives, non-profit foundations, or a writing association, the turnaround time to find out if your application was successful can take several months—but who ever said anything in publishing was quick? Eligibility is often measured by your publication track record, and in some cases, self-published works either don't qualify, or there is a caveat attached requiring a demonstrated minimum sales threshold. An excellent primer on grants and grant writing (a skill in itself) can be found on Jane Friedman's website (#AR).

Though you'll want to do further investigation, a good place to start your grant search (as noted in the previous Awards section) is the *Poets & Writers* website.

Programs

As a Canadian author, I'm aware of two programs (Public Lending Right (PLR) and Access Copyright) that offer compensation to authors, but I wasn't sure if the U.S. had anything similar. One of the benefits of belonging to an association with an online digest is the ability to post a question, and so when it came to writing this section I did just that, turning to my fellow members of the Sisters in Crime for any information they could provide. The consensus was (sadly) that no such programs existed, though it was suggested that an author might want to contact universities with large or prominent library science programs (which would be more in line with grants), and possibly even reach out to the Library of Congress.

Public Lending Right

While there were no such programs in the U.S., one Guppy noted that Australia does have a program called the Australian Lending Right Scheme (#AR). That led me to thinking that the PLR program might be available in other countries besides Canada and Australia, and it turns out there are established programs in more than 30 countries, with more in development (though still nothing in the U.S.) (#AR).

Founded in Denmark in 1946 as a way to compensate authors and other rightsholders for the free public use of their works in libraries, the program was adopted by Norway in 1947, and Sweden in 1954. Canada came on board in 1986.

While the basic principles of the PLR program are the same throughout, the method used to calculate payment varies by country. In some, payment is based on library lending (how many times the material is checked out). In others, payments are based on the total number of copies of each book held in libraries. In Canada, PLR undertakes an annual survey of library catalogues with large collections from all provinces, territories, and regions of Canada. PLR Canada does not consider the number of copies found in each library or the number of times a title has been checked out. An example of past libraries selected can be found on the PLR website (#AR). You must be a Canadian citizen or permanent resident to be eligible for Canada's PLR program, and there are also requirements for the types of books accepted, e.g., minimum page count, date published, genre, etc. All titles must have an ISBN and be published in either print or e-book. Audiobooks are eligible if they have a valid ISBN. Audiobooks created through ACX, Amazon's Audible audiobook program, are ineligible as they are not available in Canadian libraries. (Refer back to the section on Audiobooks for more information on ACX.)

Eligible genres include children's literature, drama, fiction, poetry, non-fiction, and scholarly work. Ineligible works include "practical books" (cookbooks, self-help, "how-to" guides, travel guides, manuals, reference works, etc.), educational books (textbooks, books resulting from a conference, seminar, or symposium), periodicals (newspaper, magazines), and second or subsequent editions of an eligible book, unless at least 50% of the edition constitutes completely new text. For example, all three of my Marketville mystery series titles are registered with the PLR program, however the box set of books 1-3 were considered ineligible (and fair enough). There is an appeals process, however, if you feel your title was unfairly disqualified.

In Canada, registration of titles can only be done between April 1 to May 1, after which the period is closed for another year. You'll need to complete a form with the title and all related ISBNs, as well as provide a copy of the copyright and title pages, and table of contents, if applicable.

Payments are adjusted based on the number of years a title has been registered with the program (not on its publication year) and are sent annually in mid-February to all eligible authors who meet the minimum threshold of $50. The maximum payment varies year-to-year. In 2020-21, the amount was $4,500. A T4A tax slip will be sent for payments of $500 or more, however you are still required to report any payment less than $500 on your tax return.

ACCESS COPYRIGHT

The Access Copyright (#AR) affiliate program for creators (writers, editors, translators, visual artists) is available to Canadian citizens or permanent residents (excluding Quebec) who own the reproduction rights to at least one published work in print or digital format, e.g., book, magazine, newspaper, or scholarly journal that is also commercially available. Authors in Quebec may qualify for the Copibec program, which I'll cover next.

Registration for Access Copyright is submitted through an online portal from January 1 to December 31 to be eligible for the next year's Payback (#AR), an annual payment to qualifying authors that recognizes a creator's contribution of works.

Details on the funding formula can be found the Access Copyright site under Payback FAQs (#AR), but this program works largely on trust. That means they'll take your word for the number of articles, books, and pages that you enter, though they reserve the right to audit your submission at any time. I know, firsthand, that these audits exist, but if you've been honest in your reporting, there is nothing to fear.

Once you've registered, each April 1 you'll be invited to complete an online form with the number of books, magazine, newspaper, and journal articles complete for the year two years prior, e.g., 2021 for 2023 submission. The deadline to complete is May 31, and if you miss it, you're out of luck for that particular year (there's no going back the next year and adding data). You do not need to complete a form if you have no new works to add. Payback will be calculated on the past contributions.

Access Copyright supplies T5 tax receipts, though there may be a minimal payment threshold. Whether you receive a T5 or not, you are obligated to report the income on your tax return.

COPIBEC

Copibec (#AR) collects and distributes the royalties paid when a Quebec author's published content is used by others. At present,

Copibec has reciprocal agreements with 33 organizations outside of Quebec. You'll need to create an account and provide details for all published works, including novels, poetry, magazine articles, textbooks, and scientific publications.

As the copyright holder, eligible authors are paid royalties whenever Copibec is informed that one of your works has been used. Payment is issued once an account balance exceeds $100, or every two years for balances over $10. As with all income, you'll need to declare any royalties paid on your annual tax return.

If you're a Quebec author who wasn't aware of the program, you may still be in luck. Copibec has a list of unlocatable authors and publishers whose works have been noted as reproduced. If you're on the list (#AR), there's money waiting for you.

INDY AUTHOR PROJECT

The Indie Author Project (IAP) (#AR) is a publishing community that includes public libraries, authors, curators, and readers working together to connect library patrons with indie-published books. Authors are able to submit e-books directly to their local public library to then be vetted by industry editorial partners (such as *Library Journal*, *Publishers Weekly*, and others) and regional library editorial boards. According to the IAP, being selected by these curators can lead to expanded discovery, marketing, and networking opportunities. Submissions are made through an online portal; PDF file is required.

OUT & ABOUT

Author Events

Author events can take on many forms. Many libraries, for example, will host an annual author showcase or similar multi-author forum, allowing their patrons a chance to meet and mingle with local authors. There's typically no charge to participate, though there may be a cap on the number of authors accepted, and you may be asked to donate a copy of your book for a raffle basket or door prize. Many libraries will also be grateful for a donated copy of your book to add to their collection.

What if your library doesn't offer a multi-author forum? As a debut author without massive name recognition, it's unlikely that you'll be enough of a draw to carry an event on your own. That doesn't mean you're out of options. In the spring of 2016, new to Alliston (a small town about 90 minutes northwest of Toronto) and with just two books published, I approached the Branch Manager at my local library and offered to help organize a multi-author event to be held in October during Ontario Library Week. It turned out the Branch Manager had been wanting to do something similar for some time and he took me up on my offer. Together we plotted and planned, invited other authors, and found the perfect venue.

I wish I could tell you the event was a rousing success. Unfortunately, attendance was sparse. The evening coincided with two televised events that no one could have predicted when we picked the date: the final 2016 Clinton-Trump debate and game five of the World Series semi-finals with our home team, the Toronto Blue Jays, facing elimination. (Spoiler alert: They lost.)

While the outcome of our author event wasn't exactly what we'd hoped for, my commitment to the program forever fortified my relationship with the library. It also afforded me the opportunity to get to know and network with other local authors. What can I say? You take the wins where you can get them and accept the rest for what it is. Even writers can't control everything—at least not outside the pages of our books.

Libraries aside, many writing associations also endorse or sponsor author events. During my term on the Board with Crime Writers of Canada, for example, Professional Author Members (PAMs) were invited to participate at Bouchercon Toronto (in conjunction with Sisters in Crime Toronto), Left Coast Crime Vancouver, When Words Collide Calgary, Word on the Street Toronto and Vancouver, and the Ontario Library Association's Super Conference. I know firsthand that each of these events requires many volunteers and volunteer hours because I personally led some of those initiatives and volunteered at the others. What I learned along the way was that those who stepped up benefited, not only from the relationships formed, but from the insider knowledge gained.

The bottom line? Becoming known in literary circles often means getting involved and/or stepping outside of your comfort zone. If this isn't something that comes naturally, don't worry— you'll get better at it. The first step is to try. And if an unexpected event mucks up your best laid plans, there's always ice cream.

Book Clubs

Meeting with local book club members can be a great way to become better known in your community. Most libraries have organized book clubs, some genre-based, others based on bestsellers or local history…you get the idea. Start by meeting with the librarian in charge of these groups and let them know that you'd be willing to meet with book clubs if they select your book. You might offer discounted paperback copies, free promo codes (see Apple Books), or even offer to donate a book club set (if the library has interest and shelf space).

You can also check out book clubs on social media and offer to meet virtually, an option that's become increasingly popular since the COVID-19 pandemic. Don't look at these meetings as a way to earn big bucks, but rather as a way to spread the word about your book, while also spreading your wings as an author.

Last, but not least: not everyone will love your book, and that's okay. Reading is subjective. I once attended a book club at a Senior's residence, where one member shared stories about the book she'd written about her cat ("so much better than yours, sorry, dear"), another sniffed that she didn't read "genre fiction, so just couldn't make the time for mine," and yet another regaled me with stories of Frank Mahovlich, an NHL player from the 1960s and '70s. And yes, that book club meeting will make its way into my current work-in-progress. It's just too good not to share! Besides, the herbal tea and shortbread cookies the club served were lovely.

Book Launches

It's fun to dream, right? Even pre-publication, you've probably put some thought into the kind of book launch event you'd like to have, whether virtual, in-person, or both. Here's a look at those options.

Virtual: More book launches are happening virtually, which has its benefits: no cost to rent a location or feed your guests, while broadening your potential audience from local to worldwide. You can set up a virtual book launch yourself—there's an excellent how-to tutorial on Gatekeeper Press (#AR)—or hire someone to do the work for you (most blog tour companies also offer book launch options). Prices vary widely and it can get expensive, so do your homework, get testimonials, and attend at least one virtual launch by any company you might consider hiring. Make notes on what you liked and what you didn't. Did the launch come off as amateurish or professional? Was there good audience interaction? Is it something you could do yourself just as easily? Or does the mere thought of doing it yourself make you want to run back to bed and hide your head under a pillow?

> **Pro Tip: This is also the time to manage your expectations. Virtual launches have all the benefits previously mentioned, but unless you're a known commodity with a powerful PR team behind you, chances are you're not going to get massive attendance. Inviting several other authors to participate in shifts (for example, 10-15 minutes per author) and/or offering giveaways is one way to boost your numbers.*

In-person: I held the book launch for my debut novel, *The Hanged Man's Noose*, on a warm autumn day at the home of a good friend. I supplied platters of raw veggies and dip, seasonal fruits, cheesecake bites, and cookies, along with champagne, wine, and sparkling water to celebrate the occasion. I'd purchased 25 author copies of my book, invited friends and family members, signed copies (which I sold at just above my cost), and savored every moment of it. These were people who'd been part of my journey, who had listened to my stories of world building and character arcs. It was a magical experience I'll never forget, and I'd recommend it to anyone.

> **Pro Tip: Set aside one copy of your book and ask your friends and family members to sign it for you. It will help to make your special day even more special and you'll have a keepsake to remind you of the occasion.*

Of course, if you're looking to create buzz outside of your inner circle, the family-and-friends book launch isn't going to get you there. So, what will? Again, manage your expectations. Your local independent bookstore or arts council might be willing to host you for a couple of hours, though it will up to you to provide the refreshments and generate interest by inviting friends and family. The space they provide might be free, there may be a rental fee, or they may keep a portion of any of your book sales as a consignment fee (anywhere from 20 to 40%). On the plus side, you might be introduced to new readers, and there's always the potential for local media coverage (though chances are you'll have to be the one to set that up).

> *Pro Tip: If you know another local author with a new book release, consider joining forces. You can split the expenses, double the number of friends and family, and increase the odds of connecting with a new reader.*

Consignment Sales

Consignment sales are sales where you sell author copies of your book (copies you have ordered from your POD publisher) through a third party. Sometimes you can merge an author event with a consignment sale. Sometimes you can't (or won't want to).

Here are three options to explore:

Independent Bookstores: Many indie-owned bookstores (including bookstores that sell new and used books) like to support local authors and will accept books on consignment. This isn't the sort of request you want to do by e-mail or phone, but rather in person. Bring a copy of your book and a prepared handout with your contact information and brief blurb about the book (title, ISBN, jacket copy, and a couple of one- or two-sentence reviews).

If you already have a business relationship with the store owner, all the better, as that could improve your odds. If your book is accepted, be sure to drop by every now and again to make an occasional purchase and see how things are going. The store staff is more likely to promote your book if you take an active role as author *and* customer.

Questions to Ask:

- What is the consignment fee? This can range from 20 to 40% and will determine the price you'll need to charge. Your margins will be slim, but you shouldn't lose money on the sale.
- How long will they carry the book on their shelves? Shelf space is limited, and nothing lasts forever. I've had arrangements last as little as 30 days to as long as a year.
- How will you be paid? Some bookstores (this is especially true of bookstores that specialize in used books) will reimburse you in store credit vs. cash or check.
- When will you be paid? This can vary, e.g., monthly, quarterly, at the end of the consignment period.
- Will there be a formal contract? It may not be fancy, but there should be documentation of the number of books and date delivered.
- Can you host an in-store author event? If so, what do you need to do to make that happen?

*Pro Tip: This same strategy (and the same questions) can apply to local arts councils with brick-and-mortar stores, as well as your local artisan shop.

Barnes & Noble: Many Barnes & Noble stores are open to hosting local authors for an in-store event with both print book and digital book event options. However, for your e-book to be considered, it must be available as a **NOOK** book. Contact each individual store manager directly to discuss details and availability (#AR).

Pro Tip: You will be expected to take an active role in the promotion of your event using social media, e-mail/newsletter promotions, and connecting with local news media. Demonstrate your professionalism by having a game plan in place before making contact.

Chapters Indigo: As Canada's largest independent bookstore chain, store event approval is at the discretion of the store manager, though you'll need to ask for the manager who specifically schedules local events. Unless you've made your book returnable with a Canadian price on the bar code, your only option is to do this on a consignment basis (which is what I'd recommend). Some Chapters or Indigo bookstores will allow your title to stay in-store for 30 days before you pick up your inventory.

Pro Tip: It can be fun to play "Author" at an in-store event, but you are competing with hundreds of bestselling titles (along with the deeply discounted), not to mention the candles, chocolate, and tchotchkes. Making connections, not money, should be your goal.

THINKING OUTSIDE THE BOOKSTORE BOX

As mentioned earlier, my Glass Dolphin mystery series revolves around the Glass Dolphin antiques shop and, to a lesser extent, my Marketville mystery series has a bit of an antiques angle, so approaching my local antiques mall for a consignment opportunity seemed like a possibility. Turned out the owners of the Cookstown Antiques Market (#AR) loved to support anything local, and a local author qualified. Not only were my books part of their shop for the better part of a year (before I moved out of the area), but they also promoted three "meet the author" events, in conjunction with their very popular Victorian Christmas weekend. Think outside the bookstore box. You never know where it might lead.

Pro Tip: When it comes time to pick up your inventory, you may find the book(s) show some wear from customers handling them. It's part and parcel of the consignment world. Set the book aside for an upcoming vendor event, stick a peel-off label on the cover marked "Price Reduced: Damaged Cover" (or a similar statement) and discount the book accordingly. If it's a relatively minor crease, you might discount by 10%, a larger crease or a tear by as much as 50%, though you'll want to at least recoup your initial investment. In my experience, discounted books sell quickly. Everyone loves a bargain.

WRITING CONFERENCES AND CONVENTIONS

You've probably entertained the idea of attending a writing conference or convention. You may even have asked for advice on which one to attend, unsure of what choice to make. The answer depends on you and what you're looking to gain.

While the terms are often used interchangeably, there are differences between the core objective of conferences and conventions. Let's begin by defining those differences:

Conferences: The primary purpose of an industry-specific and, in the case of writing, usually genre-specific, conference is the exchange of information with an educational component, at a venue where attendees can learn and better themselves professionally. For example, in addition to networking opportunities, a conference might offer master classes, craft-related seminars or workshops, breakout sessions, presentations, manuscript critiques, author-led panel presentations or roundtable discussions, and live agent and/or publisher pitch sessions.

Most conferences also host a debut author program or an awards banquet and dinner. Both offer excellent opportunities to meet and mingle with other authors and potential readers.

Registration for conferences is open to readers, authors, and aspiring authors, with a bestselling guest (or guests) of honor on the program to draw attendees. They typically take place over three to four days. Some offer one-day passes or fee-per-session options. Conferences are usually held in the same city each year.

Conventions: While there are more programming similarities to conferences than differences, writing conventions are billed as fan-based, meaning the primary objective is to introduce readers to authors and vice versa. In addition to author interviews, there are author-led panel discussions, the emphasis on showcasing attending authors vs. educating attendees. That said, you can and will learn from other authors and author panels, and some conventions will include an educational component, such as a workshop or seminar, though these are typically held prior to the start of the convention so as not to interfere with scheduled programming.

A key difference is that conventions are often held in a different city each year, with discounted or group sightseeing excursions offered to attendees. Conventions are more about entertainment than education.

Getting Involved

Both conferences and conventions rely heavily on volunteers, both in the planning stages and during the actual event. That means there are plenty of ways to get involved (remember, you're trying to get yourself known in literary circles).

Pro Tip: When signing up, the registration form will ask if you are willing to volunteer before or during the conference.

Planning Stages: A lot goes on behind the scenes, months, and sometimes a year or more in advance. You can learn a lot from being part of it. For Bouchercon Toronto's anthology, *Passport to Murder*, I served as the volunteer intake coordinator, ensuring that the 117 submitted stories were properly formatted and, because entries were blind judged, that they contained nothing to identify the author. I logged the entries into batches and sent the files to the judges. Once their decision was final, I sent out acceptance and rejection letters (including the humbling experience of sending a rejection letter to myself!). But the role of volunteer intake coordinator helped me to understand the many steps involved in publishing an anthology, knowledge I was able to directly apply when I decided to publish an anthology under the Superior Shores imprint.

Side Excursions: Many multi-day events offer side excursions. This is especially true of conventions that travel to a different city each year. One such excursion at Bouchercon Toronto was a Haunted Toronto tour. While the tour itself was handled by a professional organization, the starting point was a fifteen-minute walk from the host hotel. Having grown up in Toronto, I volunteered to lead the way, and was given a free ticket in exchange.

At the Event: There's always a need for volunteers to staff the registration desk (where participants pick up their badge and bag of books or other donated goodies). Every panel will also have a timekeeper, someone who flashes a sign with "5 Minutes," "3 Minutes," and "1 Minute" to the moderator. There may be other opportunities as well, including the possibility of an information table sponsored by a writing association. At Bouchercon Toronto and Left Coast Crime Vancouver, for example, Crime Writers of Canada and Sisters in Crime both had a table where members took turns fielding questions and handing out brochures.

THE BOOK ROOM

The book room is where authors can sell their books on consignment. There are usually a few vendors, with one or more accepting books direct from authors, and the others only accepting books from large publishers. The terms and conditions of the book room will be clearly outlined on the conference or convention website, such as how to contact the bookseller, the number of books allowed, etc.

> *Pro Tip: Unless you're participating on a panel, it's unlikely you'll sell any books. Even then, the big names and the guests of honor will garner the most attention. Bring no more than six copies of your book and be happy if you sell one or two.*

PANEL DO'S AND DON'TS

When you fill out your registration form as an author, you'll be asked if you'd like to be on a panel as a panelist, a moderator, or both, as well as the type of topic you'd be best suited for. While you won't know the topics when registering, you can always look up past events and go from there. For example, topics at the 2023 Malice Domestic mystery convention (#AR) included "Not Her First Crime Scene: Older Characters and Classic Tropes," "The Secret of the Old Clock: How Did Nancy Drew Influence You?", and "If It Bleeds, It Leads: Journalist Sleuths." In your registration, you might put something like, "octogenarian sleuths," "writing inspiration from classic cozies," and "newspaper reporter/sleuth."

There are typically four or five panelists and one moderator per panel. While multiple panels run concurrently to maximize the number of spots offered, there are always far more authors expressing interest than there are panels. If you don't get selected (and even if you do), attend as many panels that align with your book and/or interests as you can, and listen, watch, and learn. Here are a couple of tips:

Panelist: Some moderators will send their questions to you ahead of time, allowing you to prepare your answers in advance, but be careful here. The last thing you want to come off as is stiff and scripted, and you definitely don't want to be reading your notes!

Other moderators take a more casual approach, which can make things a bit more difficult. If it's your first panel, let the moderator know ahead of time and request that you answer the first couple of questions last or near the end (they tend to switch up the order). That way you can listen to the other authors' answers and formulate your own response. When it's your turn to go first, all you can do is your best. Remember: no one wants you to fail!

Pro Tip: Keep your answers brief and to the point, and a little bit of humor or humility never hurts. Do not, I repeat, do not be a panel hog (someone who blathers on without regard for their fellow panelists).

Moderator: Unless you've participated on a few panels or have plenty of past interview experience (in which case, you'd include those credentials on your registration form), you're better off not selecting this option.

Pro Tip: A good moderator understands that this isn't about them, it's about the authors on the panel. If you're a moderator, resist the urge to bring the questions asked back to you and your experiences.

Whether you're an audience member, a moderator, or a panelist, there's etiquette to follow. BOLO Books has a great article on this that covers the basics and then some (#AR).

Author Signing: These are usually 30 minutes and immediately follow the panels, with panelists and moderators at the table, seated in alphabetical order. If you do not have books in the Book Room, you can hand out bookmarks and offer to sign the conference program if anyone approaches you.

Note: You are not permitted to sell books outside of the Book Room.

Pro Tip: Author signings can be a humbling experience. I was once seated next to Louise Penny. Louise's line was out the door. Mine was… not.

OTHER CONSIDERATIONS

Debut Author Spotlight: If this is your first published book, an event that shines a light on debut authors, whether that be a special breakfast or some other form of recognition, is a decided plus. After all, you only get one chance to debut!

Location: Looking for something close to home? Or would you prefer to combine business with pleasure and visit a place on your travel wish list, perhaps combining it with a family or solo vacation? Your accountant can explain the ins and outs of what you can write off, but registration fees, travel, hotel accommodations for the length of the conference or convention, and a portion of meals are, in general, tax-deductible expenses. Sightseeing excursions and additional nights or expenses are not.

Total Cost: Think registration fee, travel, travel insurance, hotel, meals. Registration fees are usually tiered, with early-bird pricing that escalates as you get closer to the event. The earlier you book the less you'll pay, but be sure to check the cancellation policy. Terms and conditions vary widely. Some conferences offer scholarships based on financial need, though there will be an application process, and it's not guaranteed.

Networking: Both conferences and conventions offer networking opportunities, though a smaller venue is generally more conducive to making one-on-one personal connections, especially if you're shy, or a newbie.

Type of Event: Selecting a conference or convention with a genre-specific focus (e.g., romance, mystery, sci-fi) is probably your best bet for meeting potential readers, and you can watch and learn from authors with more experience.

Wardrobe: Find and define your own "author" style (as noted earlier, I'm a black pants/skirt/camisole/jacket/flouncy overtop type of dresser) but you can't go wrong choosing business casual with layers to accommodate unpredictable conference room temperatures, which can range from frigidly air conditioned to hot and stuffy. I'd also recommend comfortable shoes.

Bring something a bit dressier for the banquet evenings. Not formal-wedding fancy, but a step up from your daytime duds.

Virtual or Live: Many conferences and conventions now offer virtual options. The good news is the cost will be minimal (no travel-associated costs). The bad news is that networking opportunities are minimal or non-existent. That said, virtual offerings are a way to dip your toe in the water to get a feel for the experience without diving into the deep end.

Pro tip: Conference and convention organizers book a block of rooms at the host hotel to offer discounted pricing, but the number of available rooms will be limited, and advance booking is recommended. Since most networking takes place after the day's scheduled programming ends, staying at the host hotel (if financially feasible) may enhance your overall experience. At the very least it will allow you a place to take a quiet (and often much-needed) break between sessions. Don't discount this as a value-add—conferences and conventions can be exhilarating but being "on" 24/7 for three or four days can really take a toll.

Vendor Markets

These take many forms, from spring/summer/fall outdoor markets to holiday craft shows and fairs, which usually start in November through to early December. In my experience, sales tend to be best when there's a gift-giving occasion involved. Autographed books, personalized to the recipient, make great stocking stuffers or Mother's/Father's Day gifts, and it's your job as an author to point that out.

Note: Popular markets tend to sell out early, so plan ahead and register early.

Unless you're participating with other members of an arts council or association, there will be a cost involved, so you'll have to factor that in before taking the plunge. You need to sell a lot of books to break even on a $50 table, though making money shouldn't be your main priority. I've met book club organizers and PROBUS club presidents at events, which led to future opportunities. You never know where one chance meeting can lead.

An important consideration at outdoor markets is whether a tent will be supplied along with the table, because books and inclement weather don't play well together. In most cases, a tent won't be part of the deal, in which case you can take your chances, go to the expense of renting a tent, try to borrow one, or go in with another vendor who has a tent and is willing to share (perhaps you pay the cost of the table rental in exchange).

To be successful, you'll need to engage with potential customers without being pushy. I'm not a salesperson by nature, but I've learned that handing out free bookmarks is one way to gauge interest. If the person won't make eye contact or shuffles away, move on. If they accept it, point out that the books on the table were written by you and that you're happy to sign and personalize a copy. You'd be surprised at how many people are unaware that you're the actual author. Once they discover that, you'll usually get a warmer reception, and often ask what the book is about. Keep your answer short and snappy.

Fair warning: You will always get an aspiring author who wants to discuss their work-in-progress with you in great detail, thereby discouraging other potential customers from browsing. It's a delicate balance between encouraging their journey and working the table, and these folks seldom purchase a book, no matter how long you spend with them. If all else fails, journal the exchange to create a scene in your next book. Hey, everything is grist for the mill, right?

Ideally, you'll have some sort of Point of Sale (POS) system like Square to handle debit and credit (#AR). If you plan to do cash sales only (likely if it's your first event), be sure to keep the pricing simple, e.g., $15 or $20 (including tax), and have plenty of small bills to make change. I also know of vendors who will accept e-transfers. I'd recommend against accepting personal checks, but it's your call. Whatever option you choose, make sure your signage stating the price (tax included or plus tax) and payment options, e.g., Cash Only; Debit, Credit & Cash; Cash & E-Transfer, is clear.

ONE DAY AT A TIME

Doing the whole "author, author" thing, especially when it comes to going out and about, can be a scary proposition, but it doesn't have to be. Think about the day you decided to start writing your book. You understood that the process would take time, and it may even have taken longer than you expected, but the thing is, you got there in the end, and you did it by taking it one word, one sentence, and one chapter at a time.

The same holds true for every step of your author journey, including this one. Some steps will be easier, others more challenging. Many will take you out of your comfort zone, at least in the beginning. Just remember, no one wants you to fail.

So, what do you think? Are *you* ready to take the leap?

YOUR STEPS

AUTHOR, AUTHOR

No One Wants You To Fail

- Author wardrobe/look.
- Practice reading out loud.
- Request a panel spot at a conference.

Associations, Arts Councils & Awards

Associations

- Local, regional, or national?
- Prepare a wish list of benefits and compare.
- Membership fees.

Arts Councils

- Local or regional?
- Storefront (online or brick and mortar)?
- Membership fees.
- Volunteer commitment.

AWARDS

- Make a list of possibles, then add cost (including your time) and submission criteria for each.
- Read the fine print.

GRANTS & PROGRAMS

- Grants
- Project-based or professional development?
- Programs.
- Public Lending Right (Canada, excluding Quebec), Access Copyright (Canada), Copibec (Quebec).
- Indy Author Project.

OUT & ABOUT

- Look for author events (library, associations).
- Check out book clubs (online, libraries).
- Plan a book launch (virtual, live, or both?),
- Find places for consignment sales (bookstores and beyond).
- Conference or convention? Consider your criteria. Get involved (volunteer, sign up for a panel spot).
- Vendor markets (register early).

ADDITIONAL RESOURCES

GLOSSARY

ABA: American Bankers Association.

Advance Reader Copies: Also known as ARCs.

Afterword: Also known as an Author's Note, this is meant to share information that is supplementary to the main text.

Aggregator: A one-stop online distributor that will list your book with several online booksellers, as well as library and subscription services.

Alpha readers: Readers who provide detailed and constructive feedback, both positive and tactfully critical, about your book's premise, plot, characters, and other technical elements.

Assets: In Apple lingo, this refers to book details, pricing, cover art, and EPUB book files.

ASIN: Amazon Standard Identification Number.

Author copies: Paperback or hardcover copies ordered by the author from the Print on Demand (POD) publisher.

Back cover/Jacket copy/Book blurb/Retail blurb or copy: The terms used for the text on the back of your book and/or in the description box wherever your book is being sold. It's basically a sales pitch or a hook telling readers what the book is about and why they should want to read it. The terminology used depends on the publishing platform and/or the book format, e.g., paperback or e-book.

Back matter: Epilogue, afterword, author bio, and acknowledgments.

Beta readers: Readers who critique finished manuscripts before they are published.

BIC code: Business Identifier Code.

BISAC codes: Book Industry Standards and Communications codes, the U.S. categorization standard employed by online retailers, brick and mortar stores, and libraries.

Blurbs: Brief book reviews by other authors, to be used inside the book as "praise for" or on the front or back cover.

CMoS: The Chicago Manual of Style is the industry standard for style, usage, and grammar in the book publishing industry.

Comps: Comparable titles to other books in your genre.

Conference: An event with an educational component. May include agent and/or publisher pitch sessions.

Convention: Fan-based event, where the emphasis generally falls on showcasing attending authors vs. educating attendees.

Cost Per Checkout (CPC): (Also known as Price Per Unit or PPU). Allows multiple copies and multiple users to borrow your book at the same time without the library purchasing a copy.

D2D: Draft2Digital, known in the industry as an aggregator—a distributor of books to multiple sales platforms, as well as to some library and subscription services.

Digital Rights Management (DRM): Can prevent readers from copying, printing, or sharing your books by encrypting the content.

Direct deposit: Payment directly to your bank account. Also known as an Electronic Fund Transfer (EFT).

DPI: Dots per inch, a digital photo measurement.

Electronic Fund Transfer (EFT): Direct deposit payment to your bank account.

Epigraph: A quotation included at the beginning of a book.

Epilogue: A short passage added at the end of a literary work, basically a summation.

eProof: A digital copy of your print book, including cover art, to view online before approving it for sale.

EPUB: Digital file format for e-books (the file name will end in .epub). Sometimes styled as ePub.

Exclusivity: When an e-book is published exclusively on one platform, such as KDP Select for Amazon Kindle.

Foreword: A short introductory essay preceding the main text of the book.

Form 1042-S: U.S. tax form for Foreign Person's U.S. Income Subject to Withholding.

Form 1099-K: U.S. tax form for Payment Card and Third-Party Network Transactions.

Form 1099-MISC: U.S. tax form for Miscellaneous Income.

Front matter: Title page, praise for, also by, copyright page, dedication, foreword, table of contents, prologue.

Global distribution: Publishing to all countries supported by your publishing platform. Also known as "going global."

House style: Tweaks on how a publisher might display numbers or dates that vary from the template of Chicago Manual of Style.

Imprint: Publisher name.

KDP: Kindle Direct Publishing.

KDP Select: Exclusive Amazon publishing platform for e-books, auto-renewable every 90 days unless opted out.

Kindle Edition Normalized Pages (KENP): Pages read for books enrolled in Kindle Unlimited through KDP Select. Amazon only.

Kindle Unlimited (KU) Program: A subscriber-based e-book service on Amazon.

Landed prices: The total due after shipping, taxes, and any currency exchange for personal/author copies from the Print on Demand (POD) publisher.

Market manipulation: Marketing that incentivizes Kindle Unlimited customers to read your Kindle e-book in exchange for compensation of any kind.

Metadata: Data about data. Title, subtitle, series name, author, publisher name, imprint, ISBN, keywords, categories, and retail blurb.

Non-exclusivity: When a retailer allows author to "go wide" with distribution at multiple retailers.

One Copy, One User (OCOU): The library purchases a copy and lends it out in the same way physical books are handled, e.g., once the book is checked out, it is no longer available until it has been returned.

On Store: For sale (Apple Books).

Orphaned: Term for an author whose contract has been prematurely terminated by the publisher.

PDF: A file format that provides a locked version of your document pages to eliminate formatting changes when opened on different devices and programs (the file name will end in .pdf).

Pen name: The name (pseudonym) an author chooses to write under, different from their legal name.

Price Per Unit or PPU: Also known as Cost Per Checkout (CPC). Allows multiple copies and multiple users to borrow your book at the same time without the library purchasing a copy.

Primary marketplace: The country where you expect to sell the most books.

Public domain: Creative work that is no longer subject to copyright.

Public Lending Right (PLR): Established in more than 30 countries worldwide (but not the U.S.), the program compensates authors and other rightsholders for the public use of their works in libraries.

Publisher compensation: IngramSparks' term for publisher royalties.

Publishing platforms: Digital platforms where you can upload and sell your books, including Kindle Direct Publishing for Amazon, Barnes & Noble Press for Nook, etc.

Pseudonym: Another word for an author's pen name.

Ready for Store: On pre-order (Apple Books).

RGB: Red, green, blue, used in graphic design (cover art).

Routing number: Nine-digit combination of the bank institution number and transit number, required when setting up direct bank deposit.

Royalties: Monies earned from the sale of your books.

Start Reading Location (SRL): Kindle Edition Normalized Pages generally sets Chapter 1 as the first page for which you will be paid per reads by Kindle Vella readers.

Storefronts: Publishing partners that Draft2Digital (D2D-distributes to, including Amazon, Kobo, Everand, Hoopla, OverDrive, etc.

SWIFT: Society for Worldwide Interbank Financial Telecommunication, required when setting up direct bank deposit.

Target Audience: Key demographic your book and/or marketing efforts are directed to.

Tax withholding: Income tax deducted from a royalty payment.

Teasers: Short set-ups for the longer book blurb or jacket copy.

TIN: Taxpayer identification number.

TOC: Table of contents.

Track Changes: Feature in Microsoft Word that displays all additions and deletions made to help you review edits made by critique partners, alpha and beta readers, and editors.

Trade discount: Discount offered to booksellers from wholesale distributors for POD books.

Transactional: A website where people can buy your product(s), also known as e-commerce.

Trim size: The length and width of your book, e.g., 6" x 9".

Tropes: A recurring plot device or situation used in fiction.

Value per Minute Consumed (VPC): Total monthly revenue earned from all Kobo Plus subscriptions divided by the total minutes that all subscribers spent reading in that month.

W-8BEN: Certificate of Status of Beneficial Owner for United States Tax Withholding and Reporting (Entities).

Wholesale discount: The discount offered by the publisher to the wholesale distributor for POD books.

Wholesale distributor: The distributor used for wholesale distribution of POD books to retailers.

Wide: Going "wide" is the industry term for uploading content to a variety of storefronts outside of Amazon's exclusive KDP Select program.

Wire Transfer: Type of electronic fund transfer.

Writing critique group: A group of writers who meet on a regular basis to critique works in progress from other members.

RESOURCES BY SECTION

THIS IS a list of resources only; no endorsement is being made for any of the firms or services listed.

  * In some cases, an account may be required to gain access and/or the link may no longer be active. Consider this a jumping off point to undertake your own research.

READY OR NOT?

STATS, STIGMAS & FIRST STEPS

Self-published book stats: https://wordsrated.com/self-published-book-sales-statistics/

EDITING AND PROOFREADING

Chartered Institute of Editors and Proofreaders: https://www.ciep.uk/directory/

Chicago Manual of Style: https://www.chicagomanualofstyle.org

Editorial Freelancers Association: https://www.the-efa.org/

Editors Canada: https://www.editors.ca/ode/search

Building a Website

www.wpbeginner.com/beginners-guide/how-to-choose-the-best-website-builder/

Business Basics

Trademark name databases

U.S.: https://www.uspto.gov/trademarks/search

Canada: https://www.canada.ca/en/services/business/start/choosing-a-business-name-2.html

Register a Business Name

U.S.: https://www.sba.gov/business-guide/launch-your-business/register-your-business

Canada: https://www.canada.ca/en/services/business/start/choosing-a-business-name-3.html

Tax Information

Overview
U.S.: https://www.sba.gov/business-guide/launch-your-business/get-federal-state-tax-id-numbers
https://www.irs.gov/businesses/small-businesses-self-employed

Canada: https://www.canada.ca/en/revenue-agency/services/tax/businesses/topics/registering-your-business/register.html

Tax ID Number
U.S.: https://www.irs.gov/pub/irs-pdf/fw9.pdf
https://www.irs.gov/forms-pubs/about-form-w-8-ben

IRS (U.S.): https://www.irs.gov/businesses/small-businesses-self-employed/self-employed-individuals-tax-center

CRA (CA): https://www.canada.ca/en/revenue-agency/services/tax/businesses/small-businesses-self-employed-income/setting-your-business/sole-proprietorship.html

U.S Tax Forms
Form 1099-K: https://www.irs.gov/businesses/understanding-your-form-1099-k

Form 1099-MISC: https://www.irs.gov/forms-pubs/about-form-1099-misc

Form 1042-S: https://www.irs.gov/forms-pubs/about-form-1042-s

GST/HST Canada
Filing for a GST/HST number: https://www.canada.ca/en/revenue-agency/services/tax/businesses/topics/gst-hst-businesses/account-register.html

BMO article on understanding GST/HST: https://www.bmo.com/main/business/news/register-for-GSTHST/

E-Commerce / Transactional Websites

Alliance of Independent Authors (ALLi) article on the pros and cons of transactional websites: https://selfpublishingadvice.org/selling-books-on-your-author-website/

Forbes Advisor article on how to build an e-commerce website:

https://www.forbes.com/advisor/business/software/how-build-ecommerce-website/

COPYRIGHT

Berne Convention for the Protection of Literary and Artistic Works: https://www.wipo.int/treaties/en/ip/berne/

Copyright (U.S.): https://www.copyright.gov
https://www.copyright.gov/about/fees.html

Copyright (Canada):
https://www.canada.ca/en/services/business/ip/copyright.html
and
https://www.ic.gc.ca/eic/site/cipointernet-internetopic.nsf/eng/wr04196.html

BOOK BASICS

ISBNs

ISBNs (International Standard Book Number): https://www.isbn-international.org/content/what-isbn

The Bowker Agency (US ISBNs): https://www.bowker.com/isbn-us

Canadian ISBNs: https://www.bac-lac.gc.ca/eng/services/isbn-canada/Pages/isbn-canada.aspx

PREPPING FOR PUBLICATION

COVER ART & PRICING

Cover Art

Blog post, *Building a Book Cover*: http://www.judypenzsheluk.com/2022/09/03/building-a-book-cover/

Branding your book: https://www.amazon.com/stores/Judy-Penz-Sheluk/author/B00O74NX04

SelfPubBookCovers: https://selfpubbookcovers.com/

Canva: https://www.canva.com

Cool Canadian Crime monthly newsletter: https://www.crimewriterscanada.com/books/cool-canadian-crime

Pricing

IngramSpark Publisher Compensation Calculator: (POD): https://myaccount.ingramspark.com/Tools/PubCompCalculator

Technical Specifications

Color profile: https://www.howtogeek.com/343900/what-is-a-color-profile/

JPEGS vs TIFF: https://www.adobe.com/ca/creativecloud/file-types/image/comparison/jpeg-vs-tiff.html

EPUBs & PDFs

Book Formatting

Apple https://support.apple.com/en-us/HT208499

Adobe InDesign: https://www.adobe.com/products/indesign.html

Atticus: https://www.atticus.io

KDP: e-Book manuscript formatting guide: https://kdp.amazon.com/en_US/help/topic/G201723130

KDP: Convert a paperback Word file to PDF: https://kdp.amazon.com/en_US/help/topic/G202188020

KDP: What file formats are supported for e-Book manuscripts: https://kdp.amazon.com/en_US/help/topic/G200634390

Kobo Writing Life: https://kobowritinglife.zendesk.com/hc/en-us/articles/360058975512

Scrivener: https://www.literatureandlatte.com/scrivener/overview

Software options: https://selfpublishing.com/book-formatting-software/

Vellum: https://store.vellum.pub/

ARCs, Pre-orders & Publication Date

Advance Review Copies (ARCs)

Book Funnel: https://bookfunnel.com

BookLife: https://booklife.com/about-us/review-submission-guidelines.html

Goodreads Giveaway: https://www.goodreads.com/giveaway/show_create_options

Kirkus Reviews: https://www.kirkusreviews.com/indie-reviews/

Midwest Book Reviews: https://www.midwestbookreview.com/

Net Galley: https://www.netgalley.com

Reader's Favorite: https://readersfavorite.com

Hank Phillipe Ryan: https://www.jungleredwriters.com/2023/07/what-hanks-writing-most-difficult.html

Selecting Your Publication Date

Best days to publish: https://kobowritinglife.zendesk.com/hc/en-us/articles/360058975992-Picking-the-Best-Release-Day

Categories and Keywords

Categories

Book Industry Standards and Communications (BISAC) codes: https://www.bisg.org/complete-bisac-subject-headings-list

BISAC advice on how to select codes: https://www.bisg.org/selecting-a-BISAC-code

Getting Down To Business

Getting Paid

Banking: Form W-9: https://www.irs.gov/pub/irs-pdf/fw9.pdf

PayPal: https://www.paypal.com

W-8BEN: https://www.irs.gov/forms-pubs/about-form-w-8-ben

Wire transfer codes by country (SWIFT): https://wise.com/gb/swift-codes/

Metadata

Metadata Guidelines: https://kobowritinglife.zendesk.com/hc/en-us/articles/360058975792-Metadata-Guidelines

DIGITAL RIGHTS MANAGEMENT

What is DRM?: https://digitalguardian.com/blog/what-digital-rights-management

DRM downsides: https://justpublishingadvice.com/drm-is-the-biggest-downside-for-ebooks/

PUBLISHING PLATFORMS

Amazon (Kindle Direct Publishing) https://kdp.amazon.com/

A+ optional add-on: https://kdp.amazon.com/en_US/help/topic/GHL7P99B7AA543CN

Amazon ads: https://kdp.amazon.com/en_US/help/topic/G201499010

Amazon distribution: https://kdp.amazon.com/en_US/help/topic/G201834280

Amazon Prime/Prime Reading: https://www.amazon.com/amazonprime

Amazon print calculator: https://kdp.amazon.com/en_US/help/topic/GSQF43YAMUPFTMSP

Amazon Tax Central: https://taxcentral.amazon.com/tax-interview/home

Author Central: https://kdp.amazon.com/en_US/help/topic/G200644310

Author Central example: https://www.amazon.com/author/judypenzsheluk

Author copies: https://kdp.amazon.com/en_US/help/topic/GVEG4YA9G2T7N6DR#orderauthorcopies

Compensation on Kindle Vella: https://kdp.amazon.com/en_US/help/topic/G5TFR9WSHB46ZKFN

Content and language requirements: https://kdp.amazon.com/en_US/help/topic/GVEG4YA9G2T7N6DR#orderproofs

Differences for KDP POD publishing for paperbacks and laminated hardcover books: https://kdp.amazon.com/en_US/help/topic/GAVW3FZZAKA2KY3B#differences

Enroll in KDP: https://kdp.amazon.com/en_US/help/topic/GD9PMU58BV24QFZ7#enroll

Expanded Distribution: https://kdp.amazon.com/en_US/help/topic/GQTT4W3T5AYK7L45

Free Five-Day Book Promotion: https://kdp.amazon.com/en_US/help/topic/G201298240

KDP account set-up: https://kdp.amazon.com/en_US/help/topic/G200620010

KDP help section: https://kdp.amazon.com/en_US/help/topic/G200736410

KDP printing cost and royalty calculator: https://kdp.amazon.com/en_US/help/topic/GSQF43YAMUPFTMSP

KDP reports & payments: https://kdp.amazon.com/en_US/help/topic/GVTTXHKHVPAPBEDQ

KDP Select enrollment: https://kdp.amazon.com/en_US/help/topic/GD9PMU58BV24QFZ7#enroll

Kindle Countdown: https://kdp.amazon.com/en_US/help/topic/G201293780

Kindle Unlimited: https://kdp.amazon.com/en_US/help/topic/G201537300

Kindle Vella Compensation: https://kdp.amazon.com/en_US/help/topic/G5TFR9WSHB46ZKFN

Kindle Vella: https://kdp.amazon.com/en_US/help/topic/GR2L4AHPMQ44HNQ7

Royalties in Kindle Unlimited: https://kdp.amazon.com/en_US/help/topic/G201541130

Update book details: https://kdp.amazon.com/en_US/help/topic/G200736410

Ways to promote your book: https://kdp.amazon.com/en_US/help/topic/GQSKV8L8EM6APYHN

Writer Beware: https://writerbeware.blog/2023/07/07/how-scammers-are-using-amazon-and-amazon-trademarks-to-rip-writers-off/

Apple (iTunes Connect)
https://itunesconnect.apple.com/

Apple ID: https://appleid.apple.com/account

Apple Publishing Portal: https://authors.apple.com/epub-upload

Create an Apple Books Account: https://itunespartner.apple.com/books/articles/create-an-apple-books-account-2699

Create an iTunes Connect Account: https://itunesconnect.apple.com/WebObjects/iTunesConnect.woa/wa/booksApplication

iTunes Connect Help: https://itunespartner.apple.com/books/tools

iTunes Producer How to Publish: https://itunespartner.apple.com/books/articles/how-to-publish-an-ebook-with-itunes-producer-2718

Barnes and Noble (B&N Press)
https://press.barnesandnoble.com

B&N consignment events: https://help-press.barnesandnoble.com/hc/en-us/articles/5358923827867-Selling-B-N-Press-Print-Books-in-Barnes-Noble-Stores

B&N cover template: https://press.barnesandnoble.com/book-cover-template-generator

Nook App: https://www.barnesandnoble.com/h/apps

Draft2Digital (D2D)
https://draft2digital.com/

Book price calculator: https://www.draft2digital.com/podcalc

Create a Universal Book Link: https://books2read.com/links/ubl/create/

D2D channels/partners: https://draft2digital.com/partners/

Knowledge base: https://draft2digital.com/knowledge-base/

Library distribution payment types: https://draft2digital.com/library-pricing/

Refer a Friend Program: https://draft2digital.com/account/referrals/

Royalty splitting between collaborators: https://draft2digital.com/knowledge-base/

Smashwords Read an Ebook Week: https://www.smashwords.com/ebookweek

Terms and conditions: https://draft2digital.com/knowledge-base/#what-are-print-change-tokens-and-why-would-i-need-

Google Play
https://play.google.com/books/publish/

Google Play Library: https://play.google.com/books

Google Play Books Store: https://play.google.com/store/books/

IngramSpark
https://www.ingramspark.com

Account setup instructions: https://help.ingramspark.com/hc/en-us/articles/5337654132493-Instructions-for-Setting-Up-an-IngramSpark-Account

Additional currencies and payment information: https://help.ingramspark.com/hc/en-us/articles/5338720329229-Compensation-Payments-Payment-Schedule-and-Instructions-for-Updating-Payment-Information

Author copies: https://help.ingramspark.com/hc/en-us/articles/5337658492301-Placing-and-Reviewing-Orders-

Compensation earnings and payment report: https://help.ingramspark.com/hc/en-us/articles/5281192809101-Reporting-Compensation-Earnings

E-book conversion: https://help.ingramspark.com/hc/en-us/articles/5281134044685-Ebook-Creation-Services

File creation guide: https://www.ingramspark.com/hubfs/downloads/file-creation-guide.pdf

Global distribution network partial listing: https://www.ingramspark.com/how-it-works/distribute

Global print and e-book agreement: https://help.ingramspark.com/hc/en-us/articles/5281174522125-IngramSpark-Agreement-FAQs

Help center: https://help.ingramspark.com/hc/en-us/

iPage listing: https://help.ingramspark.com/hc/en-us/articles/6955373241869-iPage-Listing-Ingram-s-Online-Catalog-Booksellers-Order-From

Personalized Copies: https://help.ingramspark.com/hc/en-us/articles/5281149828109-About-our-Personalize-It-feature

Print book distribution partners: https://www.ingramspark.com/how-it-works/distribute#printbookdistributionpartners

Publisher compensation calculator (POD): https://myaccount.ingramspark.com/Tools/PubCompCalculator

Publisher compensation-e-books: https://myaccount.ingramspark.com/EbookSalesModels

Target.com program: https://help.ingramspark.com/hc/en-us/articles/6976654177933-Target-com-Program

Title setup instructions for print and e-book: https://help. ingramspark.com/hc/en-us/articles/5341507452173-Title-Setup-Instructions-and-Information-for-Print-Books-and-Ebook

User Guide PDF: https://www.ingramspark.com/hubfs/ downloads/user-guide.pdf

Wholesale discount video: https://help.ingramspark.com/hc/en-us/articles/6352130587789-VIDEO-What-is-a-Wholesale-Discount-and-Why-You-Offer-One-Length-4-47-minutes-

Kobo
http://www.kobo.com/writinglife

Choose your country: https://www.kobo.com/ca/en/choose-your-country

Help desk: https://kobowritinglife.zendesk.com/hc/en-us

OverDrive: https://www.overdrive.com

AUDIOBOOKS

AUDIOBOOK BASICS

Audio Publishers Association's (APA) audiobooks sales survey: https://www.publishersweekly.com/pw/by-topic/industry-news/ audio-books/article/89547-audiobook-growth-continues.html

Audiobook statistics: https://wordsrated.com/audiobook-statistics/

Book Riot's "The Best Places to Find Audiobook Narrator Jobs for Beginners": https://bookriot.com/audiobook-narrator-jobs-for-beginners/

Bounty Referral ACX: https://www.judypenzsheluk.com/audiobooks/

How to narrate your own book: https://youtu.be/NssisSRWHYk

How to set up a home studio: https://youtu.be/WzixwYIvMzM

ReviewMoose.ca: https://reviewmoose.ca/blog/audiobook-sales-statistics/

The Players

ACX Bounty (terms and conditions): https://help.acx.com/s/article/acx-bounty-referral-program-terms-and-conditions

ACX: https://www.acx.com/help/authors/200484540
Aggregator partners: https://draft2digital.com/digital-narration/

Apple: https://itunespartner.apple.com/books/articles/how-to-sell-audiobooks-on-apple-books-2714

Findaway Voices: https://findawayvoices.com

Google Play: https://play.google.com/books/publish/autonarrated/

Kobo Writing Life:
https://kobowritinglife.zendesk.com/hc/en-us/articles/360058976312-FAQ-Audiobooks
https://kobowritinglife.zendesk.com/hc/en-us/articles/360059385511-How-to-Upload-Your-Audiobook-Directly-on-Kobo

GETTING THE WORD OUT

ADVERTISING & PROMOTION

FREEBIES

Author Central: https://author.amazon.com/home

BookBub: https://partners.bookbub.com and https://www.bookbub.com/home/about.php and https://www.bookbub.com/settings/reading-preferences

Goodreads: https://www.goodreads.com

Pinterest: https://www.pinterest.com/

LibraryThing: https://www.librarything.com/

Shepherd.com https://shepherd.com

Shepherd for Authors: https://forauthors.shepherd.com

Shepherd lists: The best cold case mysteries with a twist…or three: https://shepherd.com/best-books/cold-case-mysteries-with-a-twist-or-three and https://shepherd.com/bboy/2023/f/judy-penz-sheluk

PAY TO PLAY

ADVERTISING COURSES & TUTORIALS

Amazon advertising: https://advertising.amazon.com/?ref_=logo https://insights.bookbub.com/category/bookbub-ads/

Bryan Cohen (Amazon ads) courses: https://advertising.amazon.com/library/case-studies/bryan-cohen and https://teamup.com/ksidaehwstpddivzpk

Meta Blueprint: https://www.facebook.com/business/learn/courses

BOOK PROMOTION SERVICES

Reedsy ratings of book promotion services: https://blog.reedsy.com/book-promotion-services/

MARKETING & PUBLICITY

MARKETING MATERIALS

Canva: https://www.canva.com

Got Print: https://www.gotprint.com/

VistaPrint: https://www.vistaprint.com/

Pens: https://www.pens.com/

NEWSLETTERS

Judy Penz Sheluk's newsletter signup form: http://eepurl.com/b4cQvP

Newsletter services: https://kindlepreneur.com/best-e-mail-services-for-authors/

Newsletters anti-spam: https://us9.admin.mailchimp.com/account/profile/

GIVEAWAYS

Goodreads Giveaways: https://www.goodreads.com/giveaway/

show_create_options

RADIO & TV

The Breakdown with Allison Dore: https://www.allisondore.com/siriusxm/the-breakdown/

House of Mystery on NBC: https://www.alanrwarren.com/house-of-mystery-radioshow

SHAMELESS SELF-PROMOTION

Judy Penz Sheluk Interviews: https://www.judypenzsheluk.com/about/

KICKSTARTER

https://www.kickstarter.com/

AUTHOR, AUTHOR

ASSOCIATIONS, ARTS COUNCILS & AWARDS

AWARDS

Writer's Digest's annual Self-Published Book Awards: https://www.writersdigest.com/writers-digest-competitions/self-published-book-awards

ASSOCIATIONS (PARTIAL LIST)

Alliance of Independent Authors: https://www.allianceindependentauthors.org

Canadian Society of Children's Authors, Illustrators and Performers: https://www.canscaip.org

Crime Writers of Canada: https://www.crimewriterscanada.com

Historical Novel Society: https://historicalnovelsociety.org

Independent Book Publishers Association: https://www.ibpa-online.org/default.aspx

Romance Writers of America: https://www.rwa.org

Science Fiction and Fantasy Writers of America: https://www.sfwa.org

Sisters in Crime: https://www.sistersincrime.org/default.aspx

Sisters in Crime Online Guppy Chapter: https://www.sistersincrime.org/page/guppy-online-chapter

Society of Children's Book Writers and Illustrators: https://www.scbwi.org/

Writers' Union of Canada: https://www.writersunion.ca
https://www.sistersincrime.org/page/guppy-online-chapter

GRANTS & PROGRAMS

GRANTS

Jane Friedman on grants and programs: https://www.janefriedman.com/grantwriting-101/

Poets & Writers list: https://www.pw.org/grants

PROGRAMS

Access Copyright: https://www.accesscopyright.ca/

Australian Lending Right Scheme: https://www.arts.gov.au/funding-and-support/australian-lending-right-schemes-elrplr

Copibec unlocatable authors: https://www.copibec.ca/en/unlocatable-copyright-owners

Copibec: https://www.copibec.ca/en/royalties

Indie Author Project: https://indieauthorproject.com/authors/

Payback: https://www.accesscopyright.ca/creators/faqs-for-creator-affiliates/

PLR (Public Lending Right) Canada: https://publiclendingright.ca

PLR Canada past examples of selected libraries: https://publiclendingright.ca/about/governance/library-sampling

PLR (Public Lending Right) programs worldwide: https://plrinternational.com/established https://plrinternational.com/indevelopment

Out & About

Book Launches

Gatekeeper Press: https://gatekeeperpress.com/virtual-book-launch/

Consignment Sales

Barnes & Noble: https://www.barnesandnobleinc.com/publishers-authors/how-to-be-considered-for-an-author-event/

Thinking Outside the Bookstore Box

Cookstown Antique Mall: http://www.
cookstownantiquemarket.com

Vendor Markets

Square Point of Sale system: https://squareup.com

Writing Conferences & Conventions

2023 Malice Domestic mystery convention: https://www.
malicedomestic.org/programming.html

BOLO Books article on the basics of panels: https://bolobooks.
com/2014/11/countdown-to-bouchercon-4/

AUTHOR'S NOTE

In February 2018, four years after signing my first publishing contract, I made the decision to start my own imprint, Superior Shores Press. It's been the right decision for me, but I would never suggest that self-publishing is the right path for everyone. In addition to traditional publishing credits, I came to the "life" following fifteen years as a freelance journalist and editor. In short, I'd learned a bit about the business before diving into the deep end solo.

I also come from a business background. Before I was a paid-for-hire writer and editor, I was employed in the corporate world, where I worked in a variety of industries as (among other things) an Office Manager, Credit Manager, and Sales and Marketing Coordinator. And yes, most of that was every bit as dull as it sounds.

The thing is, dull usually pays well, especially in the corporate world. Writing books… let's just say not too many earn what I like to call "Stephen King money." The odds of earning that kind of cash lessen with each rung down the publishing ladder. In other words, if you've decided to self-publish to get rich, you're probably in the wrong line of work.

Oh, sure, there are exceptions. Lisa Genova's *Still Alice* and E.L. James' *Fifty Shades of Grey* are two notable examples of authors going from self-published to the big time. But exceptions are never the rule, no matter how much you might will them to be so.

This book isn't meant to alter that reality, or provide false hope, but rather to guide you through the steps involved if, or when, you decide that you're ready to self-publish. Not because it's a shortcut, not because it's fast and easy, and certainly not because you think it's your only option, but because all things considered, it's the right path for you.

The right path. If, after reading this book, you realize that self-publishing isn't for you, that's okay, too. Just promise me one thing, okay? Keep writing, find another path and don't give up on your dream.

After all, dreams can't go anywhere without you. And neither can your book.

Judy Penz Sheluk
December 2023

ACKNOWLEDGMENTS

Self-publishing doesn't mean doing everything by yourself. This book would not have been possible without the assistance of many individuals. While time and space preclude me from mentioning them all, I would be remiss if I didn't acknowledge the following people:

My first readers, for the generous gift of their time and insightful feedback: Lisa Mathews, Petra Schmelzeisen, Adrienne Stevenson, Grace Topping, and Lisa Tucker.

My editorial team: Emily Nakeff, who kept me on track and accountable during a particularly challenging chapter of my life, and Ti Locke, who has remained steadfast in my corner on every step of my author journey.

I'd also like to thank Kim Burgess, Adult Programming Director at the New Tecumseth Public Library, for her ongoing support and encouragement, Sisters in Crime, WordsRated, and BISAC for permission to incorporate their data, and Hunter Martin for his creative cover art.

Last, but not least, to the authors, dreamers, and want-to-doers who read this book. Thank you for trusting me with your vision.

ABOUT THE AUTHOR

A former journalist and magazine editor, Judy Penz Sheluk is the bestselling author of *Finding Your Path to Publication: A Step-by-Step Guide*, and *Self-publishing: The Ins & Outs of Going Indie*, as well as two mystery series: the Glass Dolphin Mysteries and Marketville Mysteries, both of which have been published in multiple languages. Her short crime fiction appears in several collections, including the Superior Shores Anthologies, which she also edited. Judy has a passion for understanding the ins and outs of all aspects of publishing, and is the founder and owner of Superior Shores Press, which she established in February 2018.

Judy is a member of Sisters in Crime, International Thriller Writers, the Short Mystery Fiction Society, and Crime Writers of Canada, where she served on the Board of Directors for five years, the final two as Chair. She lives in Northern Ontario. Find her at www.judypenzsheluk.com.

www.ingramcontent.com/pod-product-compliance
Lightning Source LLC
Chambersburg PA
CBHW070858120626
46546CB00001B/51